THE FIGURE OF
THIS WORLD

Crosscurrents

Exploring the development of European thought through engagements with the arts, humanities, social sciences and sciences

Series Editor
Christopher Watkin, University of Cambridge

Editorial Advisory Board

Andrew Benjamin
Martin Crowley
Simon Critchley
Frederiek Depoortere
Oliver Feltham
Patrick ffrench
Christopher Fynsk
Kevin Hart
Emma Wilson

Titles available in the series:

Difficult Atheism: Post-Theological Thinking in Alain Badiou, Jean-Luc Nancy and Quentin Meillassoux
by Christopher Watkin

Politics of the Gift: Exchanges in Poststructuralism
by Gerald Moore

The Figure of This World: Agamben and the Question of Political Ontology
by Mathew Abbott

Unfinished Worlds: Hermeneutics, Aesthetics and Gadamer
by Nicholas Davey

The Becoming of the Body: Contemporary Women's Writing in French
By Amaleena Damlé

Forthcoming Titles:

Sublime Art: Towards an Aesthetics of the Future
by Stephen Zepke

Philosophy, Animality and the Life Sciences
by Wahida Khandker

Visit the Crosscurrents website at www.euppublishing.com/series/cross

THE FIGURE OF THIS WORLD

Agamben and the Question of Political Ontology

Mathew Abbott

EDINBURGH
University Press

© Mathew Abbott, 2014

Edinburgh University Press Ltd
22 George Square, Edinburgh EH8 9LF

www.euppublishing.com

Typeset in 10.5/13 Sabon by
Servis Filmsetting Ltd, Stockport, Cheshire.

A CIP record for this book is available from the British Library

ISBN 978 0 7486 8409 0 (hardback)
ISBN 978 0 7486 8410 6 (webready PDF)

The right of Mathew Abbott
to be identified as author of this work
has been asserted in accordance with
the Copyright, Designs and Patents Act 1988.

Contents

Acknowledgements — vi
Series Editor's Preface — vii

Introduction: The Figure of This World — 1

1. The Question of Political Ontology — 13
2. The Poetic Experience of the World — 33
3. The Myth of the Earth — 58
4. The Unbearable — 80
5. The Creature before the Law — 106
6. The Animal for which Animality is an Issue — 123
7. Understanding the Happy — 144
8. The Picture and its Captives — 162
9. The Passing of the Figure of This World — 179

Bibliography — 201
Index — 214

Acknowledgements

I gratefully acknowledge the commitment, assistance and critical acuity of John Grumley throughout this project. I would like to thank Paolo Bartoloni and Diego Bubbio for their generous help. I would also like to thank Robert Arculus, Thomas Battersby, Edward Cavanagh, Ross Grant, Fiona Jenkins, David Kishik, Paul Livingston, Nathan McGinness, Alex Murray, Benjamin Noys, Aaron Nyerges, Robert Sinnerbrink and Kedar Vishwanathan for giving advice on the material presented here. To my family and friends for helping me continue: thank you. Most of all I would like to thank my beautiful wife Emilie – your love, support, patience and humour were conditions of this book's possibility!

Material from this book was first published in *Colloquy: Text, Theory, Critique*; the *International Journal of Philosophical Studies*; *Literature and Politics: Pushing the World in Certain Directions* (edited by Peter Marks for Cambridge Scholars Publishing); *Angelaki: Journal of the Theoretical Humanities*; and *Parrhesia: A Journal of Critical Philosophy*. I thank the editors of these publications for their permission to republish.

This project was completed with the aid of a Travelling Scholarship from the Marten Bequest (Poetry).

I dedicate this book to my parents, Neil and Lindy.

Series Editor's Preface

Two or more currents flowing into or through each other create a turbulent crosscurrent, more powerful than its contributory flows and irreducible to them. Time and again, modern European thought creates and exploits crosscurrents in thinking, remaking itself as it flows through, across and against discourses as diverse as mathematics and film, sociology and biology, theology, literature and politics. The work of Gilles Deleuze, Jacques Derrida, Slavoj Žižek, Alain Badiou, Bernard Stiegler and Jean-Luc Nancy, among others, participates in this fundamental remaking. In each case disciplines and discursive formations are engaged, not with the aim of performing a pre-determined mode of analysis yielding a 'philosophy of x', but through encounters in which thought itself can be transformed. Furthermore, these fundamental transformations do not merely seek to account for singular events in different sites of discursive or artistic production but rather to engage human existence and society as such, and as a whole. The cross-disciplinarity of this thought is therefore neither a fashion nor a prosthesis; it is simply part of what 'thought' means in this tradition.

Crosscurrents begins from the twin convictions that this remaking is integral to the legacy and potency of European thought, and that the future of thought in this tradition must defend and develop this legacy in the teeth of an academy that separates and controls the currents that flow within and through it. With this in view, the series provides an exceptional site for bold, original and opinion-changing monographs that actively engage European thought in this fundamentally cross-disciplinary manner, riding existing crosscurrents and creating new ones. Each book in the series explores the different ways in which European thought develops through its engagement with disciplines across the arts, humanities, social sciences and sciences, recognising that the community of scholars working with this thought is itself spread across diverse faculties. The object of the series is therefore nothing less than to examine and carry forward the unique legacy of European thought as an inherently and irreducibly cross-disciplinary enterprise.

Christopher Watkin
Cambridge
February 2011

Introduction:
The Figure of This World

> *Not till we are lost, in other words not till we have lost the world, do we begin to find ourselves, and realize where we are and the infinite extent of our relations.*[1]

Things *are*. Philosophy is constitutively ill equipped to own up to this fact, which is both banal and singularly inexplicable.

This is because it is a very particular kind of fact. Specifically, it is not the kind of fact that can be represented, not the kind of fact that we can *know*.

Yet this is not because it is ineffably 'beyond language'. It is because our relation to it goes deeper than representation and knowing, because this very particular fact makes a particular kind of *claim* on us.

This claim is *political* in a fundamental sense. It bears on our being in common, as we share exposure to it.

In this book I define 'political ontology' as the clarification of the problems outlined in the above eight sentences. I demonstrate what such a practice of thought would entail via critical readings of a set of modern philosophers – Heidegger, Levinas, Benjamin, Nietzsche and Wittgenstein – all of whom, I work to show, deal with their consequences. Running alongside these readings, and the primary motivation for them, is a concern with presenting a defence and development of the thought of contemporary Italian philosopher Giorgio Agamben. Reading Agamben in light of these philosophers, and in the terms of political ontology, will show how his work turns on an attempt at thinking the question of being, and clarify his positive political philosophy. In this book, then, I demonstrate how and why Agamben's 'coming politics'[2] will require us to rethink our relation to the question raised by being.

The philosophical method in play here is inspired in part by

Heidegger and in part by Wittgenstein. In particular I am concerned with the Heideggerian critique of metaphysics, which term I define as follows: 'metaphysics' is a name for modes of thought that pass over, cancel out, presuppose or obliviate the question of being (Heidegger says metaphysics 'does not think the difference'[3] between being and beings). Thinking non-metaphysically, then, means thinking from out of a proper response to this question; first and foremost, this means thinking from out of a position in which one is able to let it *become* a question (acknowledging that there are not only beings, but also the fact of their being). This leads to a problematisation of the idea of foundation, because the question of being, insofar as it does not have an answer, undermines it. What I take from Wittgenstein is the idea that philosophy should be practised in an auto-critical mode, the idea that it should be concerned less with solving philosophical problems than with changing our relation to them. Yet if Wittgenstein was more concerned with traditional philosophy's desire to establish and defend claims about mind and meaning, and took his alternative philosophical practice to involve working to loosen our attachments to such metaphysical pictures (turning 'the axis of our investigations ... about the fixed point of our real need'[4]), then here I am more interested in loosening our attachment to the metaphysical schemes (pictures) that underlie certain of our political concepts, and with working to show how our relation to one very particular question might be transformed. As with Heidegger's, Wittgenstein's thought is exemplary of the attempt at thinking beyond the need to philosophically *account* for human life, beyond the mad desire to found it on certainty. The question of being, if properly faced, shows that our relation to the world is epistemically and ontologically unassured. And though this is perhaps more difficult to bring out, it also shows that this is not (does not need to be) a cause for fear or horror. Indeed, as Wittgenstein's work indicates, this lack of assurance is itself the condition of the possibility of a particular kind of happiness. If there is no reason for being, then being is gratuitous; the word 'gratuitous' shares its etymological root with 'grace'.

This book distinguishes itself from much of the literature on Agamben's work by its continuing emphasis on the 'positive' aspects of his philosophy.[5] Agamben of course is infamous for presenting a 'staggering'[6] critique of modern liberal democracies, and indeed his most trenchantly critical work – *Homo Sacer* – is his most influential.[7] Yet it is important to read Agamben's critique in light of the idea of transformation that motivates it.[8] Drawing on Benjamin, Agamben repeatedly links this with 'messianism'. Unfortunately this lends itself to hyperbolic and apocalyptic readings of his work in which the only hope for political change seems to consist in the possibility of some exceptional event that would puncture the tissue of the ordinary;[9] further, this 'saving' event appears problematically linked to the 'danger' of contemporary biopolitics.[10] If we accept such a reading, then, Agamben not only appears to leave us in a kind of obscure waiting (which itself would confirm the criticism of his work as politically paralysing), but also seems committed to a pseudo-Heideggerian dialectic in which the only way out of the worst is through. Yet this is a poor and uncharitable reading; it is too easy and too quick (it is much like existentialist readings of *Being and Time*, on which the philosopher appears to set up authenticity as the heroic task of a resolute and solitary Dasein: at first blush the text certainly lends itself to this reading, but accepting it means backing down from the real difficulties and ambiguities – as well as the real interest and philosophical insight – of Heidegger's thought[11]). If instead we meet Agamben on his real terrain – political ontology – it will become clear that redemption for him would constitute not some exceptional event of salvation, but rather a suspension of the dialectic of danger and salvation.[12] This is a way of understanding the distinction Benjamin makes in his eighth thesis on the philosophy of history, which is crucial for Agamben's thought: the '*real* state of exception'[13] would be a state in which being *as such* is lived as exceptional. What is *really* exceptional is the ordinary. 'The wise man wonders at the usual.'[14]

I do not claim to have found the idea of the exceptionality of the ordinary spelled out in Agamben's work. Indeed this book relies on a number of ideas that are not explicitly articulated in the philosopher's corpus, but which – or so I work to show – are very useful in understanding it. My intention is not to produce a systematic overview or detached scholarly appraisal of Agamben's thought; nor is it to give an exhaustive account of his influences (after all, several excellent introductions already exist in English[15]). It is to provide a defence and development of his philosophy. My turning at length to the work of Heidegger and Wittgenstein is the clearest example of this: I have not chosen these authors just because Agamben himself writes about them (he goes to Heidegger regularly and to Wittgenstein sporadically, though often at highly significant moments), but because I have found their work to be extremely helpful in clarifying and developing some of the most essential problems and ideas with which Agamben deals. If this is a work of 'Agamben scholarship', I hope it is not only that. In departing from the letter of his texts I want to engage with them in a more vital way than direct exegesis often allows, and to be doing so in the same spirit of risk and transformation with which the Italian thinker reads his own philosophical masters.

In Chapter 1 I set up my definition of political ontology, working to differentiate it from traditional political philosophy and Schmittian political theology. As with political theology, political ontology has its primary motivation not in disinterested contemplation from a rational standpoint, but in a confrontation with an existential problem. Yet while for Schmitt this is the problem of how to live and think in obedience to God, the problem for political ontology is the question of being. So the political ontologist agrees with the political theologian that the political cannot be thought without an awareness of an irreducible exigency – the fact that one thinks as situated in response to a certain moral or ethical demand – yet she takes this demand to consist not in divine revelation, but rather in the fact that the human being is a being for which being is at issue. With this definition in mind I go on to read Agamben in resolutely ontological terms, arguing that his concepts of bare life and the exception are largely unintelligible if understood ontically. Instead, these concepts are part of a critical theory that has as its primary target not the ontic political systems and material institutions of modern states but rather the (negative) metaphysical ground of those systems. Political ontology insists on the intertwining of ontology and politics, claiming theirs is a relation of mutual determination. A politics in-keeping with it would be a *subjunctive* politics, working to demonstrate practically the truth of its key claims: *no life is bare* and *the ordinary is exceptional*.

In Chapter 2 I develop Heidegger's phenomenology of poetry, articulating some of the key philosophical commitments at work in political ontology. Proceeding via an analysis of the three concepts of language operative in Heidegger's work, I demonstrate how poetic language challenges language's designative and world-disclosive functions. The experience with poetic language, which disrupts Dasein's absorption by emerging out of equipmentality in the mode of the broken tool, brings Dasein to wonder at the world's existence in such a way that doubt about its reality cannot enter the picture. A phenomenological account of this encounter with the fact of the world's existence helps clarify one of the crucial claims of this book: this fact is not 'knowable' in any of the usual or philosophical senses of the word. Our relation to it runs deeper than knowing.

In Chapter 3 I work through the political aspects of this experience, arguing that because of how it reveals the contingency of human life on something inappropriable, it sparks a desire for political grounding and justification. The problem is that this justification always involves a kind of violence, because it represents the rejection or repression of the real ontological violence – the absolute gratuity – of what is revealed in the poetic experience it rejects. This explains why Heidegger's artwork essay is riven by an ambiguity regarding earth and world, such that earth sometimes appears as the ground for world, and sometimes as a disruptive materiality that juts through it. Extending recent French critiques I show how this stems from Heidegger's attempt to collapse the distinction between the poetic and the mythic, to subsume poetic experience in mythic speech. With and against Heidegger, we must maintain the gap between the poetic and the mythic, opening the potential for another thought of the earth: one that could never act as a 'ground' for a historical people. This provides a way of understanding an important Agambenian claim: humanity has no vocation or historical destiny.

In Chapter 4 I follow up on this problem of ground, deepening the claims about the link between mythical justification and violence. I also begin to examine in more detail the nature of the political ontological shift that would allow us to think beyond it. To this end I clarify the problem of negative ground in the work of Agamben and Levinas, showing the connection between Levinas's thought of the *il y a* (the *there is*) and Agamben's political thought. This can help explain the transition in Levinas's philosophy that takes place after *Totality and Infinity*, in which the dichotomy the early works set up between being and the other breaks down. More importantly for our purposes, it can also help make sense of the positive project at the heart of Agamben's critical political ontology. Specifically it will clarify what Agamben means when he refers, in a paraphrase of an obscure text by Benjamin, to the possibility of the world's appearing 'as a good that absolutely cannot be appropriated . . .'.[16] The problem of negative ground haunts both Agamben and Levinas. Reading them together can help us understand – and potentially undo – the logic of banishment and return that defines it.

In Chapter 5 I show the biopolitical stakes of the problem of foundation. This involves rethinking life in relation to it, indicating how the political ontological change in question would transform our relationship to law by intervening into our metaphysics of human animality. I carry this out via a reading of Benjamin's important essay 'Critique of Violence', which is a crucial work for Agamben. Transforming as it does from an exemplar of meticulous philosophical analysis into an allusive political/messianic tract, the essay is representative of all that is most difficult about Benjamin's work. Against those critics who find the eschatological dimensions of his texts unpalatable and/ or philosophically bankrupt, however, the wager of this chapter is that it is possible to extract a philosophically sophisticated and politically interesting concept of the messianic from Benjamin. For it remains the case that the mortification of law carried out in the essay does not simply boil down to a naive antinomianism; that Benjamin's argument is far more subtle than any simple call for 'a radical destruction of the legal order . . .'.[17] Indeed I hope to show that if we read the text in conjunction with certain others in the Benjaminian *oeuvre* it becomes clear that it engages lucidly with a set of pressing, difficult questions about the status of law in modernity. Crucial for my argument in this book is how the essay sets up (divine) redemption in opposition to the desire for (mythical) salvation. On this reading of his work, the event that concerned Benjamin, which he defines in terms of the emergence of 'divine violence' (*göttliche Gewalt*), would represent a radical type of disenchantment. In Agamben's words, it would mean achieving 'the irreparable loss of the lost, the definitive profanity of the profane'.[18]

In Chapter 6 I place Nietzsche's philosophy of life with and against political ontology. I begin by explicating his understanding of the problem of human life. I argue that for Nietzsche, the human animal is the animal burdened by its beastliness, the animal whose entrance into society as we know it requires that it repress and/or forget aspects of its biological being. This produces two key results as evident in Nietzsche's work: the claim that illusion plays a key role for human beings, who have a tendency to obscure their being alive from themselves; and the idea that these problems are of a political character, because resentment against life is a structuring principle for politics. Agamben's approach to this Nietzschean problematic begins with an ingenious transposition of the ontological difference onto biological categories, such that the human being appears not just as a being for which being is an issue, but also as an animal for which animality is an issue. This approach, like Nietzsche's own, is predicated upon the possibility of transformation: the idea that human beings could experience a change in their relation to their lives. Against Nietzsche, however, Agamben's Pauline concept of redeemed humanity is resolutely non-hierarchical, turning on the possibility of a collective appropriation of our common consignment to unassumable animality.

In Chapter 7 I turn to the idea of happiness, working to show what it would mean to understand the happy of whom Wittgenstein speaks in his *Tractatus*. Joining the 'resolute' readers of the book – which means abandoning the idea that Wittgenstein's text somehow hints at ('shows') the ineffable – I work to demonstrate how it sets up and then undermines a picture theory of language. If successful, this undermining will make us wary of philosophical talk in which the existence of the world is passed over as a non-problem, or taken as a fact like other facts; it will shake us out of the philosophical commitments that prevent us from understanding the difference between the happy and the unhappy. Above all, 'throwing away the ladder' in the way that Wittgenstein demands means letting go of the philosophical fantasies that allow us to imagine ourselves as viewers of the world. These arguments, which turn on a deflationary interpretation of what Wittgenstein means by 'the mystical' in the *Tractatus*, consolidate recent readings that emphasise the continuity between it and the *Philosophical Investigations*. More importantly, they provide a new way of understanding the role of wonder in his work, and how it can lead us into (and out of) the kinds of unhappiness that characterise traditional philosophy.

In Chapter 8 I set these claims against Heidegger's 'The Age of the World Picture', bringing Heidegger's work together with Wittgenstein's in order to interrogate the philosophical status of the ordinary, and show how we need to work toward a broader understanding of what it would mean to become philosophically beguiled in Wittgenstein's sense. This means reading Wittgenstein in historical terms, demonstrating how his critique of the picture-concept should be understood in opposition to (what he understood as) the 'spirit' of our times. Such a reading will help indicate what it would mean to think beyond the metaphysical image of totality, allowing the question of being to emerge; it will show the instability of the dichotomy between 'everyday' and 'philosophical' life. Reading Heidegger and Wittgenstein together on the problem of the picture, then, will show how philosophical beguilement can come to penetrate the ordinary. Further, it will demonstrate how a release from the former would have to take place in the light of the latter.

In the final chapter I show how such an inquiry into the ordinary can help explain what Agamben means when he writes in *The Time That Remains* of the possibility of a people 'situat[ing] itself as a remnant, as not all'.[19] My claim is that Agamben's ontology of the remnant – of what remains after the '*Aufhebung* of the state of exception'[20] – can be understood as an attempt at thinking what it would mean to live and think beyond the picture-concept, of the world conceived as a representable totality. This must be linked with Agamben's use of Debord's concept of the spectacle which, as the ultimate form of capitalist alienation, exacerbates the problems inherent in the picture-concept in a unique and potentially transformative way. This, in turn, will show how Agamben's Benjaminian messianism saves his account from Heideggerian quietism by linking the possibility of ontological change with the concrete political struggle for common happiness. This is how we should read his repeated invocations of Paul's referring in

1 Corinthians 7:31 to 'the passing of the figure of this world': the time that remains is not what is left before the end of the world, but what remains before the end of the world picture, before the passing of the *skhēma* of the world.

Throughout this book I write with the sense that the critique of metaphysics is not – or does not have to be – primarily negative (or indeed 'deconstructive') in its basic orientation. While it is the case that large parts of it are concerned with undermining the idea that we could find or establish an ontological foundation for human life, this critique is not designed to show that we really lack something that we (sometimes) think we have, but rather that we do not need something that we (sometimes) think we lack. As Jean-Luc Nancy puts it in *The Sense of the World*, '[f]initude is not privation'.[21] My sense is that there is a thought of the good available here, because it is the ungroundedness of human lives that makes them what they are, and could become: surprising, happy, idiosyncratic. In any case, this undermining could never have been a real assault on foundation, as there was never a foundation there to destroy in the first place. Heidegger: 'This demonstration ... has nothing to do with a pernicious relativising of ontological standpoints. This destruction has just as little the *negative* sense of disburdening ourselves of the ontological tradition. On the contrary, it should stake out the positive possibilities of the tradition ...'[22] Wittgenstein: 'All that we destroy are castles in the air [*Luftgebaude*].'[23]

Running through this work is a problem regarding the relationship between theory and practice. The issue is evident in the very term 'political ontology', which to some ears may sound like something of a contradiction in terms. I do not want to downplay the status of this problem, which has a philosophical heritage that goes back at least as far as Aristotle's *Nicomachean Ethics*, with its distinction between practical life (*praxis*) and the life of contemplation (*theoria*).[24] But one of the wagers of political ontology as I want to define it (and this follows from the claim that ordinary life has, in spectacular capitalism, been penetrated by a form of philosophical beguilement) is that this distinction is fundamentally unstable. The obvious place to turn for support here is to Marxism, with its emphasis on the inextricability of theory and practice (Marx: 'The question whether human thinking can reach objective truth is not a question of theory but a *practical question*. In practice man must prove the truth ...'[25]). Specifically, however, I want to turn to a certain strain of Marxism, which has its beginnings in the young Marx and continues through Western Marxism via Benjamin and Guy Debord. In particular I want to reference György Lukács here, who is one of the most important inheritors of this Marxism, and for whom life in capitalist societies 'becomes less and less active and more and more *contemplative*'.[26] This statement, which Debord uses as the epigraph to Chapter 2 of *Society of the Spectacle*, upsets our usual understanding of the problem: it is not just that the life of contemplation is insufficiently engaged in the practical and political demands of ordinary life, but also that ordinary life has itself become marked by an alienated contemplative tendency in which human beings are separated from, and end up as distracted observers of, their own lives (Debord will put it like this: 'The whole life of those societies in which modern conditions of production prevail presents itself as an immense accumulation of *spectacles*. All that once was directly lived has become mere representation'[27]). Insisting on the mutual determination of politics and ontology, then, means insisting on the idea that thought has a political calling, and on the possibility that everyday life could have a calling in thought (and, simultaneously, that these callings can be refused or become travesties of themselves). In Greek, *theoria* literally means 'a looking at' or 'a viewing', and has its etymological root in the term *theoros*, meaning 'spectator'. If this book is successful in its critique of the picture-concept, then, it will also be successful as a critique of everyday life in the society of the spectacle. Political ontology is thus an attempt at doing for Heidegger what Marx did for Hegel: it wants to stand him on his feet. A revolution of everyday life would be an event for thought, just as everyday life – the ordinary – is both the start and the endpoint of thinking beyond metaphysics.

NOTES

1. Thoreau, *Walden*, 162.
2. Agamben, *The Coming Community*, 84.
3. Heidegger, 'Letter on Humanism', 226.
4. Wittgenstein, *Philosophical Investigations*, §108; 40e.
5. For an excellent account of the problem of negativity in recent continental theory, see Benjamin Noys's *The Persistence of the Negative*. Here Noys critiques the 'affirmationist consensus' (ix) at work in contemporary European political thought, an elision of the negative that he claims is shared (in different ways) by figures as diverse as Derrida, Deleuze, Negri, Latour and Badiou. It is perhaps unsurprising that Agamben, whose philosophy is often rejected for its extreme negativity and 'political nihilism' (Laclau, 'Bare Life or Social Indeterminacy?', 22), is not given extensive treatment in the work. Yet in the reading of Agamben I propose in this book, that critique relies on a caricature of his thinking: I argue that it is impossible to understand the grounds and stakes of his trenchant attack on capitalist modernity if it is disconnected from the philosophy of

redemption and transformation that drives it. It would seem, then, that my own account of Agamben might be open to Noys's critique of affirmationism. But the issue is complex. As I show in Chapter 6, Agambenian political ontology rejects the demand for the affirmation of life that characterises Nietzsche's work (and which, as Noys shows, is fundamental to certain forms of affirmationism, especially those of Deleuze and Derrida). I treat the issue of negativity at length in Chapter 4.

6. Prozorov, 'Why Giorgio Agamben is an Optimist', 1,054.
7. The articles in *Politics, Metaphysics, and Death* (ed. Andrew Norris) focus on *Homo Sacer* and, arguably as a result of this, many are critical of the hyperbole, lack of historical nuance and alleged pessimism of Agamben's political philosophy (see for instance Peter Fitzpatrick's 'Bare Sovereignty: *Homo Sacer* and the Insistence of Law', which argues that Agamben's own sweeping argument about the indistinction of fact and law in modernity is 'incompatible' (52) with his claims about the juridical status of the camp; see also Andrew Benjamin's 'Spacing as the Shared: Heraclitus, Pindar, Agamben', which critiques Agamben's philosophy for its 'generalising' (166) tendencies). More recent work has tended to rectify this by emphasising the continuity between Agamben's early works and the *Homo Sacer* series (see for instance the book-length studies *Giorgio Agamben: A Critical Introduction* by Leland de la Durantaye, *The Philosophy of Agamben* by Catherine Mills, *Giorgio Agamben* by Alex Murray, *Agamben and Theology* by Colby Dickinson, *The Literary Agamben* by William Watkin, and *Giorgio Agamben* by Thanos Zartaloudis). For an edited collection that takes a broader and thus generally more sympathetic view of Agamben's philosophy see *Giorgio Agamben: Sovereignty and Life* (ed. Matthew Calarco and Steven DeCaroli). A number of highly critical articles nevertheless turn up here, for instance Antonio Negri's 'Giorgio Agamben: The Discreet Taste of the Dialectic', which argues that Agamben's ontological approach to politics consigns him to a deterministic political philosophy based on 'an image of being that has been unable to become productive' (124); Dominick LaCapra's 'Approaching Limit Events', which critiques Agamben for falling into an 'apocalyptic' (151) discourse in which 'the *Muselmann* becomes a figure of sublimity and Auschwitz emerges as a transhistorical *leçon de philosophie*' (162); and Laclau's 'Bare Life or Social Indeterminacy?'. For a still more recent collection that explicitly seeks to redress these imbalances in the academic reception of Agamben's work, see *The Work of Giorgio Agamben: Law, Literature, and Life* (ed. Clemens, Heron and Murray); here, however, we find further accusations of pessimism (see 'The Role of the Shifter and the Problem of Reference', in which Justin Clemens appears to side with Alain Badiou as he declares Agamben a 'Franciscan of ontology' who glorifies an image of 'finitude at its limit' (57)). Despite recent advances, then, these issues of hyperbole, lack of nuance, and pessimism remain open ones in Agamben scholarship.

I give detailed responses to them in Chapter 1, but they are addressed implicitly throughout this book.

8. David Kishik makes a similar claim when he argues that the *Homo Sacer* series should be understood as a parable (see *The Power of Life*, 26–7). Whether this fascinating idea is right or not, I agree with the implication: the value of Agamben's work lies not only in its critical force but also – and perhaps more primarily – in its transformative potential.

9. In an interview Slavoj Žižek attacks Leftist theorists who 'adopt an attitude like Agamben's and simply wait for some magical intervention' ('Divine Violence and Liberated Territories'). While this may appear to be nothing more than a characteristically flippant off-the-cuff remark, it is nevertheless exemplary of this critique of Agamben's work (for a more sophisticated version of the argument, see Matthew Sharpe's 'Only Agamben Can Save Us?'). As I hope to show, it is based on a fundamentally flawed reading of what Agamben wants to achieve with his concept of the messianic. It is not that for Agamben the task is to prepare for an event that would somehow transform political life as we know it. Rather, the task is to own up to the fact that, to paraphrase a remark from Kafka to which Agamben repeatedly refers (*The Time That Remains*, 71; 'The Messiah and the Sovereign', 174; *Homo Sacer*, 57), the messianic event is that which comes by not coming, arriving when it is no longer needed. It is precisely not an exceptional intervention; rather what it reveals is that there will be no such intervention, and thus that political change depends entirely on us. In *Agamben and Theology*, Dickinson gives a very good account of Agamben's use of this loaded concept, showing how it differs from its employment in the 'jargon-filled discourse' surrounding it in recent continental theory (see 86–98).

10. Prozorov writes that 'Agamben paints a convincingly gloomy picture of the present state of things only to undertake a majestic reversal at the end, finding hope and conviction in the very despair that engulfs us' ('Why Giorgio Agamben is an Optimist', 1,057). As will become clear, part of what I want to challenge in this book is the ascription to Agamben of this quasi-Heideggerian concept of the messianic in which we must find our salvation in the (biopolitical) dangers of our time (such that, for instance, things are getting ontologically better whenever they are getting ontically worse). Noys has undertaken exemplary critiques of what he calls 'accelerationism' (see *The Persistence of the Negative*, 4–13; and 'Apocalypse, Tendency, Crisis'): the theoretical tradition asserting that 'the worse things get, the better the potential results' ('Apocalypse, Tendency, Crisis'). To borrow Noys's term, I want to show that it is a mistake to read Agamben as advocating any kind of biopolitical version of accelerationism. Instead, Agamben challenges the notion that we can only achieve salvation by passing through danger.

11. I develop this in more detail in Chapter 4.

12. In Chapter 5 I characterise this in terms of a 'redemption from salvation'.

13. Benjamin, 'On the Concept of History', 392 (translation modified).
14. Emerson, 'New England, Lecture III', 53. To quote at length:

> All around us, what powers are wrapped up under the coarse mattings of custom, and all wonder prevented. It is so wonderful to our neurologists that a man can see without his eyes, that it does not occur to them, that it is just as wonderful that he should see with them; and this is ever the difference between the wise and the unwise: the latter wonders at what is unusual, the wise man wonders at the usual.

15. See Durantaye, *Giorgio Agamben: A Critical Introduction*; Mills, *The Philosophy of Agamben*; and Murray, *Giorgio Agamben*.
16. Agamben, *State of Exception*, 64.
17. Hanssen, *Walter Benjamin's Other History*, 21.
18. Agamben, *The Coming Community*, 102.
19. Agamben, *The Time That Remains*, 55.
20. Ibid. 108.
21. Nancy, *The Sense of the World*, 29.
22. Heidegger, *Being and Time*, SZ 22; 20e (translation modified).
23. Wittgenstein, *Investigations*, §118; 41e.
24. See Aristotle, *Nicomachean Ethics*, Book X, Chapters VII and VIII; 343–51e.
25. Marx, *Theses on Feuerbach*, 99.
26. Lukács, 'Reification and the Consciousness of the Proletariat', 89.
27. Debord, *Society of the Spectacle*, 12.

1. The Question of Political Ontology

Those who talk about revolution and class struggle without referring explicitly to everyday life . . . have a corpse in their mouth.[1]

In his studies of the thought of Carl Schmitt, Heinrich Meier insists on a distinction he takes to be crucial for understanding the challenge posed by the jurist's 'lesson': the difference between political philosophy and political theology. If political philosophy is the study of the political good carried out 'entirely on the ground of human wisdom',[2] Meier argues, then political theology is the study of the same from the standpoint of a 'faith in revelation'.[3] In a trenchantly Straussian fashion, then, Meier understands the difference as far more than simply doctrinal, arguing instead that it 'concerns the foundation and assertion of an existential position'.[4] As he puts it: 'What could be less immaterial than the distinction between a thought that wants to move and conceive itself in the obedience of faith and one that is not bound by any authority and spares nothing from its questions?'[5]

In this chapter I want to show that a third term – political ontology – can be set against both these alternatives. We could give a preliminary definition of it as follows: the study of how our ontology – our conception of the world *as such* – conditions what we take to be the ontic possibilities for human collectives. This definition is not entirely inaccurate, but it will be immediately complicated by the fact that political philosophy makes ontological claims, and that these are sometimes claims about philosophy's relationship to ontology that upset the possibility of understanding that relation as unidirectional (such that the political ontologist could uproot the naive political philosopher by showing the contingency of his claims on an ontological picture he has failed to recognise as such). And indeed, such a definition will be complicated further still by Schmitt's own understanding of his political theological project, which he takes to involve a 'sociology of concepts'[6] grounded in the realisation that '[t]he metaphysical image that a definite epoch forges of the world has the same structure as what the world immediately understands to be appropriate as a form of its political organization'.[7] Political ontology, then, is already part of political philosophy (though it appears there with varying degrees of explicitness), and presupposed as part of the methodology of political theology, at least in its (arguably paradigmatic) Schmittian variant.

As such, I want to refine this definition by understanding political ontology in a way that is analogous to Meier's definition of political theology, as a form of thought that has its primary grounding not in disinterested contemplation from the standpoint of pure reason (Meier: 'Moral indignation is no affair of political philosophy. It constitutes no part of philosophy'[8]), but rather in confrontation with an existential problem. While for Meier's Schmitt this was the problem of how to live and think in obedience to God, the problem for political ontology is the ontological question itself. Political ontology is the study of the political stakes of the question of being. Thus the political ontologist agrees with the political theologian that thinking the political means responding to an irreducible exigency – that one thinks as situated in response to a certain moral or ethical demand – yet she takes this demand to consist not in divine revelation but rather in the fact that human beings are beings for which being is at issue. Indeed this represents a real incommensurability between political theology and political ontology, as political ontology has to work in light of a kind of atheism. This is because a proper confrontation with the ontological question requires we follow through on a certain experience of abandonment (both the abandonment of the human after the death of God and the ontological 'abandonment' of the existent by existence, what Jean-Luc Nancy will call the 'withdrawal of the cause in the thing' – I will return to this); political ontology cannot be an ontotheology. Or at least, this will be the case to the extent that the concept 'God' functions as a means of staving off the ontological question, to the extent that the existence of a creator could resolve that question (which may leave open the possibility of political ontology accommodating a different image of the divine).

This definition is significantly different from two recent characterisations of political ontology. In an ambivalent piece about the relationship between neo-left ontological thought and more traditional Marxist theory, Carsten Strathausen claims authors like Nancy, Agamben, Žižek and Laclau understand ontology as a 'de-essentialized discursive formation'.[9] According to Strathausen, post-Heideggerian political ontological thought insists on the *constructed* nature of any political ontology, and so wants to engage with material political structures by working to deconstruct and rework their ontological foundations. Immediately we can see the problem here: if Strathausen is correct in his reading, then the theorists he writes about would be in danger of working from an inflated conception of the relationship between thought and its objects, such that ontological speculation could somehow stand in for, or even become identifiable with, material political change. Oliver Marchart gives a more nuanced picture but still ends up understanding political ontological thought as stemming from a commitment to the radical contingency of political foundations, the fact that 'the political' as the ontological ground for ontic politics is in fact a groundless ground, or *Abgrund* in the terminology of the later Heidegger.[10] Neither of these pictures is entirely wrong, of course: one of the guiding claims of political ontology as I understand it is that the traditional distinction between thought and politics needs to be challenged; another is that a proper thought of the ontological difference will call all attempts at 'grounding' politics into question. But the task of political ontology is not just to insist on the contingency of ontological concepts, or to think new ones for the sake of opening up ontic political possibilities (as though by itself this would constitute anything more than melancholic and/or utopian speculation). It is to think the political through the exigency of the ontological question.

As will already be obvious, I take Heidegger's work to be crucial for political ontology (both in a positive sense as one of its enabling conditions, and in a negative sense as one of its key points of critique). Of particular importance for this project is his claim that metaphysics – his term for the trajectory of Western thought since Plato – cannot think the ontological question. Now this claim is developed and restated variously throughout Heidegger's *oeuvre*: it is present in the preface to *Being and Time*, where Heidegger famously claims our time is strangely unperplexed by its inability to understand the word 'being',[11] and continues right up to the last session of his final seminar at Zähringen in 1973, which culminates in a meditation on the difference between 'ordinary thinking and the unusual path of Parmenides' as manifested in verse one of fragment six, which Heidegger translates/paraphrases as 'being *is*'.[12] One of its clearest formulations, however, comes in the 'Letter on Humanism'. Here Heidegger claims that the defining characteristic of metaphysical thinking is that it 'does not think the difference' between being and beings; that metaphysics 'does not ask about the truth of Being itself'.[13] Indeed, not only has metaphysics failed to inquire into the truth of being itself, but 'the question is *inaccessible* to metaphysics as such'.[14] Metaphysical thinking simply cannot cope with the question of being; or, better, being is unable to *become a question* in metaphysical thought. Metaphysical thought is entirely unsurprised by being: it takes the fact that things exist for granted.

As Heidegger always insisted, metaphysical thought is perfectly equipped to inquire about beings. Depending on its founding concepts, it can think the causes of beings (Aristotle), the mathematical/geometrical structure of beings (Descartes), the conditions for our knowledge of beings (Kant), the phenomenological qualities of beings (Husserl), and so on. But the being of beings is presupposed by these modes of thought, and for an essential structural reason: these philosophies, arising as they do in the wake of the Platonic equation of being with the Idea (which Heidegger takes to have been decisive for the development of Western thought), are trapped in various versions of a representational paradigm.[15] In this paradigm, which obviously needs to be defined very broadly if it is to apply to thinkers as different as (say) Descartes and Aristotle, there is a model of truth at work in which it is a property of statements that correspond to (or correctly represent) how it is with the world. A statement, then, is a means of pointing out things about the world (including of course affective or mental states and other 'interior' events): in Aristotle's terms it is a 'saying something of something' (*legein ti kata tinos*); in Heidegger's it is a 'presentation and representation of the real and unreal'.[16] And the problem with representational models is that they cannot possibly 'point out' the fact that existence exists, because as Kant showed in his attack on the ontological proof of God, existence is not and cannot be a property of existence (it is not a 'real predicate'[17]). This is the root of Heidegger's history of being as metaphysics, under which the question of being cannot even pose itself as such. As Heidegger puts it in volume three of his *Nietzsche*, 'within metaphysics there is nothing to being as such'.[18] The history of being as metaphysics is a history of a blindness before the question of being, of representational models of truth repeatedly passing over its very status as a question.[19]

At this point, it should be clear that political ontology is (or is intended to be) post-metaphysical. This means that it will be concerned with thinking our political situation in terms of its metaphysical heritage, working from the premise that the blindness before the ontological question characteristic of metaphysics has real consequences for ontic politics. To engage in political ontology, then, means thinking from out of the idea that our conceptual systems have a deep and deeply problematic blind spot; that our representational models miss the fact of being because of a constitutive structural flaw. The claim, in other words, is that political thought has inherited the basic flaw of metaphysics, coming as it does from out of the very tradition that Heidegger worked to undermine.

Paradigmatic in this regard is the work of Agamben, which is impossible to understand except as a form of political ontology. For if we take Agamben to be a political philosopher (or a critical theorist) in anything like the traditional sense(s) then we are already at risk of misunderstanding the nature of the claims he makes. And indeed, this can help account for the ambivalent reception of his thought in English-speaking 'continental' philosophy. After all, if the political events since the beginning of the so-called 'war on terror' have made the investigations in *Homo Sacer* seem more urgent since its publication in 1995, it is arguable that they have also become more problematic and in many ways more opaque to us. The easiest criticism of Agamben's political writings is that they are marked by a deep haphazardness: important distinctions are blurred and concrete examples sublated into an essentialist, ahistorical argument that is potentially paralysing because it passes over the situational specificities that characterise real politics. My claim is that such criticisms depend in large part upon a category mistake; that Agamben's most important concepts will remain unintelligible to us until we understand their grounding in a political ontology that turns on an attempt to think the question of being.[20]

Let me explain this by turning first to the important concept of the inclusive exclusion, which Agamben invokes in order to map the paradox he finds at the heart of the Western *polis*. In this aporia, the natural life of human subjects is excluded from the city as something extraneous to political life, and yet constitutive of the city as that which must be presupposed for the construction of political life to be possible. Agamben traces this paradox as far back as the classical world, citing the Aristotelian distinction between *zoē*, as the simple fact of living common to gods, plants, animals and humans, and *bios*, or the qualified life that is the distinct property of human beings qua political creatures. He argues it 'would have made no sense'[21] in the classical world to speak of the *zoē politikē* of a citizenry, as politics was defined at the time in terms of an 'additional' (but extremely important) capacity of human existence, indeed as that which separates it from animal existence. *Zoē*, as the simple fact of living, was not considered a part of the Greek *polis*, which was concerned with the particularity of various ways of life and the relations among them. Crucial here is a movement of presupposition, in which the fact of living is presupposed by the *polis* as its unthinkable ground. For Agamben, this exclusion, in which the political subject is divided from its non-political natural life, represents the original political relation. He finds, however, that the exclusion can never quite reach completion, because it was always an 'implication ... of bare life in politically qualified life'.[22] He goes on:

> What remains to be interrogated in the Aristotelian definition is not merely – as has been assumed until now – the sense, the modes, and the possible articulations of the 'good life' as the telos of the political. We must instead ask why Western politics first constitutes itself through an exclusion (which is simultaneously an inclusion) of bare life. What is the relation between politics and life, if life presents itself as what is included by means of an exclusion?[23]

Agamben finds that the fact of living, as the unthought presupposition of the *polis*, is never successfully banished, and by the time of modernity reappears as an ambiguous political object. This can be framed in terms of the split exemplified in the title of the 1789 French Declaration of the Rights of Man and Citizen. Agamben makes very much of the equivocal use of two terms for what is supposed to be a single referent here, arguing that the introduction of the term 'man' shows what was really at stake in this founding document of political modernity: the return of natural life from the *polis* from which it was excluded and its subsequent inscription within it. This, for Agamben, represents the source of the nihilism characteristic of modernity, which he follows Foucault in defining as the period in which the life of the human being (and of human populations) takes on an unprecedented political significance.[24]

While Foucault's work plays an important role for Agamben here, this whole schema is deeply indebted to Heideggerian ontology. Consider the following from the closing pages of *Homo Sacer*, which I cite at length because it makes the extent of Agamben's debt so clear:

> In the syntagm 'bare life,' 'bare' corresponds to the Greek *haplōs*, the term by which first philosophy defines pure Being. The isolation of the sphere of pure Being, which constitutes the fundamental activity of Western metaphysics, is not without analogies with the isolation of bare life in the realm of Western politics. What constitutes man as a thinking animal has its exact counterpart in what constitutes him as a political animal. In the first case, the problem is to isolate pure Being (*on haplōs*) from the many meanings of the term 'Being' (which, according to Aristotle, 'is said in many ways'); in the second, what is at stake is the separation of bare life from the many forms of concrete life. Pure Being, bare life – what is contained in these two concepts, such that both the metaphysics and the politics of the West find their foundation and sense in them and in them alone? What is the link between the two constitutive processes by which metaphysics and politics seem, in isolating their proper element, simultaneously to run up against an unthinkable limit? For bare life is certainly as indeterminate and impenetrable as *haplōs* Being, and one could say that

reason cannot think bare life except as it thinks pure Being, in stupor and in astonishment.[25]

As this passage indicates, the basic Agambenian concept of bare life has to be understood as beginning from a transposition of Heidegger's ontological difference onto classical biological categories, where *zoē* (the fact of life) is mapped onto the fact of being *as such*, and *bios* (politically qualified life) onto the ontic level of particular beings. This allows Agamben to read the distinction between natural and political life in fundamental ontological terms, and sparks his move into the field of political ontology. As he puts it:

> [I]t may be that only if we are able to decipher the political meaning of pure Being will we be able to master the bare life that expresses our subjection to political power, just as it may be, inversely, that only if we understand the theoretical implications of bare life will we be able to solve the enigma of ontology.[26]

When Heidegger claims there is nothing to being *as such* within metaphysics, then, Agamben takes him one step further to claim that there is nothing to life *as such* within our politics. Like Heidegger, Agamben finds something like an ontological law here: that which is presupposed and passed over by a system of thought will return to that system as its unthinkable (such that any exclusion of being/life is always already an inclusion).

This explains some of the idiosyncrasies of the philosopher's style. It explains Agamben's switching of registers between concrete politics and ontology, and his tendency to finish his books with allusive gestures toward Heidegger and/or Benjamin, which may otherwise seem indicative of an inability on his part to properly cash out the real political claims of his texts, as an attempted evasion of the political quandaries into which he likes to write himself. If we read Agamben as a political ontologist, however, it will become clear that this is the natural register of his thought, the very place in which he does his thinking (and so an obvious place to return). The discussions of concrete politics, like the one that takes place in the first part of *State of Exception*,[27] will from here appear as secondary to his real aim, as functioning to illustrate an ontological point (Agamben is often read the other way around, as speciously invoking ontology as a way of bolstering his sweeping political claims). Finally, it will help explain the characteristically hyperbolic tone that marks his political writings. One could find many instances of hyperbole in Agamben, such as when he writes that '[a]ll societies and all cultures today (it does not matter whether they are democratic or totalitarian, conservative or progressive) have entered into a legitimation crisis in which law ... is in force as the pure "Nothing of Revelation"',[28] or when he pushes the argument of Benjamin's 'The Storyteller' until he arrives at the claim that experience has been destroyed in modernity.[29] Agamben's hyperbole, his tendency to pass over historical nuance ('*all* societies and *all* cultures today'), is the result of his ontological method; hyperbole, we might say, is simply what becomes of ontological thought when it bleeds into the ontic. Sociologically (that is *ontically*), Agamben's claims are exaggerations at best; ontologically however their status is yet to be properly grasped.[30] Any fair analysis of them will have to take place on their ontological terrain.

If we embark on such a resolutely ontological reading of Agamben, it will not only emerge that 'bare life' cannot function as a properly sociological category, but also that it could never be a concrete ontic potential for human beings. Instead, it is the unthought ground of the metaphysics underpinning our political systems, a presupposition that, after the failed attempt to exclude it in the classical world, has returned to haunt us in modernity. Bare life, in other words, is a metaphysical figure of (a failure of) thought, and not a category of ontic politics. This is to say that *no life is bare*: that (and indeed despite some of Agamben's own apparent suggestions to the contrary) no human form-of-life has ever been reduced to bare life. Bare life, like pure being, can never exist (has never existed). But this is not to say that it plays no role in ontic politics. On the contrary, this figure is a metaphysical condition of the possibility of those ontic spaces of domination that Agamben calls 'camps', whether they be death camps, concentration camps, refugee camps, refugee 'detention centres', Guantanamo Bay or whatever. Ontically, these spaces are all very different; however they are ruled by the same metaphysical logic. The conditions of the possibility of the inclusive exclusion of the bare life of human beings are the same as those that allow for the presupposition of pure being in metaphysics. Cancelling these metaphysical conditions, then, will require a politicised rethinking of the ontological category of pure being, and a properly *thinking* politics.

Of course, this reading of Agamben will produce its own set of problems, not the least of which is how to square it against the philosopher's own occasional tendency to invoke the category of bare life in such a way that it does in fact appear as a real ontic potential. The only strategy available is immanently critical, arguing that Agamben himself sometimes appears to make the category mistake that causes so many of his critics to miss the philosophical point. Exemplary in this regard is Agamben's *Remnants of Auschwitz*, in which the philosopher occasionally seems in danger of identifying the *Muselmann* (the 'drowned' of which Primo Levi wrote) with bare life, speaking for instance of 'the bare life to which human beings were reduced ...'.[31] The danger in this sort of talk, as Andrew Benjamin points out, is one of 'generalising',[32] such that an abstract philosophical figure comes to dominate our interpretation of the meaning of the violence and suffering of the camps. In his review of Agamben's text, Jay Bernstein makes a disturbing comparison between the 'aestheticization of horror'[33] presented in the 'atrocity photographs' of James Nachtwey and Agamben's book. He cites a review of Nachtwey's *Inferno*: '[Nachtwey] makes it far too possible for the information-deprived viewer to fall into an anguished yet impotent hopelessness: in the absence of knowledge, all starving people, all massacred people, all degraded, defeated, abject people begin to look sort of the same ...'[34] And could one not, as Bernstein implies, make exactly the same criticism of Agamben's own text, in which all the horrors of the camps are reduced to manifestations of the (in)human 'gorgon' that is bare life?[35] Is he not, then, in danger of collapsing the particularities of the testimonies of survivors into a monolithic narrative of an encounter with *nuda vita*? That there is an ethical danger here should be clear enough, but this is also another version of the political problem I invoked earlier, namely that Agamben's analysis may sublate the particularities and situational specificities that are the stuff of real politics. These are the two aspects of a problem that will emerge if we accept that the *Muselmann* and bare life are two names for the same referent.

Which is what a resolutely ontological reading of Agamben will foreclose. No life is bare in the ontic sense: rather, bare life is the figure of the return of a repressed metaphysical problem, a metaphysical image or even fantasy that haunts our politics. Nothing more, but nothing less either. Here it is worth citing Nancy: '[T]he concentration camp ... is in essence the will to destroy community. But even in the camp itself, undoubtedly, community never entirely ceases to resist this will. Community is, in a sense, resistance itself: namely, resistance to immanence.'[36] Here I would argue that Nancy's term 'immanence', which he uses to designate the metaphysical image that underlies the specific communal fantasy at work in totalitarian states, can be understood as another name for what Agamben calls 'bare life'. The concentration camp is a machine for its production, but because of the fantasmatic nature of the object in question, it is a machine that can never complete its task. Respecting this fact is not only to do justice to the victims, but carries a further recognition of the extremity of the violence: the very impossibility of creating bare life, one could say, is at the heart of the real insanity of the camp, such that the impossibility of its success is also what drives and exacerbates the whole process. The claim 'no life is bare' does not imply a commitment to the idea that there is something irreducibly human or moral that remains alive in us even in the most extreme circumstances. The claim does not say humanity is indestructible; it says there is something inhuman in it that remains. It is not identity, which can be destroyed, but the impersonal core of singularity. Someone in the late stages of Alzheimer's, for instance, can lose his very subjectivity, but not his idiosyncrasy: he may have forgotten his position in society, his name and the name of his wife, but he remains (painfully) himself; he may lose his ability to speak, but he retains something of his characteristic manner, the little gestures that make him the singular being he is. Desubjectification happens *to* someone. The unbinding of the human, the loss of identity and of linguistic capacities, makes it infantile and undignified, but it does not reduce it to the pure subsistence of naked life. That is part of what is terrible about it. 'Man is the indestructible that can be destroyed.'[37]

It is instructive to compare Agamben with Foucault here, an ostensibly crucial influence on *Homo Sacer*. The first thing to ask is this: where could a concept like 'bare life' possibly fit within Foucault's discourse? The answer, of course, is nowhere: the concept is too unwieldy, too abstract, too *metaphysical* to work in a properly Foucauldian register. If Agamben can be understood as continuing Foucault's project in *Homo Sacer* (bearing in mind that the basic problem of the text turns up in Agamben as early as *Language and Death*, which is framed in terms of the conflict between 'animal voice' and 'human language'[38] and in which Foucault is never even mentioned), then it is only via the importation of a quasi-Heideggerian concept that irrevocably changes the rules and outcomes of the game. Indeed it is telling that in 'What is a Paradigm?' – a characteristically fragmentary recent piece in which Agamben shows how important the Foucauldian concept of the paradigm (which Agamben takes as 'the most characteristic gesture of Foucault's method'[39]) has been for his own work – he does not list bare life as an example of a paradigm. While paradigms like the *homo sacer*, the *Muselmann* and the state of exception refer to real historical objects, and are used by Agamben in order to 'make intelligible a series of phenomena whose kinship had eluded or could elude the historian's gaze',[40] bare life is something very different. It is precisely *not* a paradigm: rather, it is the metaphysical problem that prompts the construction of Agamben's paradigms, which are the exemplary ontic figures that bring it to light. A rough but useful way of framing the difference between Agamben and Foucault would be to say that while the latter is concerned with the ontic biopolitical field, and the myriad concrete practical problems that arise in it, Agamben is more primarily concerned with the historically contingent quasi-transcendental conditions[41] of the biopolitical *as such*. This is why Foucault's work is so compelling in its specificity, yet so opaque when it comes to questions of social transformation; this is why Agamben's work is so compelling in its radical questioning of the very grounds of the political as we know it, yet so sweeping in its claims. It is only by recognising this difference between the ontic and ontological levels of Agamben's discourse that we can make sense of – or extract any real philosophical or political value from – his philosophy.

So what value *can* we extract from Agamben on this reading of his work? What *political* value is there in ontology and metaphysical critique? The obvious danger here is that political ontology will end up qualifying as neither a real politics (because it is not primarily concerned with ontic political matters) nor a valid ontology (because it imports political 'values' into what is meant to be disinterested philosophical speculation – think of how strange, even preposterous, the very idea of 'political ontology' would sound to contemporary metaphysicians working in the analytic tradition). In relation to the first worry (I will return to the second in the conclusion to this chapter), in which we face the problem of whether extracting Agamben's claims about bare life from a sociological register will deprive them of whatever critical theoretical relevance and concrete political purchase they may have had, I would like to turn to his essay 'Form-of-Life'. Here Agamben attempts to think the conditions of a life that would escape the metaphysical image of bare life. The concept form-of-life, which is actually a strategic ontological intervention, designates a life that can never be separated from its form, a life that exists not as faceless bare life but rather as the intelligible singularity that makes each of us ourselves. The individual, on this account, is not poised above (and therefore reducible to) the abyssal 'gorgon' of bare life, but is rather a contingent structure overlayed upon a kind of excess. The face of the individual is composed of properties (brown eyes, gold hair, large mouth, full lips, etc.), and can be constructed with an identikit in a police station. The face of form-of-life, on the other hand, is the face that the state can't see (because it can't represent it): it effects the dissolution of the face of the individual and the temporary shattering of its representational logic (it is the face of someone making a gesture, of someone laughing or of someone at the point of orgasm; it is what the painter Francis Bacon brought out of his figures). The concept form-of-life designates the impersonal (because it is pre-individual) and yet most intimate part of each of us (it is that which surprises us when we surprise ourselves). If we follow Agamben in his claim that 'political power as we know it always founds itself – in the last instance – on the separation of a sphere of naked life from the context of forms of life',[42] then the intended political import of this concept should be obvious: form-of-life is meant to function as a spanner in the works of the modern political machine, rendering inoperative every attempt to divide the human from its being. Form-of-life is unrepresentable (for it disrupts predicative logic) and yet intelligible (for we can get to know it, recognise it, and fall in love with it); it is a figure of pure equality (for it is impossible to judge or place in any hierarchy) that does not sublate difference (for it is singular, absolutely unrepeatable). The concept form-of-life, then, is designed to disrupt the metaphysical logic of presupposition, in which being *as such* can only appear as a brute, 'bare' presence. Form-of-life thus functions as a tool for bringing the intelligibility of pure being to light, for redeeming the object banished in the inclusive exclusion from the nothingness to which it was consigned. In this sense, form-of-life is an exemplary Agambenian concept, operating as it does in two registers at the same time, functioning to disrupt both the inclusive exclusion of bare life in metaphysical politics and the unthinkability of being *as such* within metaphysics. Agamben's wager, and the wager of political ontology, is that these two operations are inseparable (which is not to say they are identical).

This can help absolve Agamben from the repeated charges of extreme political pessimism that have marked his work. First of all, it is worth recognising that Agamben does not consider himself to be pessimistic at all, saying in an interview that 'I don't see myself as pessimistic ... I am sure you are more pessimistic than I am.'[43] We may wonder if this statement was made in good faith, coming as it does from a philosopher who gained international notoriety with his assertion that the camp is the *nomos* of the modern.[44] Here it is worth comparing Agamben to Adorno, who presents an apparently similar set of claims regarding the historical trajectory of modernity, and the potential for absolute domination that it contains (a potential unleashed in the twentieth-century totalitarian states). Adorno is infamous for his political pessimism, which reaches an almost lyrical height in his late book *Minima Moralia*. To pick out a striking passage:

> The admonitions to be happy, voiced in concert by the scientifically hedonist sanatorium-director and the highly-strung propaganda chiefs of the entertainment industry, have about them the fury of the father berating his children for not rushing joyously downstairs when he comes home irritable from his office. It is part of the mechanism of domination to forbid

recognition of the suffering it produces, and there is a straight line of development between the gospel of happiness and the concentration camps of extermination so far off in Poland that each of our countrymen can convince himself that he cannot hear the screams of pain. That is the model of an unhampered capacity for happiness.[45]

What strikes the reader of Adorno is a sense of the philosopher's own increasing horror at the political situation of modernity: he seems to grow ever more appalled at, but also ever more convinced of the inexorability of, the dialectical movement of his thesis. It is difficult to imagine Adorno supporting, as Agamben does, Marx's 1843 statement that the 'desperate situation' of the present 'fills me with hope'.[46] I would argue that the key to accounting for this difference is methodological: Adorno remains partially wedded to a quasi-Marxist, quasi-Weberian social scientific approach, while Agamben, with his Heideggerian/Foucauldian genealogy, does not. While Agamben ends up with a critique of modernity that is perhaps as trenchant as Adorno's, he avoids the despair with which the latter flirts because his critique aims not primarily at the structure of rationality underpinning its institutions but rather at its metaphysical basis; perhaps surprisingly, the ontologicality of Agamben's philosophy makes him more receptive to the possibility of radical change. Agamben's invocation of the concept form-of-life, for instance, *would not even be intelligible* if the figure of bare life is taken to be necessary. Part of the value of an ontological approach, then, is that it can show up the radical contingency of ontic political structures, and in doing so help illuminate the ontological figures that will play a role in a thinking politics.

Here I would like to turn to another key Agambenian concept: the exception. If it is right to say that bare life is the metaphysical figure at work in the camp, then properly thinking it will require us to understand the exception, which is the metaphysical ground of the specific legal structure of the camp (as the ontic site in which 'the exception starts to become the rule'[47]). Schmitt's equation of the exception in politics with the miracle in theology makes this clear: he writes that 'the exception in jurisprudence is analogous to the miracle in theology';[48] for him, the sovereign capacity to decide on the state of exception, which he takes to be constitutive of the normal functioning of the legal order, is the 'zenith' of the sovereign's power, who acts as 'God's highest representative on earth'.[49] As Miguel Vatter puts it: 'Schmitt shows that the analogy must be taken literally: the state of exception is a state in which miracles happen, and sovereignty belongs to the one who decides on the state of exception, that is, who decides on what counts as a miracle.'[50] Important for us here is the metaphysical status of the miracle which, following Hobbes and Spinoza, Schmitt understands as an event that contravenes the laws of nature (taking the falling away of the belief in miracles characteristic of Enlightenment rationalism as paving the way for the kind of political nihilism – liberalism – that he abhorred). Schmitt, who insisted that liberalism must face up to the problem of sovereignty if it is to resolve its political dilemmas, took the metaphysics of the miracle to have a real political significance. In these respects, he is quite close to political ontology as I am defining it. But where Schmitt critiqued liberalism for its failure or indeed constitutive inability to recognise the metaphysically necessary status of the miracle/exception, political ontology works in the opposite direction.

As Nancy (who could be seen as the other major contemporary philosopher working in the political ontological field I am working to clarify) shows in *The Experience of Freedom*, a proper following through on the ontological question results in a problematisation of the very idea of metaphysical necessity. 'That there is existence . . .' as Nancy writes, 'can only be given, freely given . . .'[51] This is to say that the very fact of existence, which is unrepresentable and therefore properly *unknowable* (at least if knowledge is taken to consist of sets of justified true beliefs),[52] comes to surprise us in and as a kind of groundlessness. The ontological question uproots all foundationalisms, precisely insofar as it doesn't (could never) lead to an answer. It is the very gratuity of existence that makes it surprising, the fact that being emerges as *unnecessary*. This is what Nancy means when he refers to a *'surprising generosity of being'*.[53] For Nancy, the 'fact of freedom' is nothing other than the fact of being itself, the very 'freedom of being'[54] that is being *as such*. When Nancy writes that '[t]*he fact of freedom is this de-liverance of existence from every law and from itself as law . . .*'[55] and describes freedom as 'the withdrawal of the cause in the thing',[56] then, we need to understand this in all its ontological radicalism: it is a claim about causality which, though left untouched at the ontic level (the level of billiard balls), can no longer be understood as ontologically necessary.[57] A proper following through on the ontological question as has become possible since Heidegger shows that there is no *reason* for being: no causal principle underlying the fact of the existence of things, which instead emerges as a pure gratuity (it is worth thinking here of the project of theoretical physics: if a 'theory of everything' is one day established, such a theory would nevertheless contain an explanatory gap – knowing exactly *how* the universe emerged does not mean knowing the reason for the fact *that* it emerged). Against Schmitt, then, the miracle is not a name for an exceptional event that contravenes the laws of nature, but rather a name for the very fact of being as that which is irreducible to any causal law. We must in other words *generalise* the Schmittian position on miracles, taking the very existing of the world to be miraculous, depending as it does on no law, no foundation.

The political ontological stakes of this have their beginning in the fact that the *leaving open* of the ontological question, our allowing it to emerge as a question (which is the key condition for ontological thinking), would mean owning up to the absolute gratuity of the world. The exception, then, represents the metaphysical residue of an inability or refusal to accept this; it emerges out of a failure to acknowledge the real exceptionality of existence *as such*.[58] The camp, as the ontic site in which the metaphysical figure of bare life is exposed through the fantasy of exceptionality, also has certain of its conditions of possibility in this failure of thought. As with bare life, the exception represents the return of the unthought presupposition of being; as with bare life, thinking beyond it will require an ontological shift whereby its metaphysical conditions are cancelled. For if the ontological question is properly confronted – if, that is, we are able to own up to the ungrounding force of it – then the miraculous will be simultaneously neutralised and generalised such that *the ordinary is acknowledged as exceptional*. This explains Agamben's references to the Benjaminian idea of a *real* state of exception that could be set against the (presumably somehow fictitious, or perhaps fantasmatic) states of exception in which we live.[59] Political ontology shows that the real state of exception would be a state in which being *as such* is collectively lived as exceptional, which is logically identical to there being no exceptions (if being *as such* is exceptional, then nothing *in particular* is). Here we see how political ontology will require us to turn not to theorising the exceptional event à la Badiou, but rather to the ordinary and the everyday, and in particular toward an idea of the ordinary as a potential political *achievement*.[60] This is to place political ontology in the tradition of the politicised aesthetics of the twentieth century's avant-gardes, with their various programmes for overcoming the distinction between art and everyday life.[61] To achieve the ordinary in this way (which would be extraordinary) would mean reclaiming the very fact of the world from the metaphysical logic that presupposes and excludes it, allowing it to become something more than a nothingness or banality. Part of my claim, in other words, is that there is a certain thought of the good available in political ontology. It is the kind of good that Nancy identifies when, in the context of an argument about the necessary relativity of all values, he writes that 'it is existence itself which is without price'.[62]

In a critique of Agamben that would be devastating if it didn't make the category mistake I am trying to identify, Andrew Norris writes the following:

> If the Bush-Cheney administration is simply providing the sovereign decisions that are metaphysically necessary to maintain public order in the United States, one cannot fault it for acting tyrannically. Conversely, if it is indeed acting tyrannically, this is something that requires not metaphysical analysis and political theology, but practical, political resistance and institutional change.[63]

A political ontological approach, which undermines the very idea of 'metaphysical necessity', will dissolve the terms of this dilemma. For if bare life and the exception are not metaphysically necessary, then we should respond to this dilemma with a *both/and* rather than an *either/or*. In other words: Guantanamo Bay is metaphysically contingent, and that is part of why it is tyrannical (it is not only a political, juridical and ethical monstrosity; it is also exemplary of a violent metaphysical logic). As such we can agree with Schmitt when he writes that 'metaphysics is the most intensive and clearest expression of an epoch'; that monarchy was 'self-evident' as a form of political organisation in the seventeenth century because it was 'in accord with the structure of metaphysical concepts' in play at the time.[64] The mistake, however, would lie in underestimating the complexity of the relationship at work here, refusing to recognise the real intertwining of politics and ontology that it represents. Political ontology does not mistake theory for practice, falling into a kind of magical thinking where the former is somehow taken to have the capacity to change the world; rather it insists on the mutually determining relation between ontology and politics, on the claim that truly radical change in one area means change in the other. The practice of thought and the critique of metaphysics have political stakes, just as properly revolutionary political action is concerned not only with ontic political change, but also with challenging the very figure of the world as we know it.

'Communism is for us not a *state of affairs* which is to be established, an *ideal* to which reality [will] have to adjust itself. We call communism the *real* movement which abolishes the present state of things.'[65] Political ontology does not hold up another world as an ideal to which the present one should be made to conform; instead it demands the abolition of the present metaphysical scheme of things, in which the natural sweetness of life, the sharing of the gratuity of the world, are voided. A political movement cognisant of this would be one that insists on – one that demonstrates in practice – the truth of the claims that *no life is bare* and *the ordinary is exceptional*. These are ontological propositions, but they are also ethical propositions; they make ontological claims, but they also make a demand on us. Gershom Scholem writes that '[m]etaphysics is a legitimate theory in the subjunctive form. This is the best definition I have found so far; it says everything.'[66] Though Scholem uses the term 'metaphysics' here, exchanging it for 'political ontology' will see his point sit perfectly with this project. Political ontology is a mode of thought in which the distinction between fact and value collapses, such that what is shown to be valuable is the *fact* of existence itself. As such, a politics in-keeping with political ontology would be a *subjunctive* politics,[67] a politics informed by an exigency. As Nancy puts it:

> [T]his means to conduct this struggle precisely in the name of the fact that this *world* is coming out of nothing, that there is nothing before it and that it is without models, without principle and without given end, and that it is precisely *what* forms the justice and the meaning of a world.[68]

Such a struggle would not be carried out in the name of another world, but in the name of this one. The 'beautiful day' of life is mundane and held in common.

NOTES

1. Vaneigem, *The Revolution of Everyday Life*, 26 (translation slightly modified).
2. Meier, *The Lesson of Carl Schmitt*, xv.
3. Ibid. xiii.
4. Ibid. xiii.
5. Ibid. xv.
6. Schmitt, *Political Theology*, 44.
7. Ibid. 46.
8. Meier, *The Lesson of Carl Schmitt*, 1.
9. Strathausen, 'A Critique of Neo-Left Political Ontology'.
10. See Marchart, *Post-Foundational Political Thought*, 11–34. Jean-Philippe Deranty makes a similar argument regarding Jacques Rancière's philosophy ('Rancière and Contemporary Political Ontology').
11. Heidegger, *Being and Time*, SZ 1; 1e.
12. Heidegger, 'Seminar in Zähringen 1973', 79.
13. Heidegger, 'Letter on Humanism', 226.
14. Ibid. 227 (my emphasis).
15. While the category of *Vorstellung* is usually associated with Heidegger's critique of modernity as the age of *Gestell* and the world picture, he nevertheless finds its roots in Platonism. As Veronique Foti puts it:

> Although Heidegger considers representation and the representative world picture to be proper to modernity and to the history of metaphysics, Plato's understanding of the being of beings as *eidos*, as their

quasi-visible aspect or image, constitutes for him, as Derrida emphasizes, the mediation and hidden presupposition of the emergence of representation. ('Representation and the Image', 67)

16. Heidegger, 'Language', 192.
17. Kant writes: '"*Being*" is obviously not a real predicate; that is, it is not a concept of something which could be added to the concept of a thing' (*Critique of Pure Reason*, A598; 504e).
18. Heidegger, *Nietzsche*, 202.
19. Heidegger writes:

    Metaphysics thinks beings as beings. Wherever the question is asked what beings are, beings as such are in sight. Metaphysical representation owes this sight to the light of Being. The light itself, i.e., that which such thinking experiences as light, no longer comes within the range of metaphysical thinking; for metaphysics always represents beings only as beings. Within this perspective, metaphysical thinking does, of course, inquire about the being that is the source and originator of this light. But the light itself is considered sufficiently illuminated through its granting the transparency for every perspective on beings. ('Introduction to *What is Metaphysics*', 277)

20. This is to say that I want to resist any attempt to separate 'the metaphysical and the political Agambens' (Watkin, *The Literary Agamben*, 2).
21. Agamben, *Homo Sacer*, I.
22. Ibid. 7.
23. Ibid. 7.
24. Foucault writes: 'But what might be called a society's "threshold of modernity" has been reached when the life of the species is wagered on its own political strategies' (*The History of Sexuality*, 143).
25. Agamben, *Homo Sacer*, 182.
26. Ibid. 182.
27. See Agamben, *State of Exception*, 1–31.
28. Agamben, *Homo Sacer*, 35.
29. Agamben writes:

    Today, however, we know that the destruction of experience no longer necessitates a catastrophe, and that humdrum daily life in any city will suffice. For modern man's average day contains virtually nothing that can be translated into experience. (*Infancy and History*, 13–14)

30. This can explain some of the impatience – and, indeed, genuine bewilderment – with which Laclau treats the *Homo Sacer* project in his short, dismissive essay 'Bare Life or Social Indeterminacy?', where the social theorist claims Agamben's method 'is not sensitive enough to structural diversity' (12). As I hope is becoming clear, I want to argue that this criticism is not wrong as much as it is beside the point.
31. Agamben, *Remnants of Auschwitz*, 69.

32. Benjamin, 'Spacing as the Shared', 166.
33. Bernstein, 'Bare Life, Bearing Witness', 11.
34. Ibid. 13.
35. Agamben, *Remnants of Auschwitz*, 52–4.
36. Nancy, 'The Inoperative Community', 35.
37. Blanchot, *The Infinite Conversation*, 135. Agamben puts it similarly: '*The human being is the one who can survive the human being*' (*Remnants of Auschwitz*, 133).
38. Agamben, *Language and Death*, 44.
39. Agamben, 'What is a Paradigm?', 17.
40. Ibid. 31.
41. I give an account of historically contingent quasi-transcendental conditions in the next chapter.
42. Agamben, 'Form-of-Life', 4.
43. Agamben, 'I am sure you are more pessimistic than I am', 124.
44. Agamben, *Homo Sacer*, 166–80.
45. Adorno, *Minima Moralia*, 63.
46. Marx, quoted in Agamben, 'I am sure you are more pessimistic than I am', 124.
47. Agamben, *Homo Sacer*, 38.
48. Schmitt, *Political Theology*, 36.
49. Schmitt, *The Leviathan in the State Theory of Thomas Hobbes*, 55.
50. Vatter, 'Strauss and Schmitt as Readers of Hobbes and Spinoza', 185.
51. Nancy, *The Experience of Freedom*, 53.
52. I deal with this idea more systematically in the next chapter.
53. Nancy, *The Experience of Freedom*, 120.
54. Ibid. 13.
55. Ibid. 30.
56. Ibid. 101.
57. As Oliver Marchart shows (see *Post-Foundational Political Thought*, 15–18), this kind of thinking is *both* historical and properly ontological: it is based on a real ontological claim, and as such should apply to any epoch of being, but is also cognisant of the fact that the possibility of a proper confrontation with it has only opened up because of particular historical (that is, ontic) forces.
58. Sergei Prozorov writes:

   One may ... reverse the commonsensical image of a stable order, traversing history in its empty sameness, only being punctured momentarily by acts of exception, and instead conceive of order itself as a momentary stabilization of generalized exceptionality of existence: every form of order is the veil that conceals precisely that there is nothing behind it to conceal, that it enfolds the void. ('X/Xs', 98)

59. As Durantaye shows, the basic task of Agamben's political philosophy is to establish a 'distinction between [the] state of exception ravaging our

political landscape and "a *real* state of exception" that would spell its end' (*Giorgio Agamben*, 351). To quote him at length:

> The question that Agamben asks then endeavors to answer is the question that every one of the theses' interpreters has endeavored to answer: What did Benjamin mean by calling for a '*real* state of exception' (in an earlier version of the theses Benjamin himself underlined the word *real* [*wirklichen*])? It is difficult to imagine that Benjamin is welcoming here a state of legal exception or emergency like the one that, at the time of his writing, had already reigned in the country of his birth for seven years. His use of the simple adjective *real* implies, however, that a clear distinction is to be made, and that the state of exception in place – which threatened to become the rule – was in one manner or another a *fictive* one. It was of course not fictive in the sense of imaginary – that state of exception was real enough – but its recourse to law and justice, its all-encompassing suspension of individual rights and incorporation of the personal sphere of the state's citizens, seemed to be based on a juridical *fiction* that was at the same time a fiction of justice. Benjamin's intention then appears to have been to stress the falseness of that fiction through the idea of a 'real' state of exception that would give the lie to the one that, for him, had become the rule ... How this '*real* state of exception' is to be distinguished from a 'state of exception' increasingly in effect is a dilemma that no commentator has yet succeeded in solving ... (343–4)

60. As Stanley Rosen writes in *The Elusiveness of the Ordinary*, though with a very different intent: 'The ordinary is something we pursue' (2). Or in Simon Critchley's words, 'the ordinary is an achievement, the goal of a quest ...' (*Very Little ... Almost Nothing*, xxiv).
61. Watkin speaks of a 'devastation of the distanciation between art and life imposed by the presence of the spectator ...' (*The Literary Agamben*, 103). I turn to the concept of spectacle in the context of the relation between the ordinary and the exceptional in the final chapter.
62. Nancy, 'The Insufficiency of Values and the Necessity of Sense', 439.
63. Norris, 'Sovereignty, Exception, and Norm', 46.
64. Schmitt, *Political Theology*, 46.
65. Marx, *The German Ideology*, 56–7.
66. Scholem, quoted in Jacobson, *Metaphysics of the Profane*, 5.
67. I intend this not in opposition but as a potential supplement to Peter Hallward's 'prescriptive' politics (see 'A Politics of Prescription').
68. Nancy, *The Creation of the World*, 54–5.

2. The Poetic Experience of the World

> From this the poems springs: that we live in a place
> That is not our own and, much more, not ourselves
> And hard it is in spite of blazoned days.[1]

In the preface to *Infancy and History*, Agamben writes that the question 'which defines the *motivum*' of his thought – the single problem he has pursued in all his works, both written and unwritten – is the following: '[W]hat is the meaning of "there is language"; what is the meaning of "I speak"?'[2] While the philosophy of language is a significant sub-field in contemporary philosophy, Agamben's way of posing his question shows how far his concerns are from those of most professional philosophers, including not only analytic but also many 'continental' thinkers. His question is not about the nature of meaning, or problems of truth and reference; nor is it necessarily about hermeneutics, semiotics, *différance* or discourse ethics. It is about the fact that language exists: the fact that one speaks and writes at all. If this strikes as a strange point of departure for an entire philosophy, it is probably because it seems relatively unremarkable – after all, we presuppose it as soon as we say 'philosophy of language', as soon as we say we are interested in language as a philosophical problem (indeed, we presuppose it as soon as we say anything). Surely the truly interesting philosophical questions have to do with how language works, with how meaning and communication are possible. Or, if that seems too academic, perhaps they have to do with the ethics and/or politics of language use, with the role of language in the constitution of the public sphere, or how different ways of speaking and writing can be used for the political purposes of exclusion and/or hegemonic struggle, and so on. Why get stuck on the apparently trivial fact that language *exists*?

Part of Agamben's interest in this question stems precisely from this apparent unremarkableness: for him, the fact that we do not consider the existence of language as a philosophical problem is itself part of what makes it philosophically problematic. He claims our typical relationship to the fact of language's existence in philosophy is one of presupposition: the fact is simply passed over as we move onto problems that seem more pressing or concrete. But again, this presuppositional character of language is part of what, for him, makes the problem essential. As he writes, 'human beings can reveal beings through language but cannot reveal language itself';[3] language is thus 'the absolute presupposition'.[4] After all, what am I actually saying when I say 'language exists'? What has been conveyed that hasn't already been presented by the fact of my speaking in the first place?

This is not to say, however, that Agamben consigns the fact that language exists to the ineffable or the unsayable. Instead, his strategy revolves around attempting to bring this fact to language – but to do so in a way that recognises its paradoxical, aporetic character. His philosophical method, as Daniel Heller-Roazen remarks, is close to the one Paul Celan set himself in poetry: '[T]o conceive of the event of language in the form not of its presupposition but its *exposition* . . .' such that the 'taking place of language . . . emerges . . . as a dimension immanent in every utterance'.[5] In this chapter, I go to Heidegger – whose own relationship to Celan and his poetry was both fascinating and extremely problematic – in an attempt at articulating the philosophical basis for this interest in the fact of language. As I work to show, it is an inquiry made possible by Heidegger's philosophical obsession with unearthing the question of being. For, in a phrase from Wittgenstein that Agamben evokes in *Infancy and History*[6] (and to which I will return): '[T]he right expression in language for the miracle of the existence of the world, though it is not any proposition *in* language, is the existence of language itself.'[7] In the early Heidegger's hermeneutic philosophy, as well as (and especially) in his late works on poetry, we find a way of understanding the philosophical obsession with the sheer fact of language.

There are three concepts of language in Heidegger. The first one – the designative concept of language – is the one whose predominance Heidegger challenged all his life. The second – what Cristina Lafont calls the world-disclosing view[8] – is the conceptualisation of language that played a key role in the hermeneutic, quasi-transcendental philosophy set up in *Being and Time*. The third, poetic concept is importantly different from both. In the experience with poetic language there is a temporary suspension of Dasein's absorption in world (understood as a historically conditioned horizon of understanding). As such, the phenomenology of poetic experience has the potential to help absolve Heidegger's philosophy of the charge of linguistic idealism (and *ipso facto* of the charges of relativism and radical incommensurabilism). This conclusion is especially interesting because the Heidegger of the late works is often read as a fetishist of language, such that any idea of the objective existence of the material world disappears behind a cloud of pseudo-poetic obscurantism (indeed Lafont's position is that it is the nascent idealism of the early works that eventually led Heidegger to linguistic dead-ends in the late texts on language). I want to show that things are less obvious than this, and the poetic experience that so obsessed the late Heidegger is best understood as an experience of the emergence of something that lies on the boundary of the linguistic/equipmental world of Dasein. Perhaps surprisingly, then, the late Heidegger's philosophy of poetry consists less in the 'reification of language'[9] than in an attempt to show how a certain experience with it can lead the human to the material edge of its linguistic encasement: the very fact of the world as that which can never form part of it.

First we need to consider the understanding of language that Heidegger worked against throughout his life. The late essay 'Language' gives perhaps his single clearest formulation of this 'current view',[10] which Heidegger says is predicated upon three core presuppositions. The first is the idea that 'speaking is expression'.[11] This is the notion that language is the means by which a subject can express mental states to other subjects. It is the ideal of intersubjective communication: I have something I want to convey, so I use language to convey this something to another, listening subject. Heidegger's point is that this presupposition itself relies upon many other presuppositions characteristic of the philosophy of consciousness (and its separation between subject and object), including the notion of a division between inside and outside, or between the interiority and exteriority of the subject. The second presupposition is that 'speech is regarded as an activity of man'.[12] A useful way of understanding this claim is to insert something like 'just another' into it: this idea is founded on an understanding of speech as *just another* activity of man, like walking, eating or picking up a pen. Such an understanding does not ascribe to language the essential import for human experience that Heidegger believes it possesses. We should also approach this claim in terms of its instrumentalism. Speaking, according to this understanding, is a thing one does, where the word 'does' is understood as an action one carries out as a means for bringing about a certain end: 'pass me the milk', 'open the door', 'fill out these forms'. Within this understanding, language is tied to will: it is something the subject uses in order to bring about certain effects in the world. The third presupposition, 'that human expression is always a presentation and representation of the real and unreal',[13] places language within the sphere of propositional truth (even commands or requests can be understood according to this paradigm as propositional: '*I want you to* pass me the milk', '. . . open the door', '. . . fill out these forms'). For reasons that will become clear, this presupposition is perhaps most problematic for Heidegger.

It is worth noting that Heidegger's critique of the 'current view' of language is a very broad one, and cannot be reduced to a specific attack on (say) referentialist, verificationist or truth-conditional theories. Heidegger's critique is instead aimed at what he takes to be the basic image of language that permeates modern philosophy. It is an attack on what one might call a 'cat is on the mat' understanding of language, in which it is assumed from the outset that language is a tool for the transmission of information. Heidegger's critique is both radical and very general, and rests on the quite counterintuitive idea that language is not primarily a means of conveying how it is with one, or how it is with the world, that language is not primarily something human beings use to communicate. Of course, this isn't to say that Heidegger fails to recognise the obvious fact that we can and indeed often do use language to communicate: he simply claims that this instrumental, communicative function of language is derivative of its more fundamental (or 'primordial') function.[14] In this chapter, I will follow Cristina Lafont in referring to the concept that Heidegger attacks as the 'designative' view of language, and his first alternative as the 'disclosive' view of language.[15]

Lafont identifies the latter idea as one of the conceptual bedrocks of *Being and Time*, claiming that the philosophical grounding for the late Heidegger's elevation of language into an object of central concern was already present in nascent form in *Being and Time*; that 'the basic premises of Heidegger's view of language . . . are already anchored' in that text's 'hermeneutic transformation of philosophy . . .'.[16] Lafont's Heidegger is a transcendental thinker who works as a strange sort of successor to Kant, inheriting and radicalising the idea that experience is conditioned by factors that are not themselves experienced. One of the basic claims of the early Heidegger is that there is no apprehension of beings without a pre-existing system of understanding. This is Heidegger giving a transcendental twist to the intentionality thesis of Brentano, who famously claimed that consciousness is always *consciousness of* something (a claim that was, of course, fundamental for Husserl): Heidegger's argument is that phenomena do not first appear as simple sense objects for the perception and/or interpretation of the human subject, but that the very condition of the possibility of their appearance is that they are always apprehended *as* something. He rejects the picture of the world as a container of physical objects available for the perception of human subjects, showing instead how every act of perception is always already predicated on a pre-existing structure of understanding (Heidegger: '"Initially" we never hear noises or complexes of sound, but the creaking wagon, the motorcycle ... It requires a very artificial and complicated attitude in order to "hear" a "pure noise"'[17]). Heidegger's inheritance from Kant, then, is what we might call the constitutivity thesis: the claim that there are deep structures forming the conditions of the appearance of phenomena that on a superficial ('pre-critical' or 'dogmatic' in Kantian terms; 'metaphysical' in the terms that Heidegger will develop after *Being and Time*) glance appear to be 'objectively' given for our perceiving.

Yet there is a caveat: where Kant was concerned with thinking the conditions of the possibility of knowledge, the Heidegger of *Being and Time* is primarily concerned with thinking the conditions of the possibility of meaning. So we have a transcendental philosophy that is also hermeneutic in its basic orientation. What allows Heidegger to make this hermeneutic turn within a broadly transcendental framework? Lafont is clear on this point: '[I]n order to bring about a hermeneutic transformation of philosophy, Heidegger substitutes the *ontological difference* for the empirical/transcendental distinction.'[18] On this reading of *Being and Time*, Heidegger's distinction between being and the multiplicity of beings grounds his version of transcendentalism. To quote from Lafont:

> The ontological difference (the distinction between being and beings) is established by Heidegger in such a way that it follows that there can be no *access* to entities without a prior understanding of their being. It is for this reason that entities appear to us as always already understood in one way or another (as thus or thus), or, as Heidegger puts it, why 'we always already move about in an understanding of being.' This is the *fact* from which *Being and Time* starts, and which lies at the basis of Heidegger's philosophy as a whole.[19]

According to this schema, Dasein's historically conditioned understanding of being is constitutive for the apprehension of particular beings. This is what Heidegger means when he speaks of 'the elemental historicity of Dasein'[20] and claims that 'Dasein is determined by historicity in the ground of its being'.[21] Heidegger's point is not just that there is no apprehension of beings without a pre-existing structure of understanding, but that this structure is itself determined historically. Here, then, we can see another point on which Heidegger diverges from Kant. For the latter the constitutive categories are universal and atemporal; for the former they are determined by the irreducible temporality of Dasein and its specific place in the history of being. Heidegger's constitutivity thesis results in a different sort of transcendentalism (one should really call it a quasi-transcendentalism, because the transcendental structures Heidegger identifies are temporal, historically conditioned categories[22]), which is perhaps more problematic than Kant's for its essential connection to historicity. As Lee Braver aptly puts it: 'Heidegger's argument takes the form of a Kantian-style idealism transcribed into a temporal key.'[23]

The keystone of Heidegger's hermeneutic quasi-transcendentalism is the claim that *understanding is constitutive*: that it is the historically conditioned understanding of being that makes the appearance of particular beings possible. Bound up in this claim, then, is a certain conception of the entity. As we have seen, the entity for Heidegger cannot be the empiricists' bundle of sense data, because *Being and Time* is built upon a foreclosure of the very possibility of a simple 'sensory' object existing in isolation from a historically conditioned system of meaning. If the condition of the appearance of objects is such a system, then each object is what it is in virtue of its place in a particular historico-temporal field (the hammer is a hammer in virtue of its specific relation to other tools, and to the referential/practical context in which tools have their place: it is what it is, in other words, in virtue of its being in relation to our dwelling). This is why Heidegger cites the ancient Greek term for things – *pragmata* – with such approval: the thing usually *is* for Dasein only because it participates in a broader structure of meaning. 'Handiness' – each being's potentiality for use as a part of Dasein's historically conditioned contexture of intentionality – thus becomes the being of the particular beings encountered by Dasein.[24] As Heidegger writes, '[t]he specific *thisness* of a piece of equipment [is] ... its equipmental character and equipmental contexture.'[25] An object is ready-at-hand for Dasein in virtue of its place in a historico-temporal context, and all objects that turn up in the referential context of Dasein's in-order-tos and for-the-sakes-of-which are by definition ready-at-hand: turning up, we might say, is just being *zuhanden*.

From here we can begin to understand the Heideggerian concept of world. Here I'll cite a key early passage from the text:

> It is not the case that human being 'is,' and then on top of that has a relation of being to the 'world' which it sometimes takes upon itself. Dasein is never 'initially' a sort of a being which is free from being-in, but which at times is in the mood to take up a 'relation' to the world. This taking up of relations to the world is only possible *because*, as being-in-the-world, Dasein is as it is. This constitution of being is not first derived from the fact that besides

the being which has the character of Dasein there are other beings which are objectively present and meet up with it. These other beings can only 'meet up' 'with' Dasein because they are able to show themselves of their own accord within a *world*.[26]

World is the opening at the heart of human being that forms the condition of the possibility of the appearance of phenomena, the historically conditioned horizon of understanding that is constitutive for the equipmental contexture in which Dasein apprehends particular entities. With this quasi-transcendental concept, Heidegger wants to sidestep the whole philosophical problematic of the existence of 'external reality'. Where for Kant the scandal of philosophy was its failure to have provided a proof of the existence of the external world, for Heidegger the true scandal of philosophy consists *'in the fact that such proofs are expected and attempted again and again'*.[27] 'Correctly understood,' he writes, 'Dasein defies such proofs, because it always already is in its being what the later proofs first deem necessary to demonstrate for it.'[28]

Yet Heidegger's deflationary attack on the problem of the external world raises some important questions for his project. First, Heidegger's quasi-transcendentalism opens up a problem of idealism: if the condition of the appearance of objects for Dasein is a historically conditioned horizon of meaning, then how can Dasein ever encounter the kind of *material resistance* that would provide a condition for establishing the correctness of its statements about those objects? Or again: if objects are what they are because of their place in a particular historico-temporal field, how can we ever claim to have knowledge of those objects, if knowledge is taken to consist of access to facts that would transcend any such field? Indeed, as Fichte's liquidation of the Kantian *Ding an sich* indicated (a liquidation that in retrospect seems inevitable, where the external world drops out like one of Wittgenstein's beetles), this is a familiar problem for any transcendental project. Herman Philipse puts it like this: 'In the past, all ... transcendental theories turned out to imply a specific variety of the problem of the external world: the problem of the *Ding an sich* ... We may wonder how Heidegger can be a transcendental philosopher and also claim that he eliminates this problem ...'[29] (indeed, Heidegger will arguably have more difficulty than Kant regarding this, for where the latter wants to save knowledge by showing the logically necessary status of a universal subject, the former's commitment to historicity bars this option from him). Of course, Heidegger takes himself to have sidestepped these questions with the claim that the very existence of Dasein always already implies its being-in-the-world, but as the continuing debates over the status of science in Heidegger's philosophy show (Philipse for instance argues against Hubert Dreyfus's claim that Heidegger 'sought to establish a robust realist account of science',[30] claiming instead that the philosophy of *Being and Time* represents an 'ontological disqualification of science'[31]), it is at the very least unclear as to whether Heidegger's system leaves room for knowledge as traditionally understood.[32]

And there is a further problem, less explored in the literature but no less interesting for that. It is that Heidegger himself admits that the problem of the external world is something more than a pseudo-problem characteristic of the philosophy of consciousness, and has consequences extending further than one may expect in light of his critique. He writes:

> It is not a matter of proving that and how an 'external world' is objectively present, but of demonstrating why Dasein as being-in-the-world has the tendency of 'initially' burying the 'external world' in nullity 'epistemologically' in order first to prove it. The reason for this lies in the falling of Dasein and in the diversion motivated therein of the primary understanding of being to the being of objective presence.[33]

Here Heidegger indicates that the tendency to objectify and then doubt the existence of the world is something inherent in Dasein itself, a tendency that coincides with its falling. This is therefore not just a problem for the establishment of knowledge, but also one that (to step out of a Heideggerian register for a moment) presents as a problem for human life. And if we take seriously Heidegger's assertion (or admission) that Dasein is 'essentially falling',[34] then it will become clear that this is a problem of some importance, indeed a problem inherent in Dasein's very being (it will also give weight to the Cavellian reading of Heidegger as a philosopher with a serious concern for the problem of scepticism, as a thinker who like Wittgenstein was concerned with 'the truth of scepticism'[35]). The urge to prove the existence of the external world may be the result of a theoretical quagmire that would in principle be resolvable with recourse to a new and more originary conception of being-in-the-world, but our falling into that quagmire is nevertheless a tendency inherent in everyday Dasein itself. As such, the problem of the external world is a real one for Heidegger, both in its epistemological variant, in which the key question is how Heidegger can ground statements of knowledge regarding things in the world, and in what we might call its 'existential' variant, in which the issue is how Dasein can extricate itself from a sceptical threat that stems from its very being as the kind of being that falls.

Lafont, who is concerned with the epistemological variant of the problem of the external world as it presents itself for Heidegger, sets up her criticisms on the basis of a reading of *Being and Time* in which the concept of world is shown to be predicated on an understanding of language as disclosive. Her claim, which is developed out of a laborious but not unpersuasive re-reading of the text in light of the later Heidegger, is that 'language alone lends plausibility to *Being and Time*';[36] that it is 'unacceptable to ascribe a minor role to language in *Being and Time*'.[37] Her argument rests on her interpretation of the key Heideggerian theme of understanding, which she takes as 'owing to the existence of a symbolic medium . . .'[38] that would distribute the various possibilities of Dasein as thrown projection: '[T]he facticity of Dasein consists in being-in-the-world, and the world as a "whole of significance" is therefore of a symbolic nature . . .'[39] For Lafont, the crucial Heideggerian claim that the condition of the possibility of our access to entities is a pre-existing system of understanding (the 'always already') is intelligible only if we take understanding to be linguistically constituted. The elevation of language characteristic of the works after Heidegger's *Kehre* was already present in nascent form in *Being and Time*, and that '[t]o see this by no means requires projecting from the later Heidegger back onto the earlier writings. *Being and Time* provides a continual stream of evidence for this claim . . .'.[40] In other words, Lafont wants to show how the understanding of language that Heidegger put forward in the later work was pre-empted in *Being and Time*. On this model, language is what gives structure to the world: it makes possible my experience of it as intelligible. As Lafont puts it, 'as a consequence of [Heidegger's] turn, the traditional view of language as a mere instrument for the designation of independently existing entities was overcome. That amounted to a recognition of the constitutive role of language for our experience and understanding of the world.'[41] There are at least three reasons why Lafont's reading of the work is persuasive: (1) it is consistent with the text, and in particular with the otherwise enigmatic section on discourse, where Heidegger asserts that '[d]iscourse is constitutive for the being of the there, that is, attunement and understanding';[42] (2) it explains something of why the later Heidegger became so obsessed with language; and (3) it produces a version of Heidegger's claims which is philosophically plausible. This last assertion is clearly the most dubious of all three, and part of the task of this chapter is to show how one might go about defending Heidegger from Lafont's own criticism of linguistic idealism (and in doing so show how her Heidegger is more persuasive than she gives him credit for).[43]

It is important that from here any strict distinction between language and equipment in the early Heidegger will start to look untenable.

This is because the equipmental context must now be understood as symbolically structured: after all, equipment is what it is because of its place within a horizon of understanding, and that horizon is itself linguistically constituted. In *The Basic Problems of Phenomenology*, Heidegger writes that '[t]he world comes not afterward but beforehand, in the strict sense of the word. Beforehand: that which is unveiled and understood already in advance in every existent Dasein before any apprehending of this or that being, beforehand as that which stands forth as always already unveiled to us.' He goes on:

> Each particular equipmental thing has ... a specific reference to another particular equipmental thing ... the functionality that goes with chair, blackboard, window is exactly that which makes the thing what it is ... The functionality whole, narrower or broader – room, house, neighbourhood, town, city – is the prius, within which specific beings, as beings of this or that character, are as they are and exhibit themselves accordingly ... A specific functionality whole is *pre*-understood.[44]

The critical point here is that what Heidegger here calls pre-understanding would not be possible without the linguistic. To claim this is not only fair to the texts themselves, but also the most philosophically plausible way of taking understanding: after all, what could a pre-existing understanding of the world conditioning our access to entities be, if not a condition for the world's intelligibility, and how could it be such a condition without being linguistic? As Heidegger puts it, the referential totality that is the equipmental contexture 'must be previously disclosed in a certain intelligibility'.[45] Importantly, this is not quite to say that particular ontic languages *themselves* are constitutive, but rather that the referential totality of a particular 'functionality whole' gets its structure from a particular ontic language. And crucially, both are constituted by *discourse*, which is the ontological ground of any particular referential totality, of that which *expresses itself* as the linguistic/equipmental contexture (as Heidegger writes, '[*t*]*he existential-ontological foundation of language is discourse*'[46]). Lafont is uncharitable to Heidegger on this point, and tries to link his understanding to the linguistic determinism characteristic of nineteenth-century German romanticism, claiming that Heidegger's own attempts at casting the ontological difference in terms of a distinction between discourse and language fail (thus leading him into a Sapir-Whorf style linguistic idealism). But this distinction, in which discourse appears as the ontological horizon expressed by an ontic language structuring a particular equipmental contexture, is very important for Heidegger. As Stephen Mulhall writes: 'At the heart of understanding we find the formal-existential framework of meaning; but this framework is bequeathed to us not through language but rather through the existential-ontological foundation of language, i.e. "discourse".[47] Discourse expresses itself as a particular ontic language in a particular locality, in a particular equipmental contexture. Mulhall again: 'Language is the way in which discourse is expressed, but it is discourse which – in grounding the intelligibility of the world – accounts for the comprehending modes of perception (the hearing of wagons and words rather than tone data) . . .'.[48]

We can now break Heidegger's position down into three basic claims: (1) world constitutes the disclosure of beings – it is 'that *in terms of which* things at hand are at hand for us';[49] (2) the linguistic horizon (discourse) is a fundamental component in this process of disclosure by which beings show themselves in language as part of a particular equipmental contexture; and (3) this contexture is always historically conditioned, because the linguistic horizon is historically contingent (Heidegger: 'Discourse is *in itself* temporal . . .'[50]). The combination of these three theses may be the most important conceptual innovation of *Being and Time*. Taken together they provide the basis of Heidegger's critique of modern philosophy in the name of a more primordial notion of being-in-the-world.

For Lafont, the problem with the project of *Being and Time* consists not in Heidegger's transcendentalism as such, but in the combination of transcendentalism and historicity that results from his commitment to the constitutive role of the linguistic horizon (to put it crudely, what troubles her is the 'quasi' nature of his transcendentalism, in which the a priori becomes historical). As she puts in a recent article, 'one may well wonder whether Heidegger's aim is really to transform the notion of apriority or rather to simply reject it altogether.'[51] Or as she argues in her book, after Heidegger's hermeneutic transformation of the transcendental '[t]here is no way to step outside of our understanding of being in order to check its validity, to test whether or not our understanding of being coincides with the being of things themselves, for there is no being without an *understanding* of being.' This is because in Heidegger understanding 'is not the (eternal) endowment of a transcendental ego (which would guarantee the objectivity of experience and, thereby, the possibility of valid knowledge for all human beings)'.[52] More specifically, Lafont's claim is that Heidegger's quasi-transcendentalism – consisting as it does of a transcendental that has been unmoored from the universal subject and placed under the condition of contingent history – results in a sort of linguistic idealism, in which '[w]hat things are becomes thoroughly dependent on what is contingently "disclosed" for a historical linguistic community . . .'. This is because 'that which constitutes the objects of experience . . . can no longer be understood as a unique synthesis of apperception, valid for all rational beings . . .' but rather simply as 'the plurality of linguistic world-disclosures resulting from the contingent, historical process of projecting meaning for interpreting the world'.[53] On this account, Heidegger inherits the obvious problem of the linguistic idealist position: a disqualification of the possibility of knowledge, and potentially a linguistic incommensurabilism that soon collapses into relativism (if my world is constituted by my language, and my language is different to yours, then we live in different worlds). While Lafont's transcendental/hermeneutic reading of Heidegger is a perceptive one, I nevertheless want to show that placing Heidegger here is to make a mistake, and that this mistake is the result of forgetting the importance for him of the question of being. Indeed, the simple question raised by the *fact that there are things* acts as a sort of counterweight to the problems stemming from Heidegger's quasi-transcendentalism, effectively pulling it toward a kind of universalism that may provide a minimally sufficient condition for establishing criteria of epistemological validity (indeed Lafont herself seems to acknowledge this: '*that* there are entities has nothing to do with us, but *what* they are depends on our prior projection of their being'[54]). The *Seinsfrage*, in other words, may provide a pathway out of the linguistic idealist tendencies implicit in Heidegger's work. To begin to understand this, we need to move toward the later Heidegger, but only after working through his phenomenology of the tool.

A defining trait of the tool is its material inconspicuousness. Handiness, or a tool's potentiality for use within a particular equipmental context, always entails a recession of the presence of the tool as object. 'What is peculiar to what is initially at hand', says Heidegger, 'is that it withdraws, so to speak, in its character of handiness in order to be really handy.'[55] A working tool is a tool that dissolves into the hermeneutic tapestry that it partly constitutes; a hammer is useful as a hammer precisely insofar as its user remains unaware of its objective presence. Heidegger goes on: 'What everyday association is initially busy with is not the tools themselves, but the work.'[56] The artisan does not busy himself with his hammer and saw; rather he uses his hammer and saw as he busies himself with his work. Graham Harman sums this up nicely, writing that in use entities are '[d]issolved into a general equipmental effect', losing 'their singularity' and operating 'in an inconspicuous usefulness, doing . . . work without our noticing it'.[57]

Yet there are moments at which Dasein is confronted by the presence of the tool. In these encounters, the handiness structure is interrupted and Dasein is temporarily thrown out of its immersion in use. Harman: 'When the tool fails, its unobtrusive quality is ruined. There occurs a jarring of reference, so that the tool becomes visible *as* what it is . . .'[58] As a brief example, the reader could consider these very pages. If all has been going well, you will not have consciously registered the presence in your hand of the pages of this book until this point in the exposition: your use of them had made them materially invisible to you. Perhaps only now will you notice their qualities: the smooth feel of their surfaces, the sharpness of their edges, the sounds they make when rubbed together (or, if you are reading this on a computer, you may now notice the feel of the keyboard or mouse against your hand, the glow of the screen in front of you, the background hum of the cooling fan, etc.). Of course, all this has been objectively present for the entire time; you had just failed to notice this fact because of your absorption in use. This is the experience of what Heidegger calls the 'broken tool'.

Here there is another important distinction to be made. On the ontic level, a broken tool is obviously just that: a tool that has for one reason or another become unusable. On the ontological level, however, any tool that draws attention to its material presence is a broken tool, because in doing so it throws Dasein out of its immersion in use. Harman again:

> [T]he visibility of Heidegger's 'broken tool' has nothing to do with equipment not being in top working order. Even the most masterfully constructed, prize-winning tools have to be regarded as 'broken' as soon as we consider them directly; the broken/unbroken distinction does not function as an ontic rift between two different sorts of entities. Thus, as ought to have been expected, Heidegger teaches us not about smashed-up blades and chisels, but only about beings in general.[59]

The experience of the broken tool is not an experience with a useless chisel, but an experience of ontological hiatus in which '[t]he contexture of reference and thus the referential totality undergoes a distinctive disturbance . . .'.[60] In these encounters, Dasein can become newly stunned by or plainly *aware* of objects, which now emerge from inconspicuousness in and as equipment to confront Dasein in their materiality. As Heidegger shows, the experience with the broken tool sees Dasein break out of the referential structure of the ready-to-hand (*zuhanden*) as objects temporarily appear in the mode of objective presence (*vorhanden*). It is an experience with what one could call the mute 'thereness' of things, in which they show up in their 'thatness' as opposed to their 'whatness'. The very *being here before me* of things jumps out in this experience, and shows itself as something with no inherent regard for or connection to human Dasein: things in their thereness, one might say, are simply there, and would still be there without us.

It is here that Heidegger clears the pathway on which he may be able to escape the idealist trappings that inhere in any theory of language as disclosive. As we saw above, the early Heidegger sets up a theory of the relation between object and language whereby the former is in a crucial way contingent on the latter: against the designative theory of language, Heidegger claims that objects do not exist for Dasein apart from the equipmental/linguistic contexture that it dwells in. They do not appear to a subject as simple 'sense objects' for interpretation because the condition of their first appearing is that they appear *as something*. The phenomenology of the broken tool, however, shows that this does not have to entail the rejection of the claim that objects have a sort of 'independent' existence (even if Heidegger's system problematises this sort of language). The salient point is that what temporarily emerges in the breakdown of the equipmental/linguistic totality occasioned by the experience of the broken tool are objects freed from their subsumption in use, objects as materially resistant to the equipmental world of Dasein. To put this in terms that I will work toward refining, what emerges in this experience of breakdown is a kind of outside in which Dasein's intentional projects lose their purchase on things. A materiality emerges here that shows itself as a kind of remainder, a residue that is left over after the world-constitutive movement of discourse. As such it is no accident that Heidegger understands science as blind before or forgetful of the referential context of Dasein, as necessarily passing over the worldliness of human life to reveal things as objective presence. Indeed, it is in exactly this sense that we can understand Heidegger as giving us a realism robust enough to account for scientific knowledge. In the event of Dasein's demise things would lose their 'whatness', but not their 'thatness': meaning that in Heidegger's system objects do have an 'objective' existence. Yet things are complex here, for in Heidegger's system science itself cannot be understood except as derivative of Dasein's self-understanding, which (as we have seen) is always primordial. In Heidegger, science has access to a reality that exists independently of Dasein's understanding (things are really real!), but that access is always already tempered by that understanding (things become what they are because of the as-structure). To put it another way: things exist independently of us, it is just impossible to escape our status as always already thrown into a particular historical world, and hence impossible for science to proceed from out of some trans-historical view from nowhere (hence Newtonian physics produces accurate predictions, but has to make those predictions from within a particular historical situation, and so ends up reproducing – and reinforcing – a particular understanding of being). Lafont, then, may be right in attributing to Heidegger the claim that there is no access to the 'whatness' of things outside of a linguistically structured equipmental world, but this needs to be supplemented with the recognition that it can be breached and temporarily suspended, such that things show themselves as existing without regard for us. In other words, the charge of linguistic idealism that she levels at Heidegger wrongly attributes to him the claim that the equipmental/linguistic contexture in which Dasein dwells is impermeable. This is not the case: the world of Dasein is not seamless and can be disrupted. My claim, upon which I hope to make good in the remainder of this chapter, is that we need to move toward Heidegger's late works if we want to understand the phenomenological structure and – most importantly for the broader purposes of this book – philosophical consequences of this rupture.

Here I want to return primarily to the essay 'Language', where we find Heidegger carrying out one of his most useful engagements with the question of language *as such*. The (apparently tautological) question guiding the inquiry is: 'In what way does language occur as language?'[61] As we have seen, Heidegger wants to move away from the 'current view'[62] of language: the instrumentalist/designative paradigm. As is the case in *Being and Time*, this isn't to say that he rejects this concept of language outright. Indeed, Heidegger does not even question the 'correctness' of this paradigm of language even in this late essay: 'No one would dare to declare incorrect, let alone reject as useless, the identification of language as audible utterance of inner emotions, as human activity, as a representation by image and by concept.'[63] Here we are reminded of the claim in *Being and Time* that the apophantic statement is itself parasitic upon the hermeneutic contexture of Dasein: the designative understanding of language is not wrong, as such, but it is an abstracted image of language that, if taken as the only one, works to conceal its other dimensions:

> We still give too little consideration, however, to the singular role of these correct ideas about language. They hold sway, as if unshakable, over the whole field of the varied scientific perspectives on language. They have their roots in an ancient tradition. Yet they ignore completely the oldest natural cast of language. Thus, despite their antiquity and their comprehensibility, they never bring us to language as language.[64]

But importantly, Heidegger is also attempting to move beyond the equipmental understanding of language that we find in *Being and Time*. As with the early criticism of the designative paradigm, Heidegger has become convinced that there is more to language than *Being and Time* may have indicated. In particular, he is concerned in this text with what he calls 'language as language', and he turns to poetry in an attempt to explicate its excesses over designation and equipment. In particular, he turns to Trakl's 'A Winter Evening'.

There is something striking about Heidegger's reading of this piece. It is that it is not primarily a 'reading', at least according to the usual understanding of the term. Of course, he does spend three paragraphs explicating the 'content' of the poem, but after doing so reneges on the project:

> The content of the poem might be dissected even more distinctly, its form outlined even more precisely, but in such operations we would still remain confined by the notion of language that has prevailed for thousands of years. According to this idea language is the expression, produced by men, of their feelings and the world view that guides them. Can the spell this idea has cast over our language be broken? Why should it be broken? In its essence, language is neither expression nor an activity of man. Language speaks. We are now seeking the speaking of language of the poem. Accordingly, what we seek lies in the poetry of the spoken word.[65]

Now there is a break in the style of the presentation, as Heidegger slips into a more allusive, metaphorical and indeed pseudo-poetic register. Tautologies appear more frequently and key phrases begin to repeat as Heidegger unfolds images from the Trakl piece and sets them alongside his own concepts, which he now introduces quite abruptly and without real explanation. It is an alienating and at times exasperating reading experience, and it is easy to see why some commentators make the mistake of either ignoring certain writings from the later Heidegger or condemning him for wilful obscurantism. Here, however, it is worth giving Heidegger the benefit of the doubt. What are the reasons for this stylistic development? Answering this question means turning first to a set of other, closely related ones: what is missed by philosophical language? What is the unrepresentable and why is Heidegger concerned with it? What does 'poetic' language do that philosophical language does not?

I would like to give the answer to the last question first, and will start by saying that for Heidegger, poetic language is potentially transformative in a way that philosophical language is not. This is because it can produce a particular sort of 'experience with language', where an 'experience' is something that 'overwhelms and transforms ... we endure it, suffer it, receive it as it strikes us and submit to it'.[66] How? First, it is clear that poetic language is able to effect such a transformation because 'man finds the proper abode of his existence in language'.[67] This metaphor of language as dwelling place is of course a very common one in the late Heidegger, but one can find its seeds in the quasi-transcendental, hermeneutic system of *Being and Time*. After all, if this reading of this text holds good, then it should be clear that its key theses are predicated upon a theory of the world-disclosing nature of language, and so on an image of the human dwelling within a hermeneutic totality that is itself (ontologically) constituted by discourse and (ontically) structured by bits of linguistic equipment. These theses spring from the same basic commitments that drive the late Heidegger's claim that the human being is 'always speaking':[68] the point is that the human is *involved* in language even when it is not literally speaking, reading or listening to speech. There is immersion in language in 'attending to some work or taking a rest',[69] because these engagements are always carried out within a wider linguistic/equipmental context. This is why Heidegger claims that 'language belongs to the closest neighbourhood of man's being'; that '[w]e encounter language everywhere'.[70] In the late and early Heidegger, language is the elemental stuff of the world. It is gear for dwelling.

Yet equipment functions only insofar as it remains inconspicuous to its user. As we have seen, this is because the broken tool calls attention away from work and toward itself, and in so doing, breaks the chain of intentionality, which functions because of a tool's referring back to other tools and projects in the linguistic/equipmental context. In this emergency, Dasein is confronted with the object freed from its equipmental background, and thus temporarily expelled from immersion in use.

This is how we should understand the poetic experience with language that so obsesses the late Heidegger. In this experience, language does not just communicate propositional content (designation) or work to constitute the equipmental contexture of a particular world (world-disclosure), but also 'brings itself to language'.[71] Heidegger's experience with language is an experience of temporary breakdown, where language draws attention to itself, and thus stops 'working' in the usual way. This is why he points out that language only functions to the extent that its essential nature remains veiled: 'Only because in everyday speaking language does *not* bring itself to language but holds back, are we able to simply go ahead and speak a language, and so to deal with something and negotiate something by speaking.'[72] Poetic language is language that draws attention to itself: it is not perfectly 'clear' and refuses the ideal of transparent inconspicuousness so as to remain and linger on the page. It is a broken language that erupts out of equipmentality, forcing Dasein into a confrontation with its sonority, its material qualities. In the terms of the artwork essay, poetic language is language that foregrounds its 'thingly character',[73] drawing attention to itself as a material thing.

This is why Heidegger became so fixated on poetic language. More specifically, it is why he is not primarily concerned with the 'content' of the Trakl piece he wants to analyse, focusing instead on what he variously calls its 'speaking',[74] 'calling'[75] and 'naming'.[76] Heidegger's claim is that language has two different and perhaps incommensurable faces; that words can disappear in communication or refuse such transparency to show themselves more essentially as the material things they are. Here we find Heidegger running up against a fundamental phenomenological limit (and thus reason to be wary of any too-neat pragmatist or reductive linguistic idealist reading of him), a point at which the linguistic context of Dasein – the structured totality of meaning in which it dwells – is disrupted by an event of exposure. In this event, words start to signify themselves, bringing attention to language as a material thing, as marks on a page or screen.[77] 'Only at the level of materiality do words connect with things,' as Gerald Bruns puts it, before going on to immediately quote Ponge: 'O infinite resources of the thickness of things, brought about by the infinite resources of the semantical thickness of words!'[78] This is what Heidegger means when he writes of the 'bidding' that takes place in the first stanza of the Trakl piece. 'Bidding', he says, 'is inviting. It invites things in, so that they may bear upon men as things.'[79] The poet's task is to invite things into a presence in which they viscerally bear upon us.

The key distinction here is between the experience of breakdown occasioned by the confrontation with the broken tool and the experience of breakdown characteristic of poetic experience. What must be explained is why poetic experience is more fundamental than the experience of the broken tool, which is not transformative for Dasein. Phenomenologically, we can identify the difference in terms of the *novelty* essential to any poetic experience with language, drawing a contrast between this and the familiar annoyance and relatively boring low-level anxiety that usually accompanies the experience of the broken tool: the difference between poetic experience and the mute experience of breakdown it so closely resembles consists in the element of astonishment inherent in the former. So there is an important structural isomorphy between these two experiences of breakdown, but in poetic experience I am able to follow the experience of breakdown to a conclusion: poetic experience, one could say, completes the experience of breakdown. Think of the difference between encountering someone speaking a language of which you have an imperfect grasp and reading a poem: in the former, there might be a sense of frustration as you do your best to understand what is being said, as the materiality of language, the sounds of the words themselves, jumps out as a disturbance.

In the experience with poetic language, there is a structurally similar encounter with the material resistance of words (with language as a broken tool), but, in the case of a successful poem at least, it appears not as a disturbance but rather as *something's becoming intelligible*, where the sound (and even physical shape) of words[80] starts to become evocative, and something previously unarticulated to you (and until now inarticulable for you) shows up and surprises. Whereas an unknown foreign word emerges materially as a disturbance, the language of a successful poem (and by successful I mean successful-for-the-reader, the kind of poem that produces a poetic experience) emerges materially in a way that grants access to the worldliness of the world, the ontological ground of intelligibility itself. If in the experience of the broken tool we are struck by a sudden awareness of the cracked hammer in our hand, then in poetry we are struck by a sudden awareness of this transcendental condition for encountering things in general. When my hammer breaks, I am jarred by the brute presence of things. In poetry, the world's existing appears as something speakable.

In one of his more enigmatic moments, we find Heidegger stating that '[t]hinging, things are things'.[81] At this point we should be able to understand both why Heidegger resorts to a tautology and exactly what he intends to 'express' by it: in everyday life, things are not truly things, because they remain inconspicuously involved in the equipmental contexture; through poetry they are able to 'thing' and become what they are. A successful poem lets language itself emerge in the mode of the broken tool and, because language is constitutive for equipmentality, allows Dasein to follow through on that experience in a novel way. A poem turns an experience of breakdown into an experience of *the intelligibility of the fact of existence* (of what J. H. Prynne calls 'the eloquence, the gentility of / the world's being . . .'[82]): it renders inoperative the chain of references that constitute Dasein's world, but at the same time lets things become things again, bringing our attention back to their existing in a way that reveals it as something other than objective presence. As Prynne writes in a prose piece: '[T]he reality of the external world may be constituted . . . on the basis of the world's perceived existence, the resistance it offers to our awareness.'[83] Poetry offers a particular kind of resistance to our awareness, a resistance that makes the 'thereness' of the world newly intelligible to us. We have to understand the later Heidegger's obsession with poetry not as the fruit of a linguistic idealism that had its roots in *Being and Time*, but rather as an attempt by him at resolving one of the basic problems of his hermeneutic philosophy. Poetic experience does not see Dasein learning that it is forever closed off in some hermetically sealed linguistic sphere;

it is an experience of a materiality that prevents that kind of closure. It provides an opening onto reality that allows for a returning to it.

The condition of the possibility of this experience is that Dasein is a being that forgets itself (a being-there that forgets its being there): the kind of being that, to use the Heideggerian term I invoked earlier, *falls* into existing as though its existing is not an issue for it. After all, something can be surprising to me only if I don't know of it, and if the fact of the world's existence can surprise me, then this fact (which in a sense is entirely 'obvious') must not be something that I can know. As Mulhall writes: '[T]he world's existence – unlike the existence of a given object in the world – is not something in which we "believe", not an "opinion" that we hold on the basis of evidence.'[84] So in the emergency of language characteristic of poetic experience, something comes to be experienced by Dasein that exceeds the form of knowledge. After all, what is imparted here is precisely not a fact about the world (a 'state of affairs') that could itself be expressed more or less accurately with a corresponding propositional claim. This fact is absolutely singular: it is the fact of the world, not a fact in the world. So it isn't quite that the world appears in poetic experience with a vividness that undermines all doubt, but that what appears here is of a wholly different order to the dialectic of doubt, belief and knowledge (encountering the world's existing is not the same as 'knowing that P', or coming to know it). What emerges in poetry is an experiential or phenomenological *proof-for-Dasein* of the existence of the world, which arises for a moment and then recedes as Dasein is reabsorbed. In the terms I introduced earlier, the poetic experience with language temporarily resolves the existential variant of the problem of the external world, leading Dasein up out of its falling and into a confrontation with that from which it fell. Of course, this experience cannot be finally or wholly transformative in its resolution of the problem (after all, it does not present any propositional content that could be retained and remembered at will). But it seems that the limitedness of this experience, the fact that the transformation it accords is temporary, is one of its conditions of possibility. After all, this is how it can be surprising each time: it is why each poem seems to be saying something new to one; the condition of poetry's imparting the kind of novelty that differentiates it from the prosaic experience of the broken tool. The speakability of the world is quite literally *renewed* with every poetic experience. This comes to more than the notion that pre-theoretical Dasein does not face the epistemological problems characteristic of post-Cartesian philosophy, beginning as they do with a passing over of being-in-the-world and a move into abstraction. The claim is not simply that the retreat into abstraction causes us to miss the richness or thickness of being-in-the-world, but that everyday being-in-the-world can itself be suspended by a poetic experience of the word/world *as such*, which is a kind of touching against the materiality of existence. What takes place in this touching is an escape from both everyday equipmentality and the philosopher's cage of representational knowledge. It is a breath of air occasioned by the poetic experience of the world.

NOTES

1. From Stevens, 'Notes Toward a Supreme Fiction'.
2. Agamben, *Infancy and History*, 6.
3. Agamben, 'The Idea of Language', 40.
4. Ibid. 43.
5. Heller-Roazen, 'Editor's Introduction to *Potentialities*', 5.
6. Agamben, *Infancy and History*, 10.
7. Wittgenstein, 'Ethics, Life and Faith', 257. I complicate this statement in Chapter 7. It should be pointed out at this stage that Wittgenstein regards it as nonsense.
8. See Lafont, *Heidegger, Language, and World-Disclosure*.
9. Ibid. 104.
10. Heidegger, 'Language', 192.
11. Ibid. 192.
12. Ibid. 192.
13. Ibid. 192.
14. *Being and Time* presents an early version of this critique when Heidegger distinguishes between hermeneutic and apophantic discourse (SZ 154–60; 144–50e). The latter functions according to designation; 'this hammer is too heavy' is Heidegger's example. Heidegger's claim is that the apophantic statement is parasitic on the hermeneutic world of Dasein: 'the statement's pointing out is accomplished on the basis of what is already disclosed in understanding . . .'; that the statement 'always already maintains itself on the basis of being-in-the-world' and 'cannot disclose entities on its own' (SZ 156; 146e). A more originary understanding of the function of language – the hermeneutic understanding – places such a statement within the equipmental contexture of Dasein (which terms I will define shortly): 'The primordial act of interpretation lies not in a theoretical sentence, but in circumspectly and heedfully putting away or changing the inappropriate tool "without wasting words"' (SZ 156; 147e). As such, the statement 'the hammer is too heavy' is not to be understood as a simple designative claim that follows the structure of 'the object X has the property Y', but rather as another part of Dasein's equipmental contexture. Its meaning, then, is best interpreted as 'too heavy, the other hammer!' (see SZ 156; 147e). This is Heidegger working to show that the designative paradigm of language is an abstraction (even if it is a sometimes useful one).

15. In using the term 'designative' to describe this theory of language I am following Lafont, who is herself following Charles Taylor in his 'Theories of Meaning'. In this important paper Taylor gives a historical account of the designative theory of language as arising contemporaneously with the scientific revolution of the seventeenth century. The reader will also note that I sometimes use the term 'instrumentalist' in this context; this is because the term 'designative', while useful in its clarity, is problematic in its exclusivity. Heidegger was concerned to critique not only the designative or predicative understanding of language, but more broadly the understanding of language as an instrument that humans use for communicating information.
16. Lafont, *Heidegger, Language, and World-Disclosure*, 1.
17. Heidegger, *Being and Time*, SZ 164–5; 153e.
18. Lafont, *Heidegger, Language, and World-Disclosure*, xiii.
19. Ibid. xiii.
20. Heidegger, *Being and Time*, SZ 20; 18e.
21. Ibid. SZ 20; 18e.
22. See *Transcendental Heidegger*, edited by Steven Crowell and Jeff Malpas, for a series of illuminating discussions of the role of the transcendental in Heidegger.
23. Braver, *A Thing of This World*, 222.
24. See Heidegger, *Being and Time*, SZ 83–9; 77–83e.
25. Heidegger, *The Basic Problems of Phenomenology*, 292.
26. Heidegger, *Being and Time*, SZ 57; 53–44e.
27. Ibid. SZ 205; 190e.
28. Ibid. SZ 205; 190e.
29. Philipse, 'Heidegger's "Scandal of Philosophy"', 178.
30. Dreyfus, 'How Heidegger defends the possibility of a correspondence theory of truth with respect to the entities of natural science', 151.
31. Philipse, 'Heidegger's "Scandal of Philosophy"', 198.
32. For a sustained and systematic contribution to this debate, see Trish Glazebrook, *Heidegger's Philosophy of Science*; I turn to Glazebrook's book again in Chapter 8.
33. Heidegger, *Being and Time*, SZ 206; 191e (translation modified).
34. Ibid. SZ 222; 204e (translation modified).
35. Cavell, *The Claim of Reason*, 241. As he puts it earlier in the book:

    > My major claim about the philosopher's originating question – e.g. '(How) do (can) we know anything about the world?' or 'What is knowledge; what does my knowledge of the world consist in?' – is that (in one or another of its versions) is a response to, or expression of, a real experience which takes hold of human beings. It is not 'natural' in the sense I have already found in the claim to 'reasonableness': it is not a response to questions raised in ordinary practical contexts, framed in a language which any master of a language will accept as ordinary. But it is, as I might put it, a response which expresses a natural experience

of a creature complicated or burdened enough to possess language at all. (140)
36. Lafont, *Heidegger, Language, and World-Disclosure*, 23.
37. Ibid. 23.
38. Ibid. 47.
39. Ibid. 48.
40. Ibid. 25.
41. Ibid. xi.
42. Heidegger, *Being and Time*, SZ 165; 154e.
43. This reading of *Being and Time* relies on a distinction crucial for Heidegger but which is not always recognised in the literature on his work: the difference between the pre-predicative and the pre-linguistic. As is well known, part of Heidegger's innovation in *Being and Time* was to show how the philosophy of consciousness passes over Dasein's being-in-the-world because it takes knowing to be fundamental, reducing human interaction with the world to propositional attitudes and missing as a result the myriad everyday practices that are not reducible to them. One of the great merits of Dreyfus's highly influential reading of *Being and Time* lies in his insistence on the importance of Heidegger's insights regarding the severely limited nature of most traditional theories of human action, and his clarity in elucidating his alternative model, which is based on a series of phenomenological descriptions of 'everyday concernful coping' (Dreyfus, *Being in the World*, 61). As he puts it in a more recent text, 'when I enter a room I normally cope with whatever is there. What enables me to do this is not a set of beliefs about rooms, nor a rule for dealing with rooms in general and what they contain; it is a sense of how rooms normally behave, a skill for dealing with them, that I have developed by crawling and walking around many rooms' (Dreyfus, 'Heidegger's Critique of the Husserl/Searle Account of Intentionality', 153). Yet Dreyfus holds onto the assumption that this coping is somehow 'prelinguistic' ('Responses', 330). Typical as this is of the various pragmatically inclined readings of Heidegger, in which our concrete worldly practices are taken to be constitutive and primordial in themselves, it is reliant on an important misreading of the text in which Heidegger's critique of the designative paradigm of language is taken as a critique of the very idea of understanding as linguistically constituted. Yet insisting on the linguistically grounded nature of our practices for our being-in-the-world does not mean falling back into a paradigm in which human action can be reduced without residue to propositional attitudes, provided we take into account Heidegger's work in establishing a concept of language that escapes the designative paradigm. In other words, while Dreyfus is right to be zealous in critiquing the propositional paradigm of human action, to claim that pre-predicative absorption is pre-linguistic is to overshoot the mark, and relies on the mistaken assumption that language always functions in its designative mode. Coping, on this reading of Heidegger, cannot be boiled down to propositional

attitudes, but nevertheless has its condition of possibility (i.e. the very intelligibility of the world in which we cope) in the discursive constitution of understanding.
44. Heidegger, *The Basic Problems of Phenomenology*, 165–6.
45. Heidegger, *Being and Time*, SZ 86; 80e.
46. Ibid. SZ 160–1; 150e.
47. Mulhall, *On Being in the World*, 118.
48. Ibid. 119.
49. Heidegger, *Being and Time*, SZ 83; 77e.
50. Ibid. SZ 349; 320e.
51. Lafont, 'Heidegger and the Synthetic A Priori', 107.
52. Lafont, *Heidegger, Language, and World-Disclosure*, xix.
53. Ibid. 7.
54. Lafont, 'Heidegger and the Synthetic A Priori', 106.
55. Heidegger, *Being and Time*, SZ 69; 65e.
56. Ibid. SZ 69; 65e.
57. Harman, *Tool Being*, 45.
58. Ibid. 45.
59. Ibid. 45.
60. Heidegger, *History of the Concept of Time*, 188.
61. Heidegger, 'Language', 188.
62. Ibid. 190.
63. Ibid. 191.
64. Ibid. 191.
65. Ibid. 194.
66. Heidegger, 'The Nature of Language', 57.
67. Ibid. 57.
68. Heidegger, 'Language', 187.
69. Ibid. 187.
70. Ibid. 187.
71. Heidegger, 'The Nature of Language', 59.
72. Ibid. 59.
73. Heidegger, 'The Origin of the Work of Art', 145.
74. Heidegger, 'Language', 195.
75. Ibid. 196.
76. Ibid. 197.
77. Maurice Blanchot's description of a particular literary strategy is relevant here. In this strategy, which Blanchot doesn't quite name as such but could be called 'poetic', the goal of the writer is to somehow present the words themselves in their materiality. Blanchot writes:

> My hope lies in the materiality of language, in the fact that words are things, too, are a kind of nature – this is given to me and gives me more than I can understand. Just now the reality of words was an obstacle. Now, it is my only chance. A name ceases to be the ephemeral passing of nonexistence and becomes a concrete ball, a solid mass of existence;

language, abandoning the sense, the meaning which was all it wanted to be, tries to become senseless. Everything physical takes precedence, rhythm, weight, mass, shape, and then the paper on which ones writes, the trail of the ink, the book. Yes, happily language is a thing: it is a written thing, a bit of bark, a sliver of rock, a fragment of clay in which the reality of the earth continues to exist. ('Literature and the Right to Death', 383–4)

78. Ponge, quoted in Bruns, *The Material of Poetry*, 83.
79. Heidegger, 'Language', 197.
80. See Prynne, *Stars, Tigers, and the Shapes of Words*.
81. Heidegger, 'Language', 197.
82. Prynne, 'On the Matter of Thermal Packing'.
83. Prynne, 'Resistance and Difficulty', 27.
84. Mulhall, 'Can There Be an Epistemology of Moods?', 33.

3. The Myth of the Earth

> [I]ntelligibility has become detached from meaning: with modern science, conceptual rationality weans itself from the narrative structures that continue to prevail in theology and theologically inflected metaphysics. This marks a decisive step forward in the slow process through which human rationality has gradually abandoned mythology, which is basically the interpretation of reality in narrative terms. The world has no author and there is no story enciphered in the structure of reality. No narrative is unfolding in nature . . .[1]

In the final paragraph of his preface to *Infancy and History*, Agamben turns Wittgenstein's statement about the right expression in language for the miracle of the world's existence on its head. Referring to it as the Viennese philosopher's version of the *experimentum linguae* – the experience with the fact of language that occupies Agamben throughout his works – he writes:

> [I]f the most appropriate expression of wonderment at the existence of the world is the existence of language, what then is the correct expression for the existence of language? The only possible answer to this question is: human life, as *ethos*, as ethical way. The search for a *polis* and an *oika* befitting this void and unpresupposeable community is the . . . task of future generations.[2]

As is clear from this passage, part of what is distinctive about Agamben's inheritance of Heidegger is how he insists on the ethical and political stakes of the question of being.[3] Yet as any attentive reader of Heidegger knows, such concerns were never far from Heidegger's mind either (even if – for a variety of reasons, some of which I articulate below – they are rarely outlined in a fully explicit way in the German philosopher's work). Indeed part of the fascinating ambiguity in

Heidegger's thinking – and, of course, part of what makes certain aspects of it so problematic – turns on such concerns, and in particular on how problems of human destiny, dwelling and being-together arise out of the experience of the *Seinsfrage*. This is why Agamben writes in *The Open* that Heidegger was the 'last philosopher to believe in good faith that the place of the *polis* . . . was still practicable, and that it was still possible for men, for a people . . . to find their own proper historical destiny'.[4] If the ethico-political stakes of the question of being were crucial to Heidegger's thinking, then at the same time this also represented a kind of blind spot for him. Turning in particular to the essay on the work of art, in this chapter I try to show how Heidegger's figuring of the relation between politics, history and fundamental ontology can be clarified – and criticised – by attending to the precise way in which he tried to politically mobilise poetic experience.

Heidegger's approach in the artwork essay is distinctive in that he wants to identify the essence of the artwork by inquiring into the artwork itself. The potential benefits of such an approach should be obvious, for it effectively saves us from the problematic structure of, say, a traditional aesthetic approach, which begins not from the artwork qua artwork but from the experience of artworks. This is a key move in Kantian transcendental methodology: one looks to and makes inferences from one's experience of the object in question, rather than inquiring directly into the object in itself. This approach, in limiting itself to inferring from experience, avoids the epistemological problems associated with any methodology that wants to go directly for the object (the obvious reference point here is Meno's Paradox). Heidegger's approach to the artwork, by contrast, assumes that '[w]hat art is should be inferable from the work'.[5] Now this confronts Heidegger with the sort of problem that the Kantian method avoids. The problem is the following: if we want to establish the essence of the artwork by inquiring into the artwork itself, then we need to first assume that we know what an artwork is (after all, we can't inquire into an object that we can't first identify). But this leaves us in a circle: to approach the essence of art with sole reference to art requires that we first presuppose an understanding of the essence of art.[6] Heidegger's move here is a provocative one: he declares the problem of circularity null. 'This', he states, 'is neither a makeshift nor a defect', claiming rather curtly that embarking on this circular path 'is the strength of thought'; that continuing on it is its 'feast'.[7] He then moves on to his inquiry, as though this obscure declaration could count as a refutation of the charge that such circularity will undermine the claims of his essay.

Of course, this would be nothing more than sophistry if Heidegger had not already faced this problem in an original way in *Being and Time*, where he showed that this circular structure is an inherent and in fact productive feature of his hermeneutic method. 'What is decisive', Heidegger argued in 1927, 'is not to get out of the circle but to get in it in the right way.' Circularity is an essential feature of 'the existential *fore-structure* of Dasein itself'.[8] If we attempt to avoid the circle, whether through Kant's transcendental method, or perhaps by philosophising from a foundation in theology or metaphysics (as in, say, a pre-critical scholastic philosophy), we miss the fundamental point that Dasein is always already interpreted and self-interpreting. Any mode of thought that takes objectivity as its goal will miss the phenomenon of Dasein by definition, as it will miss the fact that human life finds itself in a hermeneutic structure. In a move that is in many ways analogous to the Wittgensteinian appeal to the use of words in ordinary language, then, Heidegger is happy to take the everyday linguistic or hermeneutic conduct of human beings as something of a starting point. The fact that we call artworks 'artworks' should be enough to ground the analysis; we don't need to know the necessary and sufficient conditions of something's being an artwork before inquiring into it as an artwork.

From here Heidegger turns to an investigation of the thingly character of the artwork, which means something like the status of the artwork qua literal, concrete object. Obviously works of art are objects like other objects; as Heidegger says they hang on walls, are shipped from place to place and are left in storerooms as potatoes are left in cellars.[9] Nevertheless Heidegger cautions against the idea that such claims are superfluous to what it is that makes artworks artworks, arguing that 'even the much-vaunted aesthetic experience cannot get around the thingly aspect of the artwork'.[10] As Heidegger goes on to point out, we show tacit awareness of the importance of the thingly character of artworks in ordinary language, where we find ourselves saying that 'the architectural work is in stone, the carving is in wood, the painting is in color, the linguistic work in speech, the musical composition in sound'.[11] Heidegger warns against any easy dismissal of this fact on the grounds of its obviousness. His claim instead is that the thingly character of the artwork is essential to it, and that this is the case in a way that does not apply for other objects. On the face of it this is a strange claim, but it is absolutely basic to Heidegger's analysis. Indeed, we might even say that it is the guiding thread of the artwork essay. It can be clarified with a set of questions like the following: why are artworks more thingly than other things? How do they reveal their thingly character? What kind of thingliness is essential to the artwork?

In beginning to answer such questions, Heidegger characteristically turns to the conceptions of thingliness that he wants to avoid in his essay. There are, he says, three traditional modes of understanding thingliness: the object understood as (1) 'a bearer of traits'; (2) 'as the unity of a manifold of sensations'; and (3) as 'formed matter'.[12] The first understanding, which corresponds according to Heidegger with the translation of Greek thought into the subject-predicate structure of the Latin sentence, is in some ways paradigmatic of all three, in that it represents the beginnings of the conceptual movement by which the originary Greek experience of the being of beings was obliterated. '*Roman thought*', Heidegger says with emphasis, '*takes over the Greek words without a corresponding, equally original experience of what they say, without the Greek word.*'[13] It may seem that Heidegger makes this (not uncontroversial) assertion without sufficient support, but it is part of the broader confrontation with the foundational categories of Western metaphysics that takes place in his work; as such it cannot really be assessed without a proper engagement with that confrontation. What Heidegger wants to question above all are our most intuitive pictures of existence: the problem here, as in *Being and Time*, is with language's ability to condition the possibilities of thought through the naturalisation of grammatical categories. His question, and he admits that from a certain standpoint it may be properly undecidable,[14] is whether 'the structure of a simple propositional statement' mirrors the structure of the world, or whether 'the structure of the thing as thus envisaged is a projection of the framework of the sentence'.[15] The novelty of Heidegger's thought consists in his posing of this question, which could not have been asked with the same clarity without its grounding in *Being and Time*'s thesis of the essential historicity of Dasein, in which our understanding of being is contingent upon historical and linguistic community. After this thesis is established, one has to approach language with a new sort of guardedness. In this spirit, Heidegger's qualm with the subject-predicate sentence structure focuses on the fact that being *as such* cannot express itself or indeed even pose itself as a question in it. In the terms of the artwork essay, the subject-predicate sentence passes over the 'thingly character' of the object, taking its *suchness* for granted as something literally unremarkable.

The second characterisation of the object – as the unity of a manifold of sensations – is understood by Heidegger in terms of the development of this historical movement of the oblivion of being. This characterisation, which is one of the founding assumptions of empiricism, obliterates the thingly character of the thing by reducing it to an abstract object. It may be possible, as Heidegger himself concedes, to have something like a 'pure' sensation, but to the extent that this is the case it is so because human beings are able to become detached from absorption in worldly life. In worldly life, we are not first presented with two blocks of eight high-frequency sonic pulses, but rather with the sound of a ringing phone (to use one of Heidegger's own examples, we 'hear the door shut in the house' and not the 'acoustical sensations or even mere sounds'[16] produced by the clap of wood on wood). 'In order to hear a bare sound,' as Heidegger puts it, 'we have to listen away from things, divert our ear from them, i.e., listen abstractly.'[17] It is true that Heidegger doesn't consider the other mode in which we encounter bare sensations: in the experience of a sensation of unknown origin, say when hearing a low, non-carlike rumble coming from across the street. But this in no way refutes Heidegger's claim; after all, if one thing unites such experiences it is the fact that one finds oneself *investigating* when they occur: I won't be able to continue with my work undistracted until I have identified the source of the sound (it is my neighbour's metal band). A 'bare' sound is like a broken tool: it enters worldly absorption as an interruption.

So the subject-predicate object structure imposed by the Latin sentence and the empiricist concept of the object as a unity of sensations participate in the oblivion of the thingly character of the thing in different but related ways. The former is unable to grasp thingliness because thingliness (or 'existence') isn't a real predicate, because the subject-predicate sentence passes over the *as such* of the object in order to ascribe properties to it; the latter misses it because it assumes it as something that is always already objectively present in an unproblematic fashion, when in fact this thingliness, when it emerges, entails a breakdown in the functioning of Dasein's worldly life. In Heidegger's own words, the first 'keeps the thing at arm's length from us, as it were, and sets it too far off'; the second 'makes it press too physically upon us. In both interpretations the thing vanishes.'[18]

The third characterisation of the object – the thing understood as formed matter – is perhaps more ambiguous. The reference points for Heidegger here are scholastic philosophy and Kantian aesthetic theory. This understanding of the thing, Heidegger says, has its basis in an idea of creation. Whether we take the thing to be the product of God or something 'formed' by human work, the idea of formed matter conceives of the object as something *made*. Indeed Heidegger's claim is that the matter-form structure is itself a product of a theological 'idea of creation',[19] in which the material aspect of an object is subsumed under a conceptual system that places it in a secondary relationship to form, which becomes the 'whatness' of the object, that which allows one to identify it and distinguish it from other objects. 'Mere' matter is simply everything left over in the object, the opaque residue that is not 'used up' in the creative transformation of matter into a particular. On this conception of the object, if one strips away the usefulness of a piece of equipment, then the remnant left over is 'not defined in its ontological character'; thus it 'remains doubtful whether the thingly character comes to view at all . . .'.[20] What Heidegger wants to get at with his concept of thingliness is the uncanny givenness of the object; the model of creation obliterates the strangeness of the gift of being by relating it back to a human or divine creator.

Now Heidegger is not claiming that it is always possible in practice to isolate these three conceptions of the thing. After all, the first characterisation is not specific to either classical or scholastic thought, reappearing as it does with a new sort of rigour in modern logic, most notably in the works of Frege and Wittgenstein. Similarly, the second characterisation appears in empiricism but again and with more sophistication in Kant, who also utilises the form/matter distinction, and so on.[21] In these reinterpretations and combinations, Heidegger says, the three conceptions of thinghood were 'further strengthened' and have, by the time of the twentieth century, taken on a highly problematic self-evidence. For however complex and nuanced their rearticulations, all three conceptions share a disinclination or indeed perhaps a constitutive inability to properly think the thingly character of the thing: in (1) it is passed over by the predicative structure of the sentence;[22] in (2) it is assumed as objective presence; and in (3) it is subsumed beneath form on the model of creation. Heidegger's artwork essay is distinctive, then, in that in it he explicitly sets out to investigate the object *as object*, specifically in this case the artwork qua concrete thing. He is of course aware of the difficulty of doing so, and this must go some way toward explaining the fact that the style of the essay becomes more obscure from this point on. The problem is that the 'unpretentious thing evades thought most stubbornly'; that 'this self-refusal of the mere thing, this self-contained, irreducible spontaneity, belongs precisely to the essence of the thing'.[23] Heidegger's task in this essay, then, is both very simple and extremely difficult: 'to keep at a distance all the preconceptions and assaults of the above modes of thought, to leave the thing to rest in its own self . . . in its thing-being'.[24]

Here the discussion turns to the theme from *Being and Time* explored in the last chapter: equipmentality. What is interesting is that Heidegger actually chooses an artwork – one of Van Gogh's famous paintings of shoes – in his attempt to explicate once again the phenomenological role of equipment in the constitution of the worldly life of Dasein. 'The equipmental quality of equipment', Heidegger says here, 'consists in its usefulness.'[25] Heidegger's point here is a familiar one: that the essential aspects of equipment are not to be found in any inquiry into the properties of the objectively present item of equipment, but rather in and during the actual, practical use of that equipment. As in *Being and Time*, the defining trait of a piece of equipment is its inconspicuousness, which is the result of the tool's disappearing into the referential context of the world of Dasein. This is why Heidegger says that the peasant shoes are 'more genuinely' equipmental the less the peasant woman 'thinks about the shoes while she is at work, or looks at them at all, or is even aware of them'.[26] Once again, Heidegger wants to turn our attention to the role of world in constituting the condition of the possibility of the apprehension of objects: things don't appear except as parts of a wider equipmental contexture.

And yet something has changed between 1927 and the artwork essay. For Heidegger, Van Gogh's painting of peasant shoes carries out with particular clarity the task of the artwork: it foregrounds the equipmental role of shoes in the worldly life of a peasant woman, bringing to light a particular historical world, but, crucially, it also foregrounds the *earthly* materiality on which this historical world unfolds. In his words, equipment arises in the artwork from out of the 'protected belonging' of world to a 'resting-within-itself'.[27] In the artwork, the thingliness of the thing remains within itself instead of disappearing in and as equipment; the artwork has a phenomenal presence, a kind of self-showing *thereness* that ordinary objects do not. 'Earth' is the name Heidegger gives to this thereness, to this 'strange and uncommunicative feature'[28] of the thing as set forth by the artwork. It is first mentioned in the following paragraph:

> From the dark opening of the worn insides of the shoes the toilsome tread of the worker stares forth. In the stiffly rugged heaviness of the shoes there is the accumulated tenacity of her slow trudge through the far-spreading and ever-uniform furrows of the field swept by a raw wind. On the leather lie the dampness and richness of the soil. Under the soles stretches the loneliness of the field-path as evening falls. In the shoes vibrates the silent call of the earth, its quiet gift of ripening grain and its unexplained self-refusal in the fallow desolation of the wintry field. This equipment is pervaded by uncomplaining worry as to the certainty of bread, the wordless joy of having once more withstood want, the trembling before the impending childbed and shivering at the surrounding menace of death. The equipment belongs to the *earth*, and it is protected in the *world* of the peasant woman. From out of this protected belonging the equipment itself rises to its resting-within-itself.[29]

I cite the entire paragraph because the stylistic turn evidenced in it is conceptually important (even if a little kitsch). Heidegger is mobilising the sonority of language in an attempt at *showing* the reader something of the concept of earth, letting the thingly character of the text speak of the earthly materiality he wants to evoke. The earth, the thingly-quality of the thing, emerges here in distinction to the three traditional ideas of thingliness that Heidegger has described. We saw that in these ideas, the thingly character of things is passed over, contained in form or subjugated under the idea of creation. The concept of earth, on the other hand, is designed to evoke a materiality that remains with the object even after its subsumption into a worldly equipmental contexture. The artwork lets material be earth: the thingliness of things is no longer passed over, reduced to a brute meaningless presence, or made into an opaque residue left over after use, but emerges in its own right, striking yet in some sense intelligible. As Heidegger will put it, in the artwork material (whether it be paint, language, stone or sound) 'is not used up' in the way it is in other objects. The artwork, if properly executed, 'sets itself back into the massiveness and heaviness of the stone, into the firmness and pliancy of wood, into the hardness and lustre of metal, into the brightening and darkening of color, into the clang of tone, and into the naming power of the word'.[30] Important in this regard is Heidegger's concept of strife (*Streit*), which he uses to name the co-belonging of, and essential difference between, world and earth. Strife is what makes possible this phenomenological difference between the experience of breakdown that takes place in the broken tool and that which emerges in the artwork. In the experience of the broken tool materiality erupts out of use in the mode of pure disruption; it throws Dasein out of absorption, but phenomenologically speaking it usually gives nothing more than this breakdown: there is no experience of touching against the world *as such*, just a moment of annoyance and/or anxiety that fades as Dasein becomes reabsorbed. The experience of the artwork proceeds analogously, waking Dasein up out of absorption, but the foregrounding of material here takes place with a simultaneous opening up of world. What emerges in the artwork is an ontological discord, a setting forth of earth that opens world, and an opening of world that sets forth earth. 'In strife', as Heidegger puts it, 'each opponent carries the other beyond itself'; world and earth 'raise each other into the self-assertion of their essential natures'.[31] If in the broken tool the materiality of the object emerges and disrupts the functioning of world, then in the artwork this is counterbalanced by a simultaneous emergence of a particular historical horizon: strife allows Dasein to follow through on the experience of disruption. One way of framing this would be to say: the artwork provokes wonder at the existence of the world by foregrounding earth, but the world that arises is in each case historical. And yet this is perhaps inaccurate, or at least too quick, for as we have seen, the emergency of language that takes place in the poem proceeds via a *suspension* of the historical dimension of experience, effecting in Dasein a kind of waking up out of its particular historical world. We could say, then, that experience with art brings Dasein out of its world in a way that allows it to have momentary phenomenological access to the historical horizon itself: that wondering at the existence of the world allows an encounter with the historically determined conditions of the possibility of ontic appearance. This can go some way to explaining why art is linked to 'the political' (and as we will see, this link is very important and highly problematic in the artwork essay): in extracting Dasein from absorption by foregrounding earth, art allows it to come to see its world for what it is (a historically given horizon that conditions appearance). Art, then, presents the *contingency* of Dasein's historical world, which is why it is fair to say that properly executed artworks are able to interrogate or even challenge the historical circumstances in which they appear. This is the case for two reasons: (1) the world's contingency is itself a condition for the world's transformation, and the presentation of contingency is a condition for the presentation of the *possibility* of transformation; art gives possibility; and (2) this presentation of possibility is always historically localisable: the possibility presented in an artwork is not just the general idea of possibility, but also the *particular* possibilities or potentialities for transformation that exist at a specific historical moment.

So for instance Joseph Kosuth's *Five Words in Red Neon* functions both as an uncannily literal example of Heidegger's 'language brought to language' *and* as a singular intervention into the history of conceptualism; in his still lifes Cezanne brought attention to the *fact* of paint by foregrounding colour and problems of perspective, but his inquiries into form also represented a sophisticated engagement with the problems of perception and temporality as they presented themselves in the historical moment of French post-impressionist painting. And the presentation and interrogation of world carried out in art also has wider historical implications: Kosuth's art cannot be understood without reference to the linguistic turn that took place in the second half of the twentieth century (he is explicit about the influence of Wittgenstein on his work); Cezanne's painting reflects on (and could even be understood as participating in) a series of important shifts in the understanding of representation taking place at the end of the nineteenth century.[32] Art juts through the historical world, presenting it in a way that allows not only an encounter with the world *as such*, but engagement with a *particular* world's conditions of possibility.

It is important that Heidegger chooses Van Gogh's painting as his first and principal example. Most obviously, he chooses the painting because it sets up a literalised image of the claim that the artwork foregrounds the material face of equipment, presenting something that is not 'used up' in worldly absorption. Yet this is incidental to Heidegger's argument; clearly an artwork doesn't have to depict a piece of equipment for it to be able to bring to light and perhaps transform our relation to equipmentality. Secondly, though, the painting is convenient for Heidegger thanks to another literality: in presenting the world of the peasant, it is also particularly useful for presenting the materiality of earth, on which and with which the peasant makes her living. This second literality *is* of conceptual importance, for Heidegger's concept 'earth' is meant to refer to *the actual earth itself*, although it does so in a particular way and with some obliquity (after all, as with worldly equipment, the earth is presented even in paintings that do not literally depict it or reference any relation with it). Repeatedly throughout the essay Heidegger links his concept of earth with the rhythms of peasant life, with a kind of organic spontaneity, with a protective force that could provide shelter and ground for dwelling.

Such pastoral metaphors are common in Heidegger, and say more about him than simply that his tastes were provincial. In *Heidegger's Roots*, Charles Bambach launches a merciless attack on this aspect of his work, linking his discourse with that of his far less philosophically sophisticated Far Right contemporaries (including Alfred Baeumler, Franz Böhm and Ernst Krieck), showing a disturbing overlap between his metaphors and imagery and that of a certain 'Alemannic-Swabian-Bavarian form of National Socialism'.[33] While Bambach's reading of Heidegger solely in terms of the ideology of autochthony (*Bodenständigkeit*) may be too reductive (such reductionism is perhaps unsurprising considering the decision to focus exclusively on his output between 1933 and 1945), the work shows that certain questions remain as urgent as ever. It shows, for instance, how carrying out a reading of the artwork essay (and certain of the late texts on language) with attention to style and tone should require us to follow up on whether Heidegger's kitschiness is more than just a quirk, considering the extent to which it reflects an aesthetic that has its roots in a particular type of radical conservatism[34] (why, for instance, does Heidegger choose a painting of *peasant* shoes as one of his key examples?[35]). In his introduction to his translation of Philippe Lacoue-Labarthe's *Heidegger and the Politics of Poetry* (which book is attentive to the real difficulty of these issues), Jeff Fort describes the situation like this: 'Put somewhat crudely, it could be said that in response to the Nazi pathos around "Blut und Boden," although Heidegger rejects blood, his feet remain firmly on the soil for which the Nazis fought.'[36] Blunt as it may be, the pertinence of the claim is borne out by the text, in which we find Heidegger repeatedly referring to the possibility of a 'historical people'[37] coming to realise its nation's 'vocation'[38] by grounding itself on the earth in an act of primordial decision. Earth for Heidegger forms a highly ambiguous function, appearing at times as a disruptive or deterritorialising force (i.e. 'the earth juts through the world'[39]) but at others as a kind of absolute *ground* on the basis of which the (German) nation could carry out some originary act of self-appropriation (i.e. 'upon the earth and in it, historical man grounds his dwelling in the world'[40]). So the question is as follows: what makes this vacillation possible? My intention is not to carry out another critique of Heidegger by drawing a crude equation between his philosophy and his Nazism,[41] but to read him against himself, attempting to rescue the philosophically valuable aspects of his pastoral.

Badiou argues that Heidegger's understanding of the artwork 'exposes an indiscernible entanglement between the saying of the poet and the thought of the thinker'.[42] His claim is that Heidegger is guilty of linking philosophy too closely to one of its conditions (in Badiou's system these are love, science, politics and art; Heidegger is accused of tying philosophy too closely to art, specifically poetry), which always implies a handing over of key philosophical tasks and so a paralysis of philosophy proper. The easiest way to find initial support for Badiou's claim is simply to look at the style of the late texts on poetic language, or to the 'toilsome tread of the worker' paragraph from the artwork essay. In these moments Heidegger tries to work in alliance with poetry, and attempts himself to utilise the materiality of language; at times it is obvious that he wants to bring the reader to the poetic experience that concerns him. It is this thesis of the alliance between poetry and 'thought' – a mode of discourse that would plot a kind of middle ground between poetic and philosophical language – that is at the root of the much maligned obscurity of the later Heidegger. And it is an obscurity that is of an entirely different order to the difficulty of *Being and Time*: if in the 1927 text Heidegger writes in a laborious style, it is by no means the case that the text is 'poetic' in the way that certain of the late works are clearly intended to be. The style of *Being and Time* is a result of Heidegger's commitment to the thesis of the world-constituting role of discourse,[43] and represents an attempt by him at escaping the grammatical traps set by the Cartesian conceptual schema. This is not an attempt to usurp the role of the poet: it is the result of the difficulty of using language to present counterintuitive ideas about it. The first glimmers of Heidegger's suturing[44] of philosophy to poetry appeared a few years after the publication of *Being and Time*, and only in the mid-to-late thirties did it start to become decisive in determining the path of his thinking. Thus Badiou's thesis, if undeniably pertinent (and presented, it should be said, in passing while he works toward a different goal), requires significant nuancing.

In fact it is possible to isolate two different versions of the suture in the works after the turning. After all, if Badiou's thesis applies quite readily to a set of later texts – the sequence of engagements with poetry and language beginning at the end of 1946 with 'What are Poets For?' and culminating in 1959 with *On the Way to Language* – then it does so more ambiguously to the texts on the same written between 1933 and the end of the Second World War, which are problematic for a different but related set of reasons. For what takes place in this fraught period is more than the suturing of poetry to philosophy via the claim that only poetic thought can rescue being from its oblivion by technological nihilism: what takes place here is '*the suturing to the political of philosophy's suturing to the poem*'.[45] The claim, and I am following Philippe Lacoue-Labarthe in making it, is that Heidegger's suture of philosophy to the poem also involved a sleight of hand with regard to the political, which in the works of the thirties and early forties was tied into the schema in a sometimes explicit, sometimes more clandestine way. By the time of writing 'What are Poets For?' at the end of 1946, Heidegger sees the task of the poet in terms that seem, at least on the face of it, to be politically rather neutral: a work of remembrance for the departed gods, and the clearance of a space for their possible return. Just three years earlier, however, Heidegger posits an intimate link between poetic saying and the possibility of an appropriation on behalf of the German people of its own particular destiny in the historical sending of being.[46] The lines toward the closing of Heidegger's lecture on Hölderlin's 'Homecoming' makes this all too clear: here Heidegger, using Hölderlinian language, identifies the poet's 'kin' with those 'sons of the homeland, who though far distant from its soil, still gaze into the gaiety of the homeland shining toward them', willing to 'sacrifice their life for the still reserved find'[47] of a renewal of poetic dwelling. This comes four months after the Nazi defeat at Stalingrad.

What takes place in the pre-war and wartime lectures on poetry, and with more subtlety in the artwork essay, is the undermining of the distinction between poetry and myth, at least if myth is understood as 'full, original speech, at times revealing, at times founding the intimate being of a community'.[48] Myth, according to this understanding, is as a system of written or spoken works which provides a ground for the existence of the world of a historical people: it legitimates social structures, gives a foundation for tradition and custom and allows a people to come to know itself through images of historical and/or cosmogenetic events. If in poetry the world *as such* appears in all its gratuity (like the rose of Angelus Silesius), then in this deployment of myth it appears as something justified. In such an understanding, the key task of myth is to *make a figure of the origin*, to render *representable* the origin of a people. Poetry and this image of myth, then, both find their *raison d'être* in existence *as such*, but while the former works to present it in all its uncanny givenness, the latter wants to explain the existence of a people's world, to provide a reason for being and for the being of the people (here we see a glimmer of the link between *mythos* and *logos*: myth as the irrational underside of the principle of sufficient reason).

Poetry presents the thingly or earthly aspect of language in a way that wakes Dasein up out of its absorption in its historical world, provoking a confrontation with it (the artwork in general proceeds according to the same schema, though of course the material foregrounded in the earthly aspect of the work is not language but paint, wood, sound or whatever). What is presented poetically is something other to the world, a materiality that can never be made a part of it. Poetic experience is an encounter with possibility: it shows that the world does not have to be the way it is, that there is no necessity behind a particular historical formation (that there is no *reason* for being). This image of myth, on the other hand, represents the erasure – or rather the fiction of the erasure – of the gap between earth and world, such that the latter could be said to swallow the former. Earth in this myth is incorporated into, and indeed is supposed to provide the ultimate grounding for, the referential totality that is Dasein's world. So we should not be surprised to find Heidegger wavering on the precise distinction between earth and world, and on the nature of their relationship: undermining the distinction between poetry and this particular image of myth means undermining the distinction between earth and world. There are two Heideggers operating in the artwork essay: one with a genuine concern for following through on poetic experience, with thinking through the irreducibility of the strife between earth and world, and one that wants to see poetic saying become mythic speech. The latter is the Heidegger that speaks most clearly in the Hölderlin lecture, the Heidegger who echoes reactionary sentiments about the rootlessness of modern life. This Heidegger wants to establish an autochthonous connection between the German people and their historical homeland, *to ground world on earth* through the philosophical valorisation of what Ernst Bloch identified as a *pastorale militans*.[49]

No doubt such a manoeuvre was made possible by the proximity, identified by Nancy, between literature and myth, such that the former is always in danger of being identified with the latter. This potential mistake (and it is a mistake: each time the identification takes place it represents the destruction of poetry, the silencing of what it has to say) stems from the fact that 'the share of myth and the share of literature are not two separable and opposable parts at the heart of the work'.[50] This is to say that it is not usually possible to draw a strict distinction between the poetic work and the mythic work (it might be more accurate to say that the poetic and the mythic represent two tendencies in any work). However, the distinction can and should be applied to the philosophical understanding of the political role of art in modernity, and it is on this that Heidegger wavers. Heidegger's mistake, we might say, was to fall into the trap of thinking that the mythic could come to subsume the poetic, lapsing into claiming that earth can ground and properly legitimate a historical world after the death of God. The difference consists in the fact that this mythic project of ontological justification is doomed to failure, because the explanation and justification of the existence of the world is ontologically impossible. This is to say that full mythical grounding *is itself a myth* (and poetry can't justify anything). This is not a 'critique of myth' as such (whatever that would mean); rather it is a critique of a certain ideological deployment of myth, of a certain temptation to mobilise – indeed to *mythologise* – the mythic that opens up in modernity.[51]

It is possible, following Nancy, to frame the problem around the concept of work, which should be understood here in terms of the full ambiguity of the word in English (and in many of its Romance equivalents), where 'work' is both noun and verb, both the literary or artistic work and the process of labour. Myth, on this account, would be a system of written or spoken works designed to make the *community itself* work, to render it operative as a meaning-producing whole. This means covering over the original lack-of-origin, the essential dispersal, at the heart of every people: of denying the uncanny givenness and gratuity of the world. Poetry, on the other hand, gives Dasein over to exactly that: *the basic inexplicability of existence*, the fact that being *as such* cannot be legitimately put to work as part of a national historical imaginary. If mythical community in modernity is a community appropriating its own essence, whether it be framed in a discourse that is biological (as in Nazism), 'cultural' (as in the more guarded words of today's Right), productive (as in Stalinism), or linguistic and historical (as with Heidegger), then poetic community (the community of Nancy's 'literary communism'[52]) is exactly what is left over after this movement of appropriation. What we see emerging here, then, is the fundamental link between the experience of existence *as such* and community, which at its most basic is nothing more or less than the sharing of the exposure to the world's gratuity. The ambiguity in Heidegger between a proper following through on poetic experience and the mythic recuperation of that experience, then, has its basis in the double-faced nature of community, which appears at one moment as the sharing of dispersal and then at another as a deadly simulacrum of such sharing.

The violence at the heart of the mythical communal project that tempted Heidegger stems from the real *ontological* violence of the poetic experience it rejects: the violent sheerness of the existence of the world, what I have been calling its gratuity, can only be appropriated by setting off a potentially infinite process of *ontic* violence. This mythic image of community, in which the death of each member will be set to work and recuperated into the hermeneutic totality of a particular historical world, in which life (and so each death) would be given a 'meaning' shared by all the members of the community, in which the people would commune through sharing a figuration of the origin, takes the condition of the impossibility of its final realisation – the unjustifiability of existence *as such*, and of every human life in the singular – as its original provoking fact, beginning a process doomed to bad infinity.[53] One thinks again of Blanchot: 'Man is the indestructible that can be destroyed.'[54] There is a violence that takes place not in spite but because of the mutual exposure that is community, and it is no less violent for it (on the contrary). It is worth citing Jonathan Littell on this point, for if there is anything his disturbing novel shows it is the very ambiguity of the bond that ties one human being to another:

> I now thought I could understand better the reactions of the men and officers during the executions. If they suffered, as I had suffered during the Great Action, it wasn't just because of the smells and the sight of blood, but because of the terror and the moral suffering of the people they shot . . . In many cases, I said to myself, what I had taken for gratuitous sadism, the astonishing brutality with which some men treated the condemned before executing them, was nothing but a consequence of the monstrous pity they felt and which, incapable of expressing itself otherwise, turned into rage, but an impotent rage, without object, and which thus almost inevitably had to turn against those who originally provoked it. If the terrible massacres of the East prove one thing, paradoxically, it is the awful, inalterable solidarity of humanity . . . Their reactions, their violence, their alcoholism, the nervous depressions, the suicides, my own sadness, all that demonstrated that the *other* exists, exists as an other, as a human, and that no will, no ideology, no amount of stupidity or alcohol can break this bond, tenuous but indestructible. This is a fact, not an opinion.[55]

The narrator's use of the 'astonishing brutality' and 'gratuitous sadism' are telling here. One can only refuse the astonishing gratuity of being with appropriately desperate violence.

It is as though Heidegger, with his ontological approach to the work of art, discovered something that he was not quite able to countenance: that the artwork, and poetry in particular (the poem is paradigmatic of art in Heidegger), reveals nothing so much as the precariousness of human worldly life, the dependence of world on a materiality that (perhaps counterintuitively, and thus perhaps contrary to Heidegger's own expectations) cannot be incorporated into it. If the power of the artwork is to bring attention to an earthly materiality or 'thingly character' that would otherwise remain inconspicuous, then this materiality, far from providing a foundation for the dwelling of a historical people, juts through the world and renders it denaturalised, even alien (the poetic experience of the world is an experience of being suddenly unable to take the world for granted). So the earth is universal in the literal sense of the word: it is not proper to any place, and has no topological content that would allow it to play a territorialising role in the historical becoming of a particular people. It cannot become a part of world. Instead of providing a ground for it, earth prevents its closure. In terms Agamben employs in *The Time That Remains* (a text I return to later in this book), this earthly materiality announces 'the revocation of every vocation',[56] the fact that humanity has no historical destiny.

In the Hölderlin lectures, Heidegger claims that the task of the poet is to 'consecrate the soil',[57] to use language to sacralise the relationship between historical Dasein and its particular locality. This is Heidegger attempting to re-enchant the earth by returning to a mythopoetic image of it; it is a move that cannot be understood except as part of his rejection of the modern technological image of the earth as an objectively present object with the potential for exploitation. Heidegger's infamous criticism in the *Introduction to Metaphysics* of the nihilistic drive of Russia and the United States is made on these grounds: both nations, despite their obvious (ontic) political differences, were for Heidegger in thrall to the same (ontological) picture of the earth.[58] But it is possible to accept aspects of Heidegger's critique of metaphysics while refusing his reactionary anti-modernism, holding that the technological/metaphysical world picture passes over the truth that happens on earth while foreclosing any turn to re-mythologisation. So we can supplement the alternatives Heidegger envisaged (the nihilism of capitalism, the nihilism of Soviet communism or a return to a mythologised earthly dwelling) with another possibility: a post-metaphysical, non-mythological thought of the earth. Against Heidegger (and with him), we need to assert that earth grounds nothing for historical Dasein: it supplies no ordering principle, provides no direction, and cannot be appropriated. If the mistake of metaphysical thought is to pass over the earth, and so to miss the site of the only truly universal experience of community, then Heidegger's own mistake was to try to mythologise this experience, to attempt to put it to work as a foundation for worldly destiny. Forever withdrawn from meaning, the earth cannot function as a foundation for world, and a 'historical people' cannot ground its *Heimat* on it without setting off a badly infinite cycle of violence. If we are able to oppose the continued technicisation of the earth in globalisation without committing to recovering an experience of meaning that has been destroyed in modernity, then it may be possible to pose the problem anew. The task would no longer be to prepare for the return of the gods, but rather to follow through on the unfinished project of disenchantment.

This is why Agamben resists the idea of human destiny that turns up occasionally in Heidegger. The poetic experience of the earth that becomes possible in modernity, while opening an opportunity for humanity to come to terms with the history of being as nihilism, simultaneously opens the option of a violent refusal of the groundlessness that emerges in it: a refusal that, despite everything, turns to being in an attempt at finding humanity's historical vocation. This refusal, which is violent not in spite but because of the exhaustion of being's epochal figures that modernity achieves, tries to found a new history – and to consolidate a people – right when and where those concepts become philosophically and politically untenable. Part of the value of Agamben's work – and here he must be understood as an ambivalent but nevertheless faithful inheritor of Heidegger's thinking – lies in his consistent foreclosure of this option. This is part of why, for instance, he rigorously insists on the category of inoperativity throughout his thinking: what he wants to take from Heidegger's philosophy of the history of being is something that could never be set to *work* in the becoming of a historical people. What he is after, in other words, is a politics 'equal to the absence of a work of man'.[59] Or as he puts it in another context:

> The fact that must constitute the point of departure for any discourse on ethics is that there is no essence, no historical or spiritual vocation, no biological destiny that humans must enact or realize. This is the only reason why something like an ethics can exist, because it is clear that if humans were or had to be this or that substance, this or that destiny, no ethical experience would be possible – there would only be tasks to be done.[60]

We need to follow up on this problem of ground and groundlessness, turning in particular to the concepts of sacrifice and violence as Agamben presents them in *Language and Death*. For if this is the book in which Agamben's inheritance of Heidegger is at its clearest, then it is also here that he makes a break with the philosopher. Yet it is a break that is in some ways truer to Heidegger's thinking than the German philosopher himself was always able to remain.

NOTES

1. Brassier, 'I am a nihilist because I still believe in truth'.
2. Agamben, *Infancy and History*, 10–11.
3. This has been renewed in Agamben's recent text *The Sacrament of Language*. Here Agamben carries out a 'philosophical archaeology of the oath' (2), arguing that it is paradigmatic of the ways in which 'the human being must put himself at stake in his speech' (71). In the terms I am developing, we might say that the oath (which is, above all, a performative utterance that refers to its own taking place) brings to light the political and ethical aspects of the *experimentum linguae* in an exemplary way. Crucial here too is the historical element: Agamben will argue that the relatively recent decline of the oath is bound up with the declension of the history of being as nihilism. In other words, the oath will reach an end if and when metaphysics does.
4. Agamben, *The Open*, 75.
5. Heidegger, 'The Origin of the Work of Art', 144.
6. Heidegger writes: 'What art is can be gathered from a comparative examination of actual artworks. But how are we to be certain that we are indeed basing such an examination on artworks if we do not know beforehand what art is?' ('The Origin of the Work of Art', 144).
7. Ibid. 144.
8. Heidegger, *Being and Time*, SZ 153; 143e.
9. Heidegger, 'The Origin of the Work of Art', 145.
10. Ibid. 145.
11. Ibid. 145.
12. Ibid. 156.
13. Ibid. 149.
14. Ibid. 150.
15. Ibid. 149–50.
16. Ibid. 152.
17. Ibid. 152.
18. Ibid. 152.
19. Ibid. 155.
20. Ibid. 156.
21. Kant writes: 'These two concepts [matter and form] underlie all other reflection, so inseparably are they bound up with all employment of the

understanding. The one [matter] signifies the determinable in general, the other [form] its determination . . .' (*Critique of Pure Reason*, B323; 280e).
22. In Frege and Wittgenstein things are obviously more complex than this. In Frege's work, the immediate significance of which consisted precisely in its advance over syllogistic and subject-predicate logic, existence is not a property but a quantifier, and is predicated of *concepts*, not of objects. Saying that X exists is for the Frege of the *Grundlagen* akin to saying that there are one or more of X. Frege: '[e]xistence is analogous to number. Affirmation of existence is in fact nothing but the denial of the number nought. Because existence is a property of concepts, the ontological argument for the existence of God breaks down' (*The Foundations of Arithmetic*, 65). Wittgenstein was also aware of the problem of existence, which for him could not be posed in propositional language. To say that one wonders at the existence of the world is for Wittgenstein a misuse of language (see Wittgenstein, 'Ethics, Life and Faith', 255). I turn to this problem in detail in Chapter 7.
23. Heidegger, 'The Origin of the Work of Art', 157.
24. Ibid. 157.
25. Ibid. 159.
26. Ibid. 159.
27. Ibid. 160.
28. Ibid. 157.
29. Ibid. 159–60.
30. Ibid. 171. In the terms of the previous chapter, we could say that the earth is what the poem mobilises in an attempt to display the 'fact' that the world exists. The poem foregrounds the earthly aspects of language, displaying the *there is* of world.
31. Ibid. 174.
32. Like that of Van Gogh and Seurat, Cezanne's work engages with perception in a way that would have been largely unintelligible before the development of photography; similarly, it investigates time and duration from a standpoint that seems uncannily prophetic of the development of film (in this sense Cezanne's work can be placed alongside that of his contemporary Bergson); and with its commitment to inquiry it paved the way for painting's interrogation of painting throughout the twentieth century.
33. Bambach, *Heidegger's Roots*, 4. Bambach writes:

> Far from being a pastoral roundelay about the rural landscape, Heidegger's song of the earth in praise of rootedness and autochthony [*Bodenständigkeit*] is part of a martial-political ideology of the chthonic that was deployed in the 1930s in the name of German metaphysical-racial autochthony. (5)

34. Saul Friedlander's still timely *Reflections of Nazism: An Essay on Kitsch and Death* divests kitsch of whatever innocence it may have had, making clear its role in the discourse of Nazism.

35. Or, if we believe Meyer Schapiro when he claims that these may not even be peasant shoes, then why is Heidegger so inclined to take them as such (*Theory and Philosophy of Art*, 136)?
36. Fort, in Lacoue-Labarthe, *Heidegger and the Politics of Poetry*, x.
37. Heidegger, 'The Origin of the Work of Art', 167.
38. Ibid. 167.
39. Ibid. 172.
40. Ibid. 171.
41. A recent and provocative contribution to this genre is Emmanuel Faye's *Heidegger*. One of the weaknesses of Faye's book is that he bases his arguments on Heidegger's weakest texts, starting from him at his worst and attempting to work from there to tarnish his far more philosophically accomplished works (and indeed, Faye's own book is at its worst in its analysis of *Being and Time*, repeating old platitudes about irrationalism and decisionism in another attempt to show the proto-fascist nature of Heidegger's critique of the Cartesian subject; see 15–38). By concentrating on the artwork essay, on the other hand, I take myself to be engaging with Heidegger in one of his most philosophically compelling moments. Following the principle of charity in this way is not only fairer to one's subject; it is also likely to produce results of greater philosophical interest.
42. Badiou, *Handbook of Inaesthetics*, 6.
43. Lafont, *Heidegger, Language, and World-Disclosure*, 11–84.
44. Badiou gives a clear definition of what he means by 'suture' in his *Manifesto for Philosophy* (see 61–9).
45. Lacoue-Labarthe, *Heidegger and the Politics of Poetry*, 23 (my emphasis).
46. Heidegger, *Elucidations of Hölderlin's Poetry*, 43. Heidegger claims that the one who 'says the mystery again and again' is able to preserve '"the treasure", which is most proper to the homeland, "the German". . . .'.
47. Ibid. 48.
48. Nancy, 'Myth Interrupted', 48.
49. Bloch, quoted in Bambach, *Heidegger's Roots*, 5–6.
50. Nancy, 'Myth Interrupted', 63.
51. In Nancy's terms, this would be a deployment of myth that takes place in the face of the 'absence of myth' that defines the post-romantic world. As he puts it:

> It is true that we do not know very much about what mythic truth was or is for men living in the midst of what we call 'myths.' But we know that we – our community, if it is one, our modern and postmodern humanity – have no relation to the myth of which we are speaking, even as we fulfill it or try to fulfill it. In a sense, for us all that remains of myth is its fulfillment or its will. We no longer live in mythic life, nor in a time of mythic invention or speech. When we speak of 'myth' or of 'mythology' we mean the negation of something at least as much

as the affirmation of something. This is why our scene of myth, our discourse of myth, and all our mythological thinking make up a myth: to speak of myth has only ever been to speak of its absence. And the word 'myth' itself designates the absence of what it names. ('Myth Interrupted', 52)

I return at length to the concept of myth in Chapter 5.
52. See Nancy, 'Literary Communism'.
53. This is why Nancy claims that the myth of communal fusion 'contains no other logic than that of the suicide of the community that is governed by it'. He goes on:

> [T]he logic of Nazi Germany was not only that of the extermination of the other, of the subhuman deemed exterior to the communion of blood and soil, but also, effectively, the logic of sacrifice aimed at all those in the 'Aryan' community who did not satisfy the criteria of *pure* immanence, so much so that – it being obviously impossible to set a limit on such criteria – the suicide of the German nation itself may have represented a plausible extrapolation of the process . ⋯ ('The Inoperative Community', 12)

The Nazi project of communal founding was set for self destruction because according to its own criteria the *Volk* could never be whole enough, never totally purified (race, after all, is a notoriously nebulous category: at the absolute best it represents what Wittgenstein would have called a 'family resemblance' concept, which means its borders cannot be fully determined and policed without it becoming an exercise in terror). Hirschbiegel's film *Der Untergang* (*Downfall* in English), which focuses on events in the Führerbunker in the days leading up to the German surrender, depicts the outcomes of this suicidal logic.
54. Blanchot, *The Infinite Conversation*, 135.
55. Littell, *The Kindly Ones*, 147.
56. Agamben, *The Time That Remains*, 68.
57. Heidegger, *Elucidations of Hölderlin's Poetry*, 170. In another piece, Heidegger speaks of the various local dialects spoken in Germany, claiming that the differences between them 'do not solely nor primarily grow out of different movement patterns of the organ of speech'. Instead, Heidegger says, the earth itself speaks through Germany's various regional languages:

> The landscape, and that means the earth, speaks in them, differently each time. But the mouth is not merely a kind of organ of the body understood as an organism – body and mouth are part of the earth's flow and growth in which we mortals flourish, and from which we receive the soundness of our roots [*Bodenständigkeit*]. If we lose the earth, of course, we also lose the roots. ('The Nature of Language', 98–9)

Language here is not only constitutive for Dasein's dwelling: it arises from and even *as* the earth on which Dasein's historical world unfolds.
58. Heidegger, *Introduction to Metaphysics*, 31.
59. Agamben, 'The Work of Man', 10.
60. Agamben, *The Coming Community*, 43.

4. The Unbearable

The rustling of the there is ... is horror.[1]

Agamben's *Language and Death* opens with a famous passage from Heidegger:

> Mortals are they who can experience death as death. Animals cannot do so. But animals cannot speak either. The essential relation between death and language flashes up before us, but remains still unthought. It can, however, beckon us toward the way in which the nature of language draws us into its concern, and so relates us to itself, in case death belongs together with what reaches out for us, touches us.[2]

As the position of this citation makes clear, this is an important thought in *Language and Death*. Why is it, Agamben will ask, that in Heidegger's philosophy human beings are presented as 'both *mortal* and *speaking*'?[3] What is the connection between the 'faculty' for death and the 'faculty' for language, as Agamben will strikingly put it? In *Language and Death*, Agamben investigates this connection by turning to the problem of negativity as it presents in Heidegger, Hegel and Western philosophy more generally. He writes:

> In the course of our research it became apparent that, in fact, the connection between language and death could not be illuminated without a clarification of the problem of the negative. Both the 'faculty' for language and the 'faculty' for death, inasmuch as they open for humanity the most proper dwelling place, reveal and disclose this same dwelling place as always already permeated by and founded in negativity.[4]

The real starting point of the text is the claim that language and death are connected insofar as they both bring the human being into relation with a primordial or foundational negativity, which Agamben will characterise in terms of a negative ground.[5]

For Heidegger and Hegel, Agamben argues, a negativity emerges right in the very thereness or thisness of the human being, in and as the fact or site of its existence (this is why the subtitle of the text is 'the *place* of negativity'). Specifically he reads Heidegger as showing, in his analysis of being-toward-death, how the very 'there' of Dasein, the dwelling place of the human, is permeated by a radical negativity:

> [I]f being its own *Da* (its own there) is what characterizes Dasein (Being-there), [the analytic of death] signifies that precisely at the point where the possibility of being *Da*, of being at home in one's own place, is actualized, through the expression of death, in the most authentic mode, the Da is finally revealed as the source from which a radical and threatening negativity emerges. There is something in the little word *Da* that nullifies and introduces negation into that entity – the human – which has to be its *Da*. *Negativity reaches Dasein from its very Da.*[6]

And he reads Hegel as finding a crucial link between language and negativity in the analysis of sense certainty in the *Phenomenology of Spirit*: '[T]he Eleusinian mystery that opens the *Phenomenology* has for its content the experience of a *Nichtigkeit*, a negativity that is revealed as always already inherent in sense-certainty at the moment when it attempts to "take the *This*" (das *Diese* nehmen) . . .'[7] As is clear from these two citations, key for Agamben is the role of demonstrative pronouns (Jakobson calls them linguistic 'shifters') in Heidegger's Dasein (being-there, or, as Agamben will have us read it, being the there) and Hegel's analysis of *das Diese nehmen* in the first chapter of the *Phenomenology*. For the Agamben of *Language and Death*, the philosophical problem raised by demonstrative pronouns constitutes 'in some manner . . . the original theme of philosophy'.[8] This is because the demonstrative pronoun does not just denote an object, but also allows language to refer to its own taking place. When I say '*this* dog is black', for instance, I do more than just attach a predicate to an object: I attach a predicate to an object that exists before me here and now. Using a word like 'this' ties my statement to a particular spatio-temporal location, such that the meaning of my utterance is not fully ascertainable outside of the physical context in which it is uttered; the 'this' in our dog sentence is intelligible only as part of a *particular* discursive event. Demonstrative pronouns are instances of language pointing to its own taking place; as with poetry, they give 'an experience of language that speaks itself'.[9] This means that they present a version of what is for Agamben the key philosophical problem: the *fact* that language exists, a fact that is indissociable from the problem of being. As Agamben writes: 'The problem of being – the supreme metaphysical problem

– emerges from the very beginning as inseparable from the problem of the significance of the demonstrative pronoun . . .'[10]

Here Agamben asks: 'What, in the instance of discourse, permits that it be indicated, permits that before and beyond what is signified in it, it *shows* its own taking place?'[11] He answers as follows: '*The utterance and the instance of discourse are only identifiable as such through the voice that speaks them* . . .'.[12] Voice is the *material* link between discourse and its taking place: it is what binds what is said to a particular subject in a particular spatio-temporal location. To return to my earlier example, voice is what gives content to the *here and now* in which I predicate blackness of this particular dog: *here and now* always means here and now *as I speak*. Importantly, this constitutes the basic difference between human and animal voice: 'A voice as mere sound (an *animal* voice) could certainly be the index of the individual who emits it, but in no way can it refer to the instance of discourse as such, nor open the sphere of utterance.'[13] Human voice is not just the 'mere sonic flux emitted by the phonic apparatus',[14] but crucially also the opening of the possibility of meaning, a sound that is potentially significant. This is why Agamben turns to Augustine's invocation in *De Trinitate* of the experience of hearing a word from a foreign or dead language: what one hears in this case is not a pure sound, but rather a sound that shows an intent to signify. What one hears, in other words, is something on the border between sound and sense, a voice that has not yet attained the status of meaning but which nevertheless emerges as meaningful (the connection between this idea and Heidegger's phenomenology of the 'bare' sound as presented in the last chapter is clear). An animal voice, say the buzz of a cricket, does not produce the same disturbance in me as does a human voice that I cannot understand: in the latter case I will, as Augustine puts it, 'desire to know the thing of which it is a sign'.[15] If we turn to the more usual case of hearing a voice speaking a language in which one is fluent, the salient point for Agamben is that in the normal case the pure intent to signify is not itself directly experienced: in fact it disappears or as he puts it 'goes to ground' in order to make way for signification. This is not as esoteric a claim as it may sound: when someone speaks I usually listen to what they say, not to the sound of their saying it (the exception that proves the rule here might be love, where the sound of someone's voice can be captivating; notice how Augustine directly invokes the case of love in his discussion of the *verbum incognitum*, asking rhetorically whether in this case the listener 'can be said to be without love'[16] – we will come back to this). This going to ground of voice is a condition of the possibility of transcription, for what is written down and recorded from speech is, of course, the content of the signification separated from the voice that voiced it (as Daniel McLoughlin puts it, '[i]t is this ability to record the voice in writing that differentiates it from *phone*'[17]). Agamben will make very much of this disappearance of the voice in communication, using the capitalised term 'Voice' to distinguish between this voice that goes to ground and the animal voice or mere sound that could never be transcribed (except, perhaps, as an empty onomatopoeia like *bark*). He writes:

> [I]nasmuch as this Voice (which we now capitalize to distinguish from the voice as mere sound) enjoys the status of a *no-longer* (voice) and of a *not-yet* (meaning), it necessarily constitutes a negative dimension. It is *ground*, but in the sense that it *goes to ground* and disappears in order for being and language to take place. According to a tradition that dominates all Western reflection on language from the ancient grammarians' notion of *gramma* to the phoneme in modern phonology, that which articulates the human voice in language is a pure negativity.[18]

For Agamben, at work here is the fundamental movement of Western metaphysics, in which language/being *as such* is presupposed and passed over as something unremarkable, as quite literally unspeakable. As he puts it:

> [I]n metaphysics, the taking place of language (the pure fact that language is) is obliterated in favour of that which is said in the instance of discourse; that is, this taking place (the Voice) is thought only as the foundation of the said, in such a way that the Voice never truly arrives at thought.[19]

Within metaphysics, the human appears poised over an unthinkable abyss, and the self-signification of language (as takes place in demonstrative utterances) can refer only to this abyss. In this way the world's existence is consigned to the ineffable, and the human being to living in the thrall of a fundamental negativity: the very site of the human's existing appears in metaphysics as a nothingness. In *Language and Death*, Agamben will schematise his approach to this problem in terms of the logic of sacrifice, which he takes as a kind of response to this haunting of the human by the negative. The essential thing in the 'sacrificial function', according to Agamben here, is the becoming 'grounded' of 'human community': sacrifice is 'a determinate action that . . . furnishes society and its ungrounded legislation with the fiction of a beginning . . .'.[20] It is, one might say, a means of taming the negativity that plagues the very being-here of human being: human communities make sacrifices – which is to say, they consign living beings to death – as part of an attempt at covering over the abyss of negativity that haunts metaphysical thought. As Colby Dickinson argues in his excellent book on Agamben, this is a 'void so monstrous that it must be disavowed through the violent institution of political actuality intended to cover up or obscure its existence'.[21] Sacrifice is 'an exclusive or divisive action intended to ground humanity in its representative (and subsequently *legal*) forms . . .'.[22] The ritualised violence of sacrifice, in other words, is meant to *hide* the fact of '[t]he ungroundedness of all human praxis'.[23]

As the above indicates, Agamben's approach in *Language and Death* is critical: the question is not just how and why negativity emerges in the very thereness of the human being, but whether and how this negative ground could be dissolved. In the closing chapters of the text, then, we find Agamben working in an almost experimental mode as he tries to rethink this brute nothingness. The question is whether there could be an experience with the voice and language *as such* that is something other than an experience with absence: whether, in other words, we can think the human as consigned to something other than the negative. What Agamben wants to clarify, in other words, is what it would take to *break* the link between the human and negativity, which means thinking being *as such* as something other than pure nothingness. This is why Agamben defines the task of his book not primarily in terms of tracing Voice as the negative foundation of human being, but rather in terms of locating 'another experience of language . . . that does not rest on a negative foundation'.[24] Or as Mills puts it:

> The task of surpassing metaphysics leads Agamben to posit the necessity of an experiment in language, in which what is at stake in language is not the ineffable that must necessarily be suppressed in speech, but the very event of language itself, the taking place of language prior to signification and meaning.[25]

Here we can see the difference between Agamben and Derrida (or at least Agamben's own understanding of the difference[26]): if for Derrida the critique of metaphysics consists in a problematisation of every foundation, of 'radicalizing the problem of negativity and ungroundedness',[27] then for Agamben this critique remains trapped in metaphysics insofar as it continues to be in thrall to a *negative* foundation.[28] As such, I want to characterise Agamben's demand in terms of a demand for a kind of disenchantment: what is pivotal for him is the potential for de-sacralisation, with thinking the conditions of the possibility of a human community that would not be founded in sacrificial or sacred negativity. As Agamben puts it in a statement that can be understood as a summary of the critical argument of the text: '*The foundation of violence is the violence of the foundation.*'[29] Disenchantment would mean a break with the logic that instils violence at the heart of community, a proper owning up to the problem of foundation.

It is worth pausing to recognise that there is incongruence between *Language and Death* and *Homo Sacer* regarding the issue of sacrifice. In the former Agamben finds the sacrificial function at the very heart of the Western *polis* (as determined by metaphysics), while in the latter he traces the figure of *Homo Sacer*, the sacred man from Roman law who can be killed but *cannot* be sacrificed. It seems that in *Homo Sacer* the problem is no longer the sacrificial function, but rather the sacred as it is exemplified in the paradigmatic figure of the *homo sacer*. As Agamben's critique of Bataille in *Homo Sacer* makes clear, this is partly because the logic of sacrifice does not do justice to the status of the *homo sacer*, which as a being that can be killed but not sacrificed is exposed not to ritualised but rather to arbitrary violence. As Agamben writes, '[w]hat confronts us today is a life that as such is exposed to a violence without precedent in the most profane and banal ways.'[30] Or perhaps more pointedly, it is because 'the dimension of bare life that constitutes the immediate referent of sovereign violence is more original than the opposition of the sacrificable and the unsacrificable, and gestures toward an idea of sacredness that is no longer absolutely definable through the conceptual pair ... of fitness for sacrifice and immolation according to ritual forms.'[31] We could be forgiven for thinking, then, that *Homo Sacer* represents a decisive break with *Language and Death*, such that the latter would be of limited use in working to explicate the philosopher's more recent writings. Yet in a paragraph that could have been lifted straight from the earlier text, Agamben writes in *Homo Sacer* that:

> [O]nly language as the pure potentiality to signify, withdrawing itself from every concrete instance of speech, divides the linguistic from the nonlinguistic and allows for the opening of areas of meaningful speech in which certain terms correspond to certain denotations ... The particular structure of law has its foundation in the presuppositional structure of human language.[32]

If in the transition between the two texts we see a move away from the concept of sacrifice toward a concept of the sacred, then the Agamben of *Homo Sacer* is still working to critique the presuppositional structure of metaphysics, which rears its head both in the metaphysical understanding of language, in which the fact of language goes to ground, and in the metaphysically determined *polis*, in which the fact of living is both presupposed and excluded according to the paradoxical structure of the inclusive exclusion. Indeed, we might say that the logic of the sacred at work in *Homo Sacer* represents not a repudiation as much as a refinement of the concept at work in *Language and Death*. As McLoughlin argues: '[W]hat remains consistent is the role of the sacred as that which constitutes law governed community through its being separated, abandoned to itself and therefore unspeakable.'[33] Or as Agamben puts it in the more recent text, '[t]he question "In what way does the living being have language?" corresponds exactly to the question "In what way does bare life dwell in the *polis*?"'[34] In both cases there is a critique of metaphysics' failure to grasp the very fact – the *as such* – of the object in question; what remains consistent across the early and late works is a diagnosis of the fundamental metaphysical problem in terms of negative foundation. Consistent too is the understanding of the legal order as partaking in a secret violence as its means of support. 'Sacrifice' may be too overdetermined a concept to grasp the nature of this violence, especially in modernity, but the underlying presuppositional movement that sparks it is the same whether it is language, life or being *as such* that is passed over and subsequently banished. In each case the oblivion of the fact of being results in its haunting of the ontic as its abyssal ground.

By now we should be able to understand what Agamben means when he writes in *The Coming Community* that the contemporary political situation can be understood in terms of a 'devastating *experimentum linguae* that all over the planet unhinges and empties traditions and beliefs, ideologies and religions, identities and communities'.[35] In the terms of *Language and Death*, this experience would represent the epochal limit of the history of being as metaphysics, a coming to light of the negative foundation that haunts our political space. It is a figure of nihilism understood in the Heideggerian sense as the historical result of the forgetting or oblivion of being, as what emerges when the being of beings is revealed as nothingness. As Agamben puts it in an essay published a few years after *Language and Death*: '[Nihilism] interprets the extreme revelation of language in the sense that there is nothing to reveal, that the truth of language is that it unveils the Nothing of all things.'[36] The experience in question is devastating, then, because it represents the revelation of the fact that there is no firm ontological ground for human action, that our practices do not get their 'meaning' from and are not justifiable with reference to some ultimate foundation (Wittgenstein: 'If I have exhausted the justifications, I have reached bedrock and my spade is turned. Then I am inclined to say: "This is simply what I do."'[37]). This is why Agamben characterises this experience in terms of the unhinging of traditions, beliefs, ideologies, religions and communities: it is an experience that reveals human forms-of-life as founded on an abyss. The implicit question, then, is as follows: what are the conditions of the possibility of a transformation of this experience, such that it no longer exposes the human to a brute negativity?

I want to clarify this question before trying to answer it. To do so I will turn to the early Levinas, and in particular to his thought of the *il y a*, which is probably the most important moment in the early texts, and certainly one which can help illuminate Agamben's project. Toward the outset of his inquiry in *Time and the Other*, Levinas provides a useful thought experiment to explain the concept:

> Let us imagine all things, beings and persons, returning to nothingness. What remains after this imaginary destruction of everything is not something, but the fact that there is [*il y a*]. The absence of everything returns as a presence, as the place where the bottom has dropped out of everything, an atmospheric density, a plenitude of the void, or the murmur of silence. There is, after this destruction of things and beings, the impersonal 'field of forces' of existing. There is something that is neither subject nor substantive. The fact of existing imposes itself when there is no longer anything. And it is anonymous: there is neither anyone nor anything that takes this existence upon itself. It is impersonal like 'it is raining' or 'it is hot.' Existing returns no matter with what negation one dismisses it. There is, as the irremissibility of pure existing.[38]

The *il y a* is existence devoid of existents, being without beings, the naked fact that *there is*. This notion of existence stripped bare provides something of a key to Levinas, because it is crucial to understanding his deeply ambivalent relation to the thought of Heidegger. For though Levinas's body of work can quite fruitfully be understood in terms of a critical response to a certain reading (or indeed productive misreading) of Heidegger's work, the early texts are testaments to a philosopher working to come to grips with the impact of the Heideggerian thought of a distinction between the multiplicity of beings and the being of those beings. And Levinas does not reject this core Heideggerian division (though he does draw some radically 'un-Heideggerian' conclusions from it). On the contrary, it is the nexus around which the early works turn, with Levinas claiming that it is something 'one cannot ignore',[39] that it is 'the most profound thing about *Being and Time* . . .'.[40] I will come back to these claims. For now, it is worth starting where Levinas himself does in *Time and the Other*: in the phenomenological description of the existent's experience of (or, better, exposure to) the *il y a*.

The description of the experience of the insomniac appears first in *Time and the Other* as an example of the existent's exposure to the naked fact of existence. Insomnia is the experience of lying awake in darkness and silence, of being unable to either tie one's consciousness to any particular intentional object or quell its murmurings in sleep. As he lies awake, the insomniac is unsettled not by any particular object but by the pure *fact* of presence itself: he opens and closes his eyes to find that the world looks the same in both instances. In his analysis of this theme in Levinas, Critchley refers to the night of insomnia as one in which 'we no longer regard things, but where they seem to regard us . . .'. He goes on: '[T]he *il y a* is the experience of consciousness without a subject . . . In the *il y a*, I am neither myself nor an other, and this is precisely the abject experience of horror . . .'.[41] The insomniac is caught in the paradox of being both radically desubjectivated and unable to lapse into unconsciousness: simultaneously deprived of all mastery over being and all possibility of escape from it through sleep, the insomniac is exposed to the naked fact of existence. The distinction Levinas makes between vigilance and attention in *Existence and Existents* is informative here. Attention is exercised by a subject in relation to particular objects (it is, roughly speaking, what the phenomenological tradition understands by 'intentionality'); vigilance, on the other hand, is a desubjectivating absorption in 'the rustling' of 'unavoidable being'.[42] Attention, as consciousness of a discrete object, has no way of accessing the *il y a*. Vigilance, as the experience of existence without existents, is the impossibility of escaping it. This is why Levinas describes insomniac experience in terms of an 'anonymous vigilance':[43] the paradox of insomnia is that the insomniac loses his very selfhood and yet remains fiercely awake. Vigilance is an experience of consciousness without subjectivity.

The relation between the *il y a* and impossibility, hinted at above, becomes more pressing in Levinas's further description of it in terms of the existent's experience of its own inability to die. The thought of the *il y a*, Levinas says, 'consists in promoting a notion of being without nothingness, which leaves no hole and permits no escape'.[44] The experience of it thus deprives the existent of the possibility not only of escape in sleep, but of escape in death as well. The experience of the *il y a* robs the existent of all mastery, including the possibility of suicide as the 'final mastery one can have over being'.[45] Here, as is often the case, Levinas is close to Blanchot, who was himself quite obsessed with the thought of the *il y a*. In 'Thomas the Obscure', he provides us with an unparalleled description of the impossibility of death in terms of a man attempting to hang himself who,

> [a]fter kicking away the stool on which he stood, the final shore, rather than feeling the leap which he is making into the void feels only the rope which holds him, held to the end, held more than ever, bound as he had never been before to the existence he would like to leave . . .[46]

The experience of the *il y a* undermines the possibility of all virility, of the suicide's every pretension toward a tragic-heroic leap into the void.

The *il y a* reveals what Levinas calls, in a famous reversal of Heidegger, the impossibility of possibility.[47]

It is this sense of absolute passivity that unites Levinas's various descriptions of the experience of the *il y a*. In *Existence and Existents*, Levinas will refer to it in terms of 'condemnation to being'[48]; in *On Escape*, Levinas describes the subject's experience of pure being in terms of the simultaneous necessity and impossibility of escaping it: the subject, confronted with pure being, finds itself backed up against something that it both must and cannot bear. This is why Levinas links the passivity he finds in the subject exposed to the *il y a* with horror. 'The rustling of the *there is* . . .' as he says in *Existence and Existents*, 'is horror.'[49] Here we should understand 'horror' not just in terms of revulsion or nausea (though, as *On Escape* testifies, it has important links to both), but in terms of the moment of impossibility it reveals. Horror for Levinas is an experience of unbearable exposure.

This partly explains why the early Levinas will characterise his phenomenology of ethical experience in terms of the possibility of an *escape* from being, working to illuminate the possibility of the subject's evading the evil of existence in favour of the singular existent – the (in)famous 'other' – that is always otherwise than being. A key term here is *transcendence*. For Levinas, the other is emphatically 'not of this world', and cannot become part of anything resembling a Heideggerian equipmental contexture. The other does not appear 'for' the subject in the mode of the tool: the other, as unassimilable and unknowable, cannot be fully integrated into my worldly intentional projects. To invoke one of Levinas's favoured metaphors, the other is foreign to all light (which for him is synonymous with knowledge). In the latter pages of *Time and the Other*, Levinas describes the subject's (non)relation with the other in terms of an encounter with the feminine, which Levinas understands in terms of its 'modesty',[50] its 'mystery',[51] its constant 'slipping away'.[52] As Adriaan Peperzak writes: 'With regard to being, the first task and desire is to escape or "evade" it. The source of true light, meaning, and truth can only be found in something "other" than Being.'[53] For the early Levinas, the other represents a breach in the brute totality of bare existence, and to experience its 'ethical' claim is not only to undergo an experience of radical responsibility, but also to be granted a kind of *salvation* from the anonymous clutches of the *il y a*, such that '[a] plurality insinuates itself into the very existing of the existent . . .'.[54] Salvation and responsibility are thus posited as two sides of the same coin: the event of the salvation of the subject by the other is also the event of the subject's realisation of its utter indebtedness to it. To be saved from being is to be responsible for the other; to be responsible for the other is to be saved from being.

Any reader familiar with Heidegger will be struck by the difference between this and his concept of the concern for the being of beings, and his understanding of the proper role of Dasein in terms of its relation to the ontological difference. Take for instance the *Letter on Humanism*, in which Heidegger sets out something like an ethics of Dasein as the being for which being itself is an issue:[55]

> Man is . . . 'thrown' from Being itself into the truth of Being, so that ek-sisting in this fashion he might guard the truth of Being, in order that beings might appear in the light of Being as the beings they are . . . Man is the shepherd of Being. It is in this direction alone that *Being and Time* is thinking when ecstatic existence is experienced as 'care.'[56]

We could say that for Heidegger, ethics consists in a keeping open of the originary openness in which beings come to show themselves. This keeping open, which Heidegger characterises in terms of a primordial 'letting be' (*Gelassenheit*), is for him the proper dwelling place or *ethos* of Dasein. In deliberate contrast to this, Levinas puts forward a phenomenology of ethical experience as a kind of escape from being. What lies at the basis of this conflict? For Heidegger, Dasein dwells in the space of rending that is the difference between being and beings and finds its calling in the possibility of a proper relation to this rending. As the reading of *Time and the Other* presented above shows, this is, interestingly enough, very close to Levinas, who (though he would never use these terms) also finds that the space created by the difference between being and beings is always an 'ethical' one. For Levinas, as for Heidegger, the fact of the ontological difference places a demand on us; it requires a response. The point of contention between these two thinkers lies in their conceptions of the nature of this difference and the resulting disparity in their understanding of what an 'ethical' response to it might look like. So we should hone our question: what is the disparity between the Heideggerian and Levinasian conceptions of the difference between being and beings?

Levinas himself actually provides us with a perfectly clear answer to this question: 'The most profound thing about *Being and Time* for me is this Heideggerian distinction. But in Heidegger there is a distinction, not a separation.'[57] The difference between Levinas and Heidegger is that the former works to push the latter's thought of an ontological difference to its most extreme point. While Heidegger thinks being as that which reveals itself in beings and thus the ontological difference as a kind of fracture at the heart of each entity, Levinas instead thinks this difference in terms of a separation. *Time and the Other*, then, is an attempt at thinking through the implications of the radicalisation of the ontological difference in the thought of an absolute schism between the multiplicity of beings and the being of those beings. Levinas's critique of the Heideggerian project is based upon his understanding of pure being in terms of generality and anonymity, his equation of being with a brute impersonality that must be transcended for the sake of the other. But crucially, it is the thought of a separation between being and beings that brings Levinas to equate being with the anonymous in the first place. In other words: the *il y a*, the notion of a pure *factum brutum* of existence, is the necessary result of Levinas's radicalisation of the ontological difference. After such a radicalisation, the Heideggerian ethic of the truth of being starts to look like a 'guarding' of a radically impersonal 'being in general' that threatens to engulf every otherness.

At this point, we can turn to the reading of Levinas carried out by Critchley in his *Very Little . . . Almost Nothing*. Critchley is concerned with the possible ambiguity in Levinas between the *il y a* and the alterity of the other, highlighting three moments in his texts in which he himself declares that it becomes phenomenologically difficult to distinguish between them. Briefly, these are: the similarity between 'the night of the *il y a* and the night of the erotic'[58] as presented by Levinas in *Totality and Infinity*; the possibility Levinas mentions in 'God and Philosophy' of confusing the transcendence of the other with the *il y a*; and the claim at the end of 'Transcendence and Intelligibility' that the alterity of the infinitely other could be said to 'announce itself in insomnia'.[59] Yet for Critchley, the ambiguity between the alterity of the other and the *il y a* problematises the Levinasian analysis, but does not undermine it: '[W]hat continues to grip me in Levinas', he says at the end of his analysis, 'is the attention to the other, to the other's claim on me and how that claim changes and challenges my self-conception.'[60] To this, one might raise the following question: doesn't this breakdown represent a loss of the very otherness of the other in the first place? Indeed, we can only understand what Critchley is saying here if we realise that he continues to understand the *il y a* itself as a space of alterity (this is made clear when he speaks of the 'possible confusion that the subject might have in distinguishing between the alterity of the *il y a* and that of illeity'[61]). But it is difficult to find a textual precedent for such an understanding of the *il y a* in the early Levinas, who always thinks pure being in terms of an anonymous force that must be evaded for an experience of and relation to alterity to become possible ('it is anonymous . . . it is impersonal like "it is raining" or "it is hot"';[62] 'All civilisations which accept Being . . . merit the name of barbarian';[63] 'None of the generosity which the German term *es gibt* is said to contain revealed itself between 1933 and 1945'[64]). Indeed, Levinas's attacks on Heidegger's project would immediately lose all pertinence if the relation to the *il y a* could become a relation of responsibility. It is worth asking, then, if the appearance of the *il y a* on the face of the other would not be more problematic for Levinas.

Here I want to venture an answer to the question Critchley raises about Levinas's work (and which also seems to have plagued Levinas himself): 'Why does the *il y a* keep returning like the proverbial repressed, relentlessly disturbing the linearity of the exposition?'[65] Because the early Levinas, in his isolation of the *il y a* and his attempt to think ethics in response to the stark separation of being and beings, is repeating the metaphysical logic of oblivion that Agamben has identified. 'Existing returns', as Levinas himself says, 'no matter with what negation one dismisses it.'[66] Or as he puts it in *Otherwise than Being* in a statement that is uncannily reminiscent of Agamben's own claims in *Language and Death*: 'The *there is* fills the void left by the negation of Being.'[67] The problem, to put it summarily, is one of presupposition: once pure being has been presupposed, it can only present as a horrifying negativity. This means that it has to be banished, but this banishment can never be fully complete, meaning that the banished ontological 'object' remains to haunt the ontic. The early Levinas's work shows that pure being, once it is set up as that which must be escaped or transcended for the ethical experience of the other to become possible, has a tendency to return right when and where we least expect it: on the face of the other who was supposed to represent my salvation from it. This is to say that Levinas's early writings present a particularly lucid description of the phenomenological structure of the paradoxical logic of the inclusive exclusion; that the *il y a*, once it has reared its faceless head, cannot be escaped. This underscores Levinas's texts, and may account for the sense of desperation his writing sometimes evokes. Consider:

> Prior to any particular expression and beneath all particular expressions, which cover over and protect with an immediately adopted face or countenance, there is the nakedness and destitution of the expression as such, that is to say extreme exposure, defencelessness, vulnerability itself. This extreme exposure – prior to any human aim – is like a shot at point blank range ... From the beginning there is a face to face steadfast in its exposure to invisible death, to a mysterious forsakenness.[68]

Levinas is describing in this passage the vulnerability of the other as revealed in the experience of the face-to-face, but with its depiction of an 'extreme exposure ... to invisible death' and 'a mysterious

The Unbearable

forsakenness' it could easily be mistaken for an Agambenian description of the *homo sacer* abandoned to sovereign violence. Indeed, perhaps there are echoes of Levinas in Levi's description of the *Muselmann*:

> They crowd my memory with their faceless presence, and if I could enclose all the evil of our time in one image, I would choose this image which is familiar to me: an emaciated man, with head dropped and shoulders curved, on whose face and in whose eyes not a trace of thought is to be seen.[69]

This can help explain what is perhaps the key difference between the early and late Levinas. In early works Levinas presents us with a sequential phenomenology, tracing the experience of the subject as it moves from the clutches of being toward the other. For the early Levinas, subjectivity begins in the impersonal and *moves toward* ethical experience. As he says at the outset of *Time and the Other*, 'it is *toward* a pluralism that does not merge into unity that I should like to *make my way* and, if this can be dared, break with Parmenides.'[70] As this citations indicate, we could in fact venture to describe this ethical subjectivity in terms of a being-toward-alterity: ethics, for the early Levinas, is synonymous with a movement away from anonymous being that is for him always already a movement toward otherness.

This aspect of the early work changes in *Otherwise than Being*. Here Levinas works to undermine this progressive (even narratival) model, ending up with a more complex and difficult thesis regarding the claim of the other on the subject. As Levinas himself writes, in a critique of a certain 'narrative, epic, way of speaking': 'The infinite does not signal itself to a subjectivity, a unity already formed, by its order to turn toward the neighbour.'[71] By the time of *Otherwise than Being*, then, Levinas has abandoned the progressive model that underlies his earlier works. Take for example the following image from the late text, where Levinas asks us to imagine the 'emptiness of space filled . . . with invisible air, hidden from perception . . . but penetrating me even in the retreats of my inwardness'.[72] He goes on:

> That this invisibility is non-indifferent and obsesses me before all thematization, that the simple ambience is imposed as an atmosphere to which the subject gives himself and exposes himself in his lungs, without intentions and aims, that the subject could be a lung at the bottom of its substance – all this signifies a subjectivity that suffers and offers itself before taking a foothold in being. It is a passivity, wholly a supporting.[73]

This image of the subject as lung, as exposed flesh, is designed to elucidate two things: first, that the subject's exposure is inescapable; second, that this exposure is always already a responsibility. This is to say that in the late works the subject *cannot not* be exposed to the other, that it *cannot not* be responsible. According to the image Levinas presents here, the subject is exposed and responsible 'before taking a foothold in being'.[74] Responsibility starts, in other words, with the subject's first breath: it is not something that somehow comes about after the encounter with the alterity of the other; it is not as though the subject only becomes responsible when presented with the vulnerability and alterity of the Other; it is not as though there are responsible and irresponsible subjects, such that the ethical task is to transform from the latter into the former. For the later Levinas, we might say, ethics does not consist in a shouldering of responsibility, but rather in the subject's response to the fact that it is always already shouldering a responsibility.[75] This strange but compelling reversal shows the difficulties of assimilating the later Levinas's phenomenology of ethical experience to any standard model of moral behaviour, for the ethical demand that he discovers is not one that has any *necessary* connection to ethical action. What Levinas discovers is something like an originary claim or bond at the heart of the human being, a bond that precedes any ability on the part of the subject to accept or refuse it. This means that an evil act is not one that takes place in indifference toward the ethical demand (which is impossible), but is rather the (always already failed) attempt at negating what cannot be negated, assuming what cannot be assumed. The ethical claim that the later Levinas discovers, then, is the condition of the possibility of evil as well as good, which is to say that in *Otherwise than Being* there is an absolute rejection of the (Augustinian) model of evil as a privation or absence of the good. If in the early works there is such a thing as an egoistic subject, a subject that exists for itself alone until its solitude is broken in the experience of the other's alterity, then in *Otherwise* this egoism is shown to be something like a fantasy. Evil is not the privation of the good, but positively the *hatred* of the good, a kind of railing against one's absolute passivity before the other. The later Levinas might therefore agree with Nancy when he writes that evil is 'the ruin of the good as such, not its privation . . .';[76] that '[e]vil does not impair the good (it could not be impaired), nor does it disregard it (for evil knows and wills itself as evil and is therefore knowledge of the good), but it refuses its coming to life';[77] that '[e]vil is the *hatred* of existence as such'.[78]

In *Totality and Infinity*, Levinas tells us that he wants to show the 'philosophical primacy'[79] of the latter over the former by proceeding 'from the experience of totality back to a situation where totality breaks up . . .'.[80] As we have seen, the problem with this basic movement is that the *il y a* – the totality of being without content – remains to haunt the subject, thus threatening not only its worldly engagements but also (and this for Levinas is far more worrying) the very otherness of the other itself. This is why, by the time of *Otherwise than Being*, we find Levinas enacting a more radical ontological strategy in his attempt at thinking through (or beyond) the problem of pure presence, questioning the idea that it has to be (indeed that it ever could be) escaped. Instead, the very idea of pure presence is itself slowly undermined, with Levinas attempting to show, via something that resembles a transcendental argument, how difference is in fact an essential and primordial condition for subjectivity as such. As Alphonso Lingis puts it in his introduction to the text: 'The present work now relates the notion of the immediate, obsessive contact with alterity and the notion of immersion in the sensuous element in such a way as to make the first the basis for the second.'[81] This is what Levinas means when he writes that, after considering the dilemma between death anxiety and the 'horror of fatality' as revealed in the experience of the *il y a* (Hamlet's problem, which recurs in Levinas's work), the text 'calls into question this reference of subjectivity to essence which dominates the two terms of the alternative'.[82] The basic thought in *Otherwise than Being* is summed up perfectly in its title and subtitle: the idea is to think otherwise than being as totality, to think beyond the '[e]ssence stretching on indefinitely' that presents as 'the horrifying *there is*'.[83]

Establishing whether Levinas is finally successful in this attempt is beyond the scope of this chapter (such an attempt would require, as Riera argues, attention to the startling and uncanny language of the text[84]). But there are some fundamental lessons here regarding the problem of negative ground. First of all, and perhaps most importantly, there is a lesson here about presupposition. It is that to set up the *il y a* as that which must be escaped, as Levinas does in his early books, is to have already presupposed it, and so to set to work a logic of banishment that can never fully complete itself. Overcoming the problem of negative ground requires not that we think the conditions of the possibility of a breach in its totality (whether it be the totality of pure being or the pure *factum brutum* of bare life), but rather that we try to think what it would mean to undermine the category in its very ground. The second lesson is that such a rethinking of totality will require a different image of the subject, which can now no longer be seen as an isolated monad existing against the background of being-in-general. Instead, and this is what I take Levinas's image of the lung to require of us, we need to think the subject as primordially exposed to a certain ethical exigency. This thought, in turn (this would be the third lesson of Levinas's text), will require us to think the subject in terms of a 'passivity without any assumption',[85] as primordially exposed to a demand that it cannot fully assimilate.

These three lessons are all at work in Agamben's various attempts to rethink the category of potentiality. In 'The Passion of Facticity', for instance, Agamben asks us to note that Heidegger employs the eponymous term in ways that are fundamentally different from the use of it by philosophers such as Husserl and Sartre. The latter uses the word to signify the meaningless givenness of existence, the brute set of facts that each human being finds itself forced to confront. Existence comes before essence in Sartre, and thus the problem the human being must ceaselessly face is how to somehow 'give a meaning' to that brute given. Heidegger, on the other hand, uses the term to signify the intimate co-belonging of existence and essence that for him is the decisive trait of Dasein. This difference forms the basis of Heidegger's criticism of Sartre in the 'Letter on Humanism':

> ... Sartre expresses the basic tenet of existentialism in this way: Existence precedes essence. In this statement he is taking *existentia* and *essentia* according to their metaphysical meaning, which from Plato's time on has said that *essentia* precedes *existentia*. Sartre reverses this statement. But the reversal of a metaphysical statement remains a metaphysical statement.[86]

If it is true that facticity in Heidegger represents the irreducible thrownness of the human being, then for him this thrownness does not, as Sartre thought, entail Dasein's forced confrontation with the *factum brutum* of existence (as when Roquentin, confronting a chestnut tree, finds himself to be 'alone in front of this black, knotty mass, entirely beastly, which frightened me'[87]). If we are able to properly (that is, non-metaphysically) rethink the opposition between existence and essence as Heidegger asks us to, then it will represent instead Dasein's irretrievable consignment to its own singular *Seinscharakter* ('character of Being') or *weise* (guise, fashion).[88] Why?

Here Agamben points to those moments in Heidegger's texts in which, perhaps despite himself, he affirms the necessarily 'fallen' status of Dasein. Heidegger's claims in these moments, Agamben shows, are the result of his commitment to the fact that the inescapable consignment that is facticity represents the 'constitutive non-originarity'[89] of Dasein; that facticity is 'characterized by the same co-belonging of concealment and unconcealment that, for Heidegger, marks the experience of the truth of being'.[90] In a passage that should compel us not to underestimate the ontological implications of the concept, Agamben writes that the 'first trait of facticity is *die ausweichende Abkehr*, "evasive turning-away." Dasein's openness delivers it over to something that it cannot escape but that nevertheless eludes it and remains inaccessible to it in its constant distraction . . .'[91] This 'something' that Dasein cannot escape or forget is the being of beings, which means that the falling of Dasein represents the ultimate impossibility for it of ever fully or 'properly' appropriating this being (being is not a property of being). Agamben, we can see, is working to emphasise the thought of passivity that shows itself in Heidegger. This remains the case when he turns to Heidegger's later work, and in particular to the concept of *Ereignis*, the 'enowning' or 'event of appropriation' (as it has been variously translated). Agamben's claim is that we should understand this event not in terms of Dasein's mastery or grasp of being, but rather in terms of Dasein's exposure to the *impossibility* of such mastery: *Ereignis*, as the event in which 'Being itself is experienced as such',[92] reveals to Dasein the impossibility for Dasein of ever properly owning or getting a hold of being. This is why *Ereignis* is not 'an extinguishing of the oblivion of Being, but placing oneself in it and standing within it'.[93] In *Ereignis*, what finally reveals itself is the fact that being will never fully reveal itself; what is unconcealed is the necessity of concealment. The importance of this thought is that the finitude it reveals is not only that of Dasein before being, but that of the 'finitude of being'[94] itself: the experience of *Ereignis* is the experience of being in its difference from itself. In *Ereignis*, Dasein finds itself exposed to the fact that being cannot ever fully coincide with itself, the fact that in a sense being can never fully *be itself*. Dasein is always already fallen, then, because being itself is always already falling away from itself. To invoke a Levinasian idea in a way that he may have rejected, being itself is otherwise than being.

This fallenness of being means that being is always already its manners of being, that being is always already a plurality of singularities. Singularity, in other words, is the result of being's own passivity with regard to itself, of its own inability to properly coincide with itself.[95] Here we should recall Agamben's reflections in *The Coming Community* on the 'irreparable'. This ontological concept, just like the political concept form-of-life, is intended to show that each being is *irreparably* consigned to its own singularity, or what Agamben calls in this text its 'being-thus':[96] 'Irreparable means that these things are consigned without remedy to their being-thus, that they are precisely and only their *thus*.'[97] Being for Agamben is always already its own 'manner of rising forth'.[98] Agamben's point is that it is this fundamental, inescapable passivity of the being before its being that constitutes, ontologically speaking, the originary source of potentiality. It is the impossibility of ever closing the order of signification with a definitive statement or set of statements that compels me to keep speaking; it is the impossibility for the poet of ever writing a work in which everything is finally said that constitutes the condition of the possibility of poetry. The potential of Dasein stems, in other words, from its constitutive inability to fully appropriate its being. Potential is your singular mode of being unable to get a hold of yourself.

This means that we may also be able to speak of the experience of *Ereignis* in terms of an experience of something unbearable. In *Ereignis* we find that being cannot bear itself, that Dasein cannot bear being, and that this means that being and Dasein are always already improper and fallen, that pure being is always already its manners and potentialities of being. Metaphysics interprets this unbearable in terms of a horror without reserve, but the cruel truth of such logic is that the attempt to avoid such horror (by banishing it according to the metaphysical logic Agamben identifies, and which haunts the early Levinas) actually exasperates it. The experience of the potential at the very heart of being always involves an exposure to an unassumable passivity, an absolute impotential; for this reason it 'marks what is, for each of us, perhaps the hardest and bitterest experience possible . . .'.[99] And indeed, it is here, in my response to my irreparable consignment to an assumable passivity, that we can locate something resembling an Agambenian ethics (an ethics which echoes aspects of that of the later Levinas):

> We know that Heidegger explains the word *Ereignis* on the basis of the term *eigen* and understands it as 'appropriation,' situating it with respect to *Being and Time*'s dialectic of *eigentlich* and *uneigentlich*. But here it is a matter of an appropriation in which what is appropriated is neither something foreign that must become proper nor something dark that must be illuminated.[100]

The experience of *Ereignis* is an experience of an exposure to something I cannot appropriate, but I *can* appropriate my response to this fact of inappropriability. This is how we should understand Agamben's claim that '[b]eings that exist in the mode of potentiality *are capable of their own impotentiality*'.[101] Agamben, we might say, places a space at the centre of the word 'cannot', turning 'I *cannot* bear it' into 'I *can not* bear it'. As Thomas Carl Wall puts it: 'It is part of our effort here to show that what Blanchot will describe as an "inability to say I," Agamben will describe as an "ability to not say I."'[102] That such an ethics does involve something like an originary affirmation is made clear in the following passage, in which Agamben describes evil in terms of a certain sort of bitterness toward one's own passivity before the *thus*:

Fleeing from our own impotence, or rather trying to adopt it as a weapon, we construct the malevolent power that oppresses those who show us their weakness; and failing our innermost possibility of not-being, we fall away from the only thing that makes love possible.[103]

Factical life is life exposed to the inappropriable, and this exposure presents itself in the other through its characteristic gestures and comportments (its smile, its voice, its particular way of laughing, etc.). The exposure to the inappropriable, then, represents not (just) the destitution of Dasein, but also what makes it lovable, and humans are unique amongst creatures in that they *'fall properly in love with the improper'*.[104] The smile of a baby is not an 'expression' but an imitation of the person looking down at it, but this does not make it any less lovable. On the contrary: we fall in love with a face not in spite of the fact that it is exposed to the inappropriable, but because of how it exposes itself in its impropriety. The only thing that makes love possible, then, is a mode of being that lets the unmasterable *thusness* of being show itself, on one's own face and on the face of the other. For Agamben love and ethics are intertwined.

'The Passion of Facticity' begins with the assertion that despite what seems to be a striking absence of any analysis of the *Stimmung* of love from Heidegger's work, his analytic of Dasein nevertheless represents an unprecedented investigation into the ontological status of love, which may actually form something like 'the central problem of *Being and Time*'.[105] Hopefully now we can understand these provocative claims, for the ethic of the unbearable sketched above is exactly what is worth rescuing from Heidegger. Such an ethics has nothing to do with the tragic pathos of a solitary Dasein pulling itself out of an entanglement in *das Man* for the sake of a proper or authentic relation with the Nothing (granted, this was always a straw Heidegger anyway); more importantly, after a proper thinking through of *Ereignis*, the notion of a nation's collective move into 'the originary realm of the powers of being'[106] appears deeply misguided at the absolute best. Instead, such an ethics requires us to abandon ourselves to the improper: 'If what human beings must appropriate here is not a hidden thing but the very fact of hiddenness, Dasein's very impropriety and facticity, then "to appropriate it" can only be to be properly improper, to abandon oneself to the inappropriable.'[107] '[A]*uthentic* existence', as Heidegger himself says (almost despite himself), 'is nothing which hovers over entangled everydayness, but is existentially only a modified grasp of everydayness.'[108]

Unbearable being is unbareable being. Metaphysics tries to bare the unbareable, and we can understand the logic of the camp in terms of the attempt to *make being be itself*, to reduce being to a pure, contentless 'thereness' and in turn to force Dasein to bear that bare thereness. The fact that being cannot coincide with itself represents the ultimate impossibility of completing this task, but this does not, in fact, deter the logic in operation; rather it exasperates it, meaning that the process, once set in motion, never has to stop, that this infinitely violent task is itself infinite. Agamben, then, is calling upon us to stop trying to bear/bare being. Such a mode of being is capable of its own incapacity; it does not recoil before its consignment to passivity. This does not mean that Agamben is calling for an affirmation of the totality of existence (this is the source of his critique of the Nietzschean concept of the eternal return[109]), because just as no one has ever fallen in love with an 'identity', no one could ever fall in love with 'being in general': love is always love for some*one*, for *this* one, for the particular one that shows itself in an idiosyncratic mannerism. Metaphysics obliviates the unbearable fact of being, only to have it return to haunt it as naked presence (or naked life); the ethical task is to appropriate being *as* unbearable, such that it becomes impossible to isolate any nakedness. The experience of impropriety, when properly followed through, reveals being not as the brute and meaningless 'thereness' that horrifies Roquentin, but rather as always already fallen into its manners of being. Meeting this demand, then, does not require of us any heroism, or anything resembling a courageous and tenacious stare into the Nothing.[110] This is why Agamben suggests at the end of *Language and Death* that human beings 'are even poorer than they supposed in attributing to themselves the experience of negativity and death . . .'.[111] If, as Heidegger sometimes appears to indicate, a fully appropriated human Dasein is one that has been able to face up to the non-relational possibility of its own certain death, then claiming that human beings are irreducibly improper entails a rejection of the very idea that they can somehow become *capable* of dying in the way Heidegger seems to demand. As Levinas's work attests, then, a proper thought of passivity (which is always already a thought of potentiality) requires that I accept that death is something for which I have no faculty. I am incapable of dying, and yet I must die. Being able to be unable is the difficult beginning of the ethics of potentiality.

At this point, we should be able to understand what Agamben means when he alludes in *State of Exception* to the possibility of the world's appearing as a good that absolutely cannot be appropriated. The conditions of the possibility of this would appear to be twofold: that the world appear not as a brute 'there is' that pins me to an existence without exits, but rather as an inappropriable, indeed unknowable fact that undoes me in my very being; and that I am able to respond to this fact without recoiling and setting the logic of banishment back to work. And yet, it might be more accurate to say that these two conditions represent two aspects of the same thing, such that my ability to be unable to appropriate being is what allows for it to emerge as a good (and vice versa). Thus it is an experience not of 'being in general', but of the absolute *particularity* of the world, where the fact of existence does not appear a *factum brutum*, but rather as the most ordinary and yet most uncanny thing. In the linguistic sphere, this is an experience of a language that has been forever disconnected from every idea of the sacred, the ineffable and the unsayable, an experience of speakability *as such* that has an important precedent in Levinas's idea of 'the saying' as distinct from the said, as an experience of the exposure entailed by the very fact of speech (Levinas: 'Saying is communication, to be sure, but as a condition for all communication, as exposure'[112]). This is an experience of the fact of speech and the fact of the world, but one in which these two facts are shown to coincide. It reveals the human not as consigned to living on a negative ground that it can never entirely banish, but absolves it of the need for ground. Being is unbearable, life is unbearable, and being and life are therefore *unbareable*. It might be worth thanking God for this fact if approaching it did not require us to come to terms with our abandonment by the divine. If there is a certain sobriety or even disillusionment in this experience, then, it is just because it discloses the pure gratuity of existence, and the impossibility of ever finding someone or something to thank for it.

NOTES

1. Levinas, *Existence and Existents*, 55.
2. Agamben, *Language and Death*, xi.
3. Ibid. xii.
4. Ibid. xi.
5. Zartaloudis gives an excellent analysis of these claims in *Giorgio Agamben* (221–38).
6. Agamben, *Language and Death*, 5.
7. Ibid. 15.
8. Ibid. 14.
9. Watkin, *The Literary Agamben*, 15.
10. Agamben, *Language and Death*, 16–17.
11. Ibid. 32.
12. Ibid. 32.
13. Ibid. 35.
14. Ibid. 35.

15. Augustine, quoted in Agamben, *Language and Death*, 33.
16. Ibid. 33.
17. McLoughlin, 'The Sacred and the Unspeakable'.
18. Agamben, *Language and Death*, 35.
19. Ibid. 102.
20. Ibid. 105.
21. Dickinson, *Agamben and Theology*, 57.
22. Ibid. 64.
23. Agamben, *Language and Death*, 105.
24. Ibid. 66.
25. Mills, *The Philosophy of Agamben*, 9.
26. Adam Thurschwell has undertaken lucid critical readings of Agamben's relationship to Derrida. See for instance 'Cutting the Branches for Akiba: Agamben's Critique of Derrida' and 'Specters of Nietzsche: Potential Futures for the Concept of the Political in Agamben and Derrida'.
27. Agamben, *Language and Death*, 85.
28. See Agamben, *'Pardes'*.
29. Agamben, *Language and Death*, 106.
30. Agamben, *Homo Sacer*, 114.
31. Ibid. 114.
32. Ibid. 21.
33. McLoughlin, 'The Sacred and the Unspeakable'.
34. Agamben, *Homo Sacer*, 8.
35. Agamben, *The Coming Community*, 83.
36. Agamben, 'The Idea of Language', 46.
37. Wittgenstein, *Philosophical Investigations*, §217; 72e.
38. Levinas, *Time and the Other*, 46–7.
39. Ibid. 42.
40. Ibid. 44.
41. Critchley, *Very Little . . . Almost Nothing*, 67.
42. Levinas, *Existence and Existents*, 61.
43. Levinas, *Time and the Other*, 51.
44. Ibid. 50.
45. Ibid. 50.
46. Blanchot, 'Thomas the Obscure', 73.
47. Levinas, *Time and the Other*, 70.
48. Levinas, *Existence and Existents*, 24.
49. Ibid. 55.
50. Levinas, *Time and the Other*, 87.
51. Ibid. 87.
52. Ibid. 86.
53. Peperzak, *To the Other*, 18.
54. Levinas, *Time and the Other*, 75.
55. For a reading of the ethical implications of this essay and in Heidegger's late philosophy more generally, see Nancy's 'Originary Ethics'. Nancy's

reading of Heidegger, which emphasises the ethical dimensions of Heidegger's ontology, is very similar to my own.
56. Heidegger, 'Letter on Humanism', 234.
57. Levinas, *Time and the Other*, 46.
58. Critchley, *Very Little . . . Almost Nothing*, 9.
59. Ibid. 91.
60. Ibid. 97.
61. Ibid. 91.
62. Levinas, *Time and the Other*, 46–7.
63. Levinas, *On Escape*, 73.
64. Levinas, 'Signature', 292.
65. Critchley, *Very Little . . . Almost Nothing*, 90.
66. Levinas, *Time and the Other*, 47.
67. Levinas, *Otherwise than Being*, 4.
68. Levinas, 'Ethics as First Philosophy', 83.
69. Levi, quoted in Agamben, *Remnants of Auschwitz*, 44.
70. Levinas, *Time and the Other*, 42 (my emphasis).
71. Levinas, *Otherwise than Being*, 13.
72. Ibid. 180.
73. Ibid. 180.
74. Ibid. 180.
75. This transition is made clear on the formal level as well. As Gabriel Riera argues, this late text actually 'lacks a progressive sequential narrative organization' (*Intrigues*, 138). Or again: 'In this later work Levinas replaces a logic of binary oppositions – being/entity, totality/infinity – with that of the amphibology of being, according to which language is conceived as a dual structure' (91).
76. Nancy, *The Experience of Freedom*, 126.
77. Ibid. 126.
78. Ibid. 128 (my emphasis).
79. Levinas, *Totality and Infinity*, 26.
80. Ibid. 24.
81. Lingis, in his introduction to *Otherwise than Being*, xxxiv. Or as Mary-Jane Rubenstein puts it:

> [T]he most radical philo-ethical move that *Otherwise* makes is its interiorization of alterity . . . In *Totality and Infinity* otherness came from outside to shatter the self's laboriously constituted interiority. In *Otherwise Than Being*, far from relying upon a previously consolidated subject into which it might make its entrance, the other prevents all such interiority from the very beginning: the other is *already within* the 'subject' itself. (*Strange Wonder*, 86–7)

82. Levinas, *Otherwise than Being*, 176.
83. Ibid. 163.
84. Riera, '"The Possibility of the Poetic Said" in *Otherwise than Being*'.

85. Levinas, *Otherwise than Being*, 164.
86. Heidegger, 'Letter on Humanism', 232.
87. Sartre goes on:

    > It left me breathless. Never, until these last few days, had I understood the meaning of 'existence.' I was like the others, like the ones walking along the seashore, all dressed in their spring finery. I said, like them, 'The ocean *is* green; that white speck up there *is* a seagull,' but I didn't feel that it existed or that the seagull was an 'existing seagull'; usually existence hides itself ... And then all of a sudden, there it was, clear as day: existence had suddenly unveiled itself. It had lost the harmless look of an abstract category: it was the very paste of things, this root was kneaded into existence. Or rather the root, the park gates, the bench, the sparse grass, all that had vanished: the diversity of things, their individuality, were only an appearance, a veneer. This veneer had melted, leaving soft, monstrous masses, all in disorder – naked, in a frightful, obscene nakedness. (*Nausea*, 127)

88. See Agamben, 'The Passion of Facticity', 194.
89. Ibid. 189.
90. Ibid. 190.
91. Ibid. 193.
92. Heidegger, quoted in Agamben, '*Se*: Hegel's Absolute and Heidegger's *Ereignis*', 128.
93. Heidegger, *On Time and Being*, 30.
94. Ibid. 54.
95. In the terms of the final chapter, this would be another way of describing Agamben's commitment to a paraconsistent dialetheist logic. To say that being itself is otherwise than being is to ascribe a certain type of inconsistency to it.
96. Agamben, *The Coming Community*, 39.
97. Ibid. 39.
98. Ibid. 28.
99. Agamben, 'On Potentiality', 178.
100. Agamben, 'The Passion of Facticity', 202.
101. Agamben, 'On Potentiality', 182.
102. Wall, *Radical Passivity*, 178.
103. Agamben, *The Coming Community*, 32.
104. Agamben, 'The Passion of Facticity', 204.
105. Ibid. 187.
106. Heidegger, *Introduction to Metaphysics*, 41.
107. Agamben, 'The Passion of Facticity', 202.
108. Heidegger, *Being and Time*, SZ 179; 167e.
109. For a very useful discussion of Agamben's engagements with Nietzsche's concept, see Durantaye, *Giorgio Agamben*, 314–23. I return to it in Chapter 6.

110. This should entail the rejection of the fierce attack on Agamben attempted in a recent article by Jeffrey Librett. Agamben, Librett claims, ends up enacting not a critique or overcoming but rather a continuation of metaphysics, exhibiting an 'impatience with endless finitude' that results in a philosophy geared toward a state of being in which 'there is no longer any lack, isolation, or inauthenticity' ('From the Sacrifice of the Letter to the Voice of Testimony', 13). As my analysis should indicate, this is a gross caricature of Agamben's project, which is geared instead toward inauthenticity and everydayness. The question for Agamben is not how to turn the improper into the proper, but rather how to establish a proper relation to our irreducible impropriety.
111. Agamben, *Language and Death*, 96.
112. Levinas, *Otherwise than Being*, 48.

5. The Creature before the Law

> Leopards break into the temple and drink to the dregs what is in the sacrificial pitchers; this is repeated over and over again; finally it can be calculated in advance, and it becomes a part of the ceremony.[1]

The previous analyses of the problem of foundation have important implications for how we understand the question of law in Agambenian political ontology. As I show in this chapter, this is because the problem of foundation goes to the heart of the concept of legitimation, throwing light on the secret connection established in modernity between life, authority and violence. I achieve this by carrying out an extended analysis of an essay that is pivotal for Agamben's own engagements with these issues: Benjamin's early essay 'Critique of Violence'. A key thesis of Benjamin's piece is that there is no stable opposition between lawmaking and law-preserving violence (or in more recent terms between constituting and constituent power): that every legal order, and indeed every judgement passed within a legal order, always contains within it something of the original founding violence that occasioned the positing of the order as a whole. Legitimation is not just something achieved in the past, say with the writing of a constitution – rather, every legal order is always already engaged in a process of re-legitimation, such that the original lawmaking moment is renewed with every decision. Importantly for our purposes, Benjamin invokes the figure of 'mere life' here as the bearer of the secret violence that is exposed in this slippage between lawmaking and law-preserving violence: this violence, which Benjamin will call 'mythical',[2] is something like the residue or remainder of this oscillation in the legal order, and its object is the sheer fact of living. The connection between mythical violence in Benjamin and sacrifice in *Language and Death* is unmistakable: what is crucial in each case is how a legal order contains within itself a hidden support, a kind of (failed) attempt at solving the problem of foundation. What Agamben calls the sacrificial function, Benjamin will call 'bloody power over mere life for its own sake'.[3] In each case, a particular kind of violence arises as part of a metaphysically determined attempt at grounding the legal order. Bare life, like pure being, is presupposed by metaphysics only to be subsequently exposed to an obscure, secret violence. Giving an account of this allows me to clarify an infamous Benjaminian concept that is key to Agamben's understanding of redemption: divine violence.

Benjamin begins his argument in 'Critique of Violence' like a good Kantian: two opposing positions, axiomatically consistent in themselves, are shown to have constitutive blindspots, each of which corresponds to that of the other in a perfect, paradoxical symmetry. The natural law tradition, predicated on the claim that there is a transhistorical Good toward which human action can and should comport itself, finds the justification (or otherwise) of the use of violence in whether it is deployed for the sake of these just ends. Violence operates here as a sort of 'raw material',[4] a natural fact of life that is not itself interpretable in terms of justice, legitimation or legality; just means (violent or otherwise) are simply those that correspond to just ends. Positive law, on the other hand, is predicated on the claim that there is no natural or *given* Good to which the human being has access, is thus unable to justify violence with reference to the justness of ends, and so instead looks to the means themselves for legitimation of human action. Just means will produce just ends as a matter of course, and positive law therefore finds itself embroiled in a series of questions on the historical foundations and legal legitimation of state violence.

Having set up the two sides of his antinomy, Benjamin moves to the claim that both positive and natural law are dependent on a paradox. It runs as follows: in both cases, justice must be found in an alignment between means and ends, where the attainment of one will establish legitimation through the guaranteed attainment of the other. And yet in either case, this can only be obtained through inquiry into one half of the nexus at the expense of leaving the other entirely undetermined. Both traditions are for Benjamin engaged in a kind of sleight of hand whereby a relation is claimed to be established between two terms, when what in fact takes place is simply the elimination (or bracketing out) of one of them. '[If] positive law', as Benjamin puts it, 'is blind to the absoluteness of ends, natural law is equally so to the contingency of means.'[5] There is a double circularity in operation here that undermines the claim of either party to a coherent concept of justice. Benjamin's strategy, then, is to 'break' this 'circular argument'[6] of the justification of means through sole reference to ends or the justification of ends through sole reference to means. Importantly, though, Benjamin does privilege one side of the antinomy: natural and positive law may be tied up together in double circularity, but Benjamin will nevertheless find his way through this circle by radicalising the basic theses of positive legal philosophy. This is because the distinction in positive law between sanctioned and unsanctioned violence is 'meaningful',[7] or at least that it is so in a legal sense. The real question for Benjamin is what light the very intelligibility of this distinction throws upon the original problem of violence. His interest in this text is not in the justification or justifiability of violence, then, but rather in the questions raised by the very fact that we make a distinction between just and unjust violence in the first place. His desired goal is not to resolve the antinomy of means and ends but rather to deploy it in the development of a 'philosophico-historical view of law'[8] that would dissolve it.

This is why the discussion turns to legal problems surrounding the legitimation of certain forms of violence. 'It can be formulated as a general maxim of present-day European legislation', says Benjamin, 'that all the natural ends of individuals must collide with legal ends if pursued with a greater or lesser degree of violence.'[9] Individuals do not possess the legal right to use violence for the sake of their own ends; as in the Hobbesian vision, it is the right to the use of force in obtaining its ends that the citizen gives up to the sovereign for the sake of its own protection. So the state sets up, 'in all areas where individual ends could be usefully pursued by violence',[10] a legal system in which these ends can be pursued by non-violent, sanctioned means. Benjamin goes on: 'From this maxim it follows that law sees violence in the hands of individuals as a danger undermining the legal system.'[11] The use of violence by individuals must be curtailed by the state because only the state may have the monopoly on violence: '[V]iolence, when not in the hands of the law, threatens it not by the ends that it may pursue but by its mere existence outside the law.'[12] Law must maintain the monopoly on violence if it wants to preserve its status as law, its very claim to legitimacy. Violence threatens law not in spite but because of the fact that law has its origins in violence.[13] Benjamin points to the figure of the great criminal and explains its historical ability to both horrify and captivate the masses in these terms. Such figures confront the violence of law 'with the threat of declaring a new law'.[14] This link between the violence of acting 'outside' or 'above' the law and the foundational violence of positing a new legal order makes such figures intolerable to the state. It is what sees them exert their strange fascination over ordinary citizens.

Here we see one of the central oppositions of the text beginning to come to light: the distinction between lawmaking and law-preserving violence. Lawmaking violence is foundational; it is the performative violence of a new constitution or a declaration of independence. The violence here is that of inauguration, of the law's original setting-into-force. It is the violence of self-positing, the violence of an emergence *ex nihilo* of a legal/social/political system. This violence operates, as Derrida points out, in the future anterior: it is violence that finds legitimation not in the past but in a not-yet-realised legal order on behalf of which it claims to speak.[15] It is violence that *will have been* just. Law-preserving violence, on the other hand, is violence carried out by an already-founded state: it is conservative and protective, designed to defend or fortify a pre-existing legal order. It is violence that is deployable against uprising or a potentially lawmaking insurrection, but also simply the basic form of the day-to-day functioning of the legal system. Law is fortified every time a judge's gavel comes down.

The key point at this stage of Benjamin's analysis is that these two forms of violence are not rigorously separable.[16] The argument here is that law can never be fully constituted; that the process of legitimation can never reach an end; that every new legal event or legal decision works not just to preserve law but engages each time in a renewal of the inaugural lawmaking moment. The foundation of a legal order, on this account, would not only be a historical event that grants legitimation to the present, but rather the law's hidden, constant accompaniment. Part of the argument here is that legitimation is contingent upon a foundation of historically determined, potentially contestable power structures; this means there is always the possibility, however small, of an uprising of lawmaking violence against the legal order. Each act of law-preserving violence, then, contains within it a defensive moment of lawmaking violence, where the legitimated regime re-posits itself as such. Law doesn't quite shake its original founding violence. It is always engaging in a kind of secret re-legitimation.

Of course, this problem runs in both directions, for the purity of lawmaking violence can itself be contaminated by the practical and administrative constraints of law-preserving violence.[17] Benjamin critiques the decline of parliamentary democracy on these grounds, arguing that '[w]hen the consciousness of the latent presence of [lawmaking] violence in a legal institution disappears, the institution falls into decay'. Parliamentary democracies, Benjamin says, 'offer the familiar, woeful spectacle because they have not remained conscious of the revolutionary forces to which they owe their existence'; they 'lack the sense' of the violence of their own origins, unsettled by the pure positing force of their own inauguration.[18] Lawmaking violence can call legitimation into question because it reveals the violence at its heart, so law-preserving violence turns away from its own original lawlessness, from the antinomian (in a sense *prenomian*) force at its origin, fearing its potential for appropriation by insurrectionist forces.[19] Law-preserving forces thus find themselves in conflict with their own original principle: parliamentary democracy contains an unresolved, indeed irresolvable contradiction that over time has an entropic effect on its institutions.

Benjamin points to the police as the modern face of this mutual infection between lawmaking and law-preserving violence. If lawmaking violence is required to prove itself with political victory, and law-preserving violence is 'subject to the restriction that it may not set itself new ends',[20] then the singular violence of the modern police force consists in its partial emancipation from both of these conditions: ostensibly, the police are simply representatives of law-preserving violence, but the specificity of the situations in which they intervene means that they must inevitably employ lawmaking violence on a situational basis. The refrain that 'it depends on the cop' comes to mind here: there are countless legal situations in which police must exercise a certain discretionary power, making decisions on the ground that may exceed strict legality, but that *will have been* legitimated (if, for instance, an inquiry takes place in future). Or, in a perhaps more insidious register, we should think here of the 'special powers' that have been granted to police on the basis of the supposed exceptionality of the terrorist threat: '[T]he police intervene "for security reasons" in countless cases where no clear legal situation exists.'[21] It is worth re-emphasising that this is a particularly modern phenomenon, relating as it does to the separation of powers (and indeed to the ultimate impossibility of a pure separation). The gap between the legislative and executive, between lawmaking and law-preserving power, only truly opens in modernity with the decline of the absolute sovereign. For Benjamin, this gives the modern police force a paradoxical sort of brutality:

> And though the police may, in particulars, everywhere appear the same, it cannot finally be denied that their spirit is less devastating where they represent, in absolute monarchy, the power of a ruler in which legislative and executive supremacy are united, than in democracies where their existence, elevated by no such relation, bears witness to the greatest conceivable degeneration of violence.[22]

The police, crossing the boundaries between lawmaking and law-preserving violence, exemplify the decay of law in modernity, revealing precisely what is 'rotten'[23] in it (one thinks here of 'the filth' – a Cockney slang term for the police).

It is very important that Benjamin employs these motifs of rottenness and decay in making his critique of the disavowed violence of law. One is reminded in particular of Kafka. And of course, Benjamin himself wrote what remain some of the most perceptive works of Kafka criticism. In the most notable example of this work, he identifies Kafka's world as 'the world of offices and registries, of musty, shabby, dark rooms'.[24] Benjamin's Kafka is the obscene Kafka, the Kafka who has Joseph K. discover his judge's store of pornography in the courtroom, who has him seduced by his lawyer's petite, syndactylous mistress. 'Filth is the element of officials,'[25] says Benjamin, and what he finds in Kafka is a commitment to developing the implications of the thesis of a fundamental link between modern law and filth, decay, rottenness. Importantly, the claim is not as simple as 'the law is rotten' – this would be one way of framing the argument of the 'childish anarchism'[26] that Benjamin himself ridicules – but rather relies on a more sophisticated argument about the relation between modern law, sovereignty and citizens. We can begin to see its outlines if we turn to the section in 'Critique of Violence' on the death penalty. Speaking of those who opposed critics of the death penalty, Benjamin writes that they 'felt, perhaps without knowing why and probably involuntarily, that an attack on capital punishment assails, not legal measure, not laws, but law itself in its origin'.[27] He goes on:

> For if violence, crowned fate, is the origin of law, then it may be readily supposed that where the highest violence, that over life and death, occurs in the legal system, the origins of law jut manifestly and fearsomely into existence . . . For in the exercise of violence over life and death more than in any other legal act, law reaffirms itself.[28]

In the terms Benjamin will introduce a few pages later, the death penalty is perhaps the most brutal example of mythical violence, or violence that is immediate and in an important sense 'bloody'.[29] In mythical violence, or 'bloody power over mere life for its own sake',[30] what shows itself is the original hold law has over life itself. Mere life in Benjamin is a figure of fallen life, of sinful, dirty life; it is the distorted life of the hunchback, bent down by some unnameable cosmic burden. Benjamin's claim here is that the space opened up in modernity at the heart of law (as exemplified in the impossibility of any full exclusion or full inclusion of lawmaking violence from/into law-preserving violence) is in fact the site of a particular form of our subjection to it. Eric Santner, whose recent work on political theology represents a singularly clear and refreshing approach to Benjamin's philosophical project, provides a useful explication of these arguments:

> What manifests itself as the law's inner decay is the fact that the rule of law is, in the final analysis, without ultimate justification or legitimation, that the very space of juridical reason within which the rule of law obtains is established and sustained by a dimension of force and violence that, as it were, holds the place of those missing foundations.[31]

This 'dimension of force and violence' represents the obscene dimension of law, the zone in which there is a slippage between law-preserving and lawmaking violence.[32] This is the site of what Santner will call our 'creaturely' tie to law (another way of framing the subjection of mere life as described by Benjamin), which is something more than our simple answerability to or responsibility before the legal order. Following both Beatrice Hanssen and Julia Lupton,[33] Santner points out that the word 'creature' derives from the Latin *creatura*, which signifies a being undergoing a process of creation. It is, Santner says, 'not so much the name of a determinate state of being as the signifier of an ongoing *exposure*, of being caught up in the process of *becoming creature* through the dictates of divine alterity'.[34] The theological dimension of the term is important: a creature is first and foremost a *created* being, a being that lives in thrall to a sovereign (the German *Kreatur* has similar connotations). As the history of the term progressed, however, it came to be synonymous not simply with God's creations but rather with particularly monstrous strains of those creations: in this usage, it can evoke compassion, pity or even horror; it signifies a being marked by an indeterminacy that puts the borders between particular life forms in question. The creature thus becomes a being that dwells in the gaps between species, a threat to the very system of classification. And it is this double meaning that Santner works with, developing a Benjaminian concept of the creature as a liminal being (and indeed as a being that emerges in liminal, exceptional situations) that finds itself biologically tied to sovereign power.

A key claim here is that this particular form of creatureliness is particular to humans; that human beings are not 'just creatures among other creatures' but are in a sense 'more creaturely'[35] than non-human animals. This is because the creaturely dimension of life opens up contemporaneously with the dimension of sovereignty and law. Indeed, one could make a case for the argument that modern humans are themselves more creaturely than pre-moderns, because of the particular tensions instilled by Enlightenment secularism. Remember Benjamin's remark on the particular violence of the modern police force, whose spirit is more devastating because it does not represent the will of any absolute sovereign. As with Freud's primal father who becomes more powerful in his absence, whose death casts a shadow of guilt upon all of his descendants, secular law has a peculiar biopolitical hold over its subjects not in spite but because of its lack of ultimate foundation. Or rather: secular law captures the mere life of its subjects in a novel way, forcing it to stand in as its new, highly ambiguous foundation. Human life itself is forced in modernity to bear the burden of the law's own ungroundedness.

In a neat double pun, Santner refers to the 'ibidinal'[36] economy of the law and its 'ex-citational' power over the human creature, arguing that there is a dimension of disavowed obscenity operating alongside or beneath those performative events by which a human being is initiated into a particular symbolic economy. Citation is understood here in terms of the problem of authority and its relation to desire; the claim is not only that the human creature is wracked by 'ibidinal' urges that it can never properly satisfy, but that this basic impossibility gives institutions a paradoxical violent power. Think here of military hazing, the Russian *Dedovschina*, the fagging system in British public schools or even the obscure sexuality of an academic degree-granting ceremony: these exemplify the way in which institutional systems discharge the tensions created by the ungroundedness of law. Law in modernity constitutes itself on the basis of an originary violence in which 'the very resources of legitimacy' link up with 'a power of suspension and disruption'.[37] In this paradoxical moment, the law traverses an intimate zone at the heart of the human and captures something there that the subject itself cannot. This is why Agamben writes that 'a theory of the state of exception is the preliminary condition for any definition of the relation that binds, and, at the same time, abandons the living being to law.'[38] Mere or creaturely life is life that *pleads guilty* for the sake of sustaining the law, providing a hidden support for its obscene, exceptional dimension.[39]

As always with Benjamin, one has to make some difficult interpretive decisions regarding the status of 'Critique of Violence'. The piece is explicitly political, but as it progresses it enters a theological register, and ends with an unsettling paean to the power of 'divine violence' (*göttliche Gewalt*). Derrida (and he is far from alone in doing so) responds to this invocation of the bloodless yet expiatory powers of divine violence and its capacity to disrupt the workings of mythical violence with a kind of horror. What he finds 'perhaps almost unbearable in this text'[40] is the possibility that it could tempt the reader to interpret the Nazi 'final solution' in terms of a manifestation of this divine violence. 'When one thinks of the gas chambers and the cremation ovens,' says Derrida, 'this allusion to an extermination that would be expiatory because bloodless must cause one to shudder.'[41] He goes on to invoke both Schmitt and Heidegger, and asks whether there could be complicity between their discourses, that of Benjamin, and 'the worst'.[42] Yet if one considers the fact that Benjamin spent his life in a sustained and explicit intellectual struggle against fascism, indeed that Benjamin probably committed suicide to avoid being captured by the Gestapo, then this starts to look like a strange move on Derrida's part (and one that betrays an uncharacteristic lack of charity). At the same time, however, it is nevertheless the case that Benjamin's rhetoric still has the power to induce a kind of terror in even the most sympathetic reader, as when Benjamin, now identifying mythical violence 'with all legal violence',[43] defines its divine antithesis as follows:

> This very task of destruction poses again, in the last resort, the question of a pure immediate violence that might be able to call a halt to mythical violence. Just as in all spheres God opposes myth, mythical violence is confronted by the divine. And the latter constitutes its antithesis in all respects. If mythical violence is lawmaking, divine violence is law-destroying; if the former sets boundaries, the latter boundlessly destroys them; if mythical violence brings at once guilt and retribution, divine power only expiates; if the former threatens, the latter strikes; if the former is bloody, the latter is lethal without spilling blood.[44]

First of all, it is worth contextualising this rhetoric of destruction, coming as it does from a young Benjamin writing in the politically, economically and culturally virulent environment of Weimar Berlin. Perhaps more importantly, however, the metaphysical and speculative language of the text itself actually precludes any neat reduction to a concrete political programme, and, with its denunciation of myth, especially any Far Right appropriation. Similarly, it seems naive or simply too easy to read Benjamin's account of divine violence in terms of the glorification of the purifying powers of mass violence or a call to arms against the legal institutions of liberal democracy.[45] The text is far too ambiguous, far too esoteric in both style and content for it to be reducible to a manifesto for any concrete politics. My claim, then, is that 'Critique of Violence' is both *less and more* 'political' than it may seem on a first reading: less because it is not reducible to any concrete politics; more because, unlike any simple glorification of mass violence or call for the destruction of law, it actually has interesting (if largely implicit) political consequences.

The best place to turn here is back to Benjamin's Kafka essay. In particular, we can turn to its passages on Kafka's animals and creatures, embedded in which is a complex and compelling theory of the relation between animality and creatureliness that can help us work through the implications of Benjamin's theory of law. On Kafka's animals:

One can understand, then, why Kafka never tired of hearing about the forgotten from animals. They are not the goal, to be sure, but one cannot do without them.[46]

Can't one see the animal in 'The Burrow' or the giant mole ponder as they dig in? Yet this thinking is extremely flighty. Irresolutely, it flits from one worry to the next; it nibbles at every anxiety with the fickleness of despair ... This much is certain: of all of Kafka's creatures, the animals have the greatest opportunity for reflection. What corruption is in the law, anxiety is in their thinking. It messes a situation up, yet it is the only hopeful thing about it.[47]

On his creatures:

Odradek 'stays alternately in the attic, on the staircase, in the corridors, and in the hall.' So it prefers the same places as the court of law which investigates guilt. Attics are the places of discarded, forgotten objects. Perhaps having to appear before a court of justice gives rise to a feeling similar to that with which one approaches trunks in the attic which have been locked up for years.[48]

Odradek is the form which things assume in oblivion. They are distorted. The 'cares of a family man', which no one can identify, are distorted; the bug, which we know all too well represents Gregor Samsa, is distorted; the big animal, half lamb, half kitten, for which 'the butcher's knife' might be 'a release', is distorted. These Kafka figures are connected by a long series of figures with the prototype of distortion: a hunched back.[49]

The animal has an essential flightiness, a constant flitting of consciousness that prevents it from concentrating its attention. This is illustrated by Kafka in 'The Burrow', whose protagonist lives in a continuous state of anxiety.[50] And yet, as Benjamin indicates, Kafka's animals seem to possess a wisdom that is fascinating despite its near total inaccessibility to human reflection. This wisdom, it seems, is part of the happiness of Kafka's animals, and it sits uneasily against their anxious dispositions: 'Sometimes', says the protagonist of 'The Burrow', 'I lie down and roll about in the passage with pure joy.'[51] Animals are exceptional in Kafka because they display a joy in pure existing that is not readily available to the other figures in his taxonomy (his creatures, humans, angels and gods all carry various burdens). This beatific wisdom is what makes animals a crucial part of Benjamin and Kafka's modernist messianism, for it represents a sort of untapped possibility for human life. Kakfa's animals are the repository of what Benjamin calls 'the forgotten', and the ethical demand he finds in Kafka emanates from this forgotten animal substratum.

Kafka's creatures are distinct from animals in that they are figures of distortion. Odradek – an apparently immortal creature – is paradigmatic here, both for its uncanny appearance and for the sense of quiet foreboding it brings with it. 'Can he possibly die?' asks the narrator who appears to be its owner (or who appears, at least, to have taken on a burden of responsibility for the creature). 'Anything that dies has had some kind of aim in life, some kind of activity, which has worn out; but that does not apply to Odradek.'[52] If one considers the 'half kitten, half lamb'[53] crossbreed that plagues another of Kafka's narrators, which seems to possess only those talents of the cat and the sheep that cancel each other out in practice, then it becomes clear that this dreadful absence of purpose may be a common property shared by his creatures. The other is quasi-humanity, as displayed in the crossbreed's 'look of human understanding'[54] and indicated by Odradek's ability to speak. Kafka's creatures, Benjamin argues, are linked to the hunchback, a figure that is always present but never directly mentioned in his works. The link here is burden, and Benjamin will draw an analogy between the distorted life of creatures like Odradek, the repeated images in Kafka of 'the man who bows his head far down on his chest: the fatigue of the court officials, the noise affecting the doormen in the hotel, the low ceiling facing the visitors in the gallery'[55] and the severe heaviness of what drives his human protagonists.[56]

One could schematise the relation between these figures by saying: *the creature is the result of the forgetting of the animal.* On this account, the creature is the offspring of a lack of or failure in relation: not simply a halfway point between human and animal, but rather a figure of the human's denial of its own animality, a kind of return of the repressed in intensified form. The human, on this account, possesses an animality that it cannot fully assimilate, a life that is unforgettable to the extent that it is impossible to remember. The animal subsists in the opacity of the body, in one's obscure encasement in a biological system; the creature is what emerges as a result of the refusal of this haunting animal life.[57] This is why we find Benjamin characterising the Kafkan ethic in terms of *attentiveness*, understood as a particular sort of relation with the animal substratum of everyday life. Attentiveness would be the name for the maintenance of this relation to the opacity of one's own animal life: a 'prayer of the soul' made on behalf of all living beings.[58]

What does this tell us about the theory of law at work in this model? As we have seen, Benjamin's claim is that the exceptional dimension of law finds its support in mere life, which stands in and pleads guilty to supply its missing foundation. We can now supplement this claim by saying that the refusal or failure of relation between human and animal

– which is what provokes the emergence of mere or creaturely life – operates as the other side of this subjection to the disavowed violence of law. In fleeing or refusing animal life, we become creaturely subjects tied to the exceptional dimension of law. This is to say that the denial of the animal is a condition of the support of the law's exceptionality; that we are subject to the obscene, supplementary dimension of law insofar as we fail to maintain the proper relation to our own animality. Which is itself to say: if the obscene dimension of law is supported by creaturely life, and creaturely life emerges out of a failure in, or refusal of, the relation between human and animal, then it follows that an intervention into our ontology of human and animal life could be the catalyst for a new, non-violent relation to law. This would represent a release not from law as such, but from our biopolitical tie to the law's exceptional dimension.

We are now in a position to understand what Benjamin elucidates with his concept of divine violence. Key here is the claim (which is actually a microcosm of his entire theory of divine violence) that the hunchback will 'disappear with the coming of the messiah'.[59] The hunchback, as we have seen, appears in Benjamin's work as the paradigm of mere or creaturely life. Its life is distorted, fallen: the clearest possible exemplification of the creaturely dimension of the human, weighed down by the obscene dimension of law. Divine violence, synonymous with the coming of the messiah, would therefore represent an intervention into this dimension of human subjectivity. This is why it does not bring either guilt or retribution (which is part of the dialectic of mere or creaturely life), and instead only expiates. It also explains why it is a pure and bloodless violence: if mythical violence seizes human subjectivity through the 'bloody' capture of mere life, then divine violence intervenes into this seizure and releases human life from its subjection to the rottenness of law. When Benjamin refers to divine violence as law-destroying, then, it is important to realise that what is destroyed here is not law *in toto* but simply our biopolitical attachment to it. Thus too the link, clear in Benjamin and insisted upon by certain of his commentators, between redemption and a fundamental change in the human/animal relation. One thinks here in particular of Hanssen's claim that 'humanity itself might be rescued in the image of animality',[60] or the assertion from Agamben that 'on the last day, the relations between animals and men will take on a new form, and ... man himself will be reconciled with his animal nature'.[61] Divine violence would redeem humanity from the obscene dimension of law through a suspension of the creaturely dimension of human subjectivity. It is the figure of a release effected by a reconfiguration of the relation between human and animal.

There is something unexpected about Benjamin's messianism. It is that the messianic in Benjamin is a figure not simply of redemption, but of redemption from salvation (Dickinson: 'there is something within the theological . . . that goes even further than the secular in eradicating the presence of a (false) sacrality'[62]). Like that of Kafka's, Benjamin's messiah is the messiah who comes by not coming, who comes 'only when he is no longer necessary'.[63] Divine violence, that is, represents not the arrival of the divine on earth, but rather the earth's abandonment by the divine (hence Agamben's image of an earth consigned to an 'absolutely empty sky'[64]). The transformation of the relation between human and animal that takes place in divine violence is the precise opposite of a rescue of the former from the latter; divine violence would not redeem the human *from* its animality as much as *redeem it to* its animality. What Benjamin seeks is not a passage from earthly oblivion into the Kingdom but rather an earthly redemption from the desire or need to enter it. One could even say that there is a definite (if decidedly postsecular) atheism in Benjamin's messianism.[65] Divine violence represents a kind of cut whereby the profane world finally separates from the transcendent. As Agamben writes in *The Coming Community*, it is 'not an event in which what was profane becomes sacred and what was lost is found again', but 'the irreparable loss of the lost, the definitive profanity of the profane'.[66] Or, as he puts it in *State of Exception*: '[D]isenchantment does not restore the enchanted thing to its original state . . .' but only gives it 'the possibility of reaching a new condition'.[67] Divine violence is disenchanting because it severs the nexus between law and violence; in letting the violent gratuity of the world emerge – the 'violence outside the law'[68] inherent in the anomie of being *as such* – it suspends the fantasmatic process by which we are subjectively invested in sovereign power. It effects not the destruction of law in general but the cutting of our subjective ties to its obscene underside. In the terms of Hölderlin's couplet, the spirit of this historical-philosophical theory of law can be summarised as follows: if it is true that the saving power grows alongside the danger, then the danger also grows where the saving power lies. Redemption consists in a release from this very dialectic of danger and salvation.

NOTES

1. Kafka, 'Leopards in the Temple'.
2. Benjamin, 'Critique of Violence', 249.
3. Ibid. 250.
4. Ibid. 237.

5. Ibid. 237.
6. Ibid. 237.
7. Ibid. 238.
8. Ibid. 238.
9. Ibid. 238.
10. Ibid. 238.
11. Ibid. 238.
12. Ibid. 239.
13. Derrida writes:

   What the state fears . . . is not so much crime or robbery, even on the grand scale of the Mafia or heavy drug traffic, as long as they transgress the law with an eye toward particular benefit . . . The state is afraid of *founding* violence – that is, violence able to justify, to legitimate, or transform the relations of law, and so to present itself as having a right to right and to law. ('Force of Law', 268)

14. Benjamin, 'Critique of Violence', 241.
15. Derrida, 'Force of Law', 269.
16. 'That which threatens the law already belongs to it, to the right to law, to the origin of law' (Derrida, 'Force of Law', 269).
17. 'There can be no rigorous opposition between positing and preserving, only what I will call (and Benjamin does not name it) a *differential contamination* between the two, with all the paradoxes that this may lead to' (Derrida, 'Force of Law', 272).
18. Benjamin, 'Critique of Violence', 244.
19. Werner Hamacher writes: 'In order to remain what it is . . . law-imposing violence must become law-preserving, must turn against its original positing character' ('Afformative, Strike', 111).
20. Benjamin, 'Critique of Violence', 243.
21. Ibid. 243. See also Derrida:

   For today the police are no longer content to enforce the law and thus to preserve it; the police invent the law, publish ordinances, and intervene whenever the legal situation is unclear to guarantee security – which is to say, these days, nearly all the time. ('Force of Law', 277)

22. Benjamin, 'Critique of Violence', 243. One also thinks here of the 'spirit' of those in modern law enforcement that possess less real authority than the police force, such as customs officers or even inspectors on public transport: on certain occasions it is possible to observe an inverse relationship between the level of authority possessed and its potential for becoming Kafkaesque in application.
23. Benjamin, 'Critique of Violence', 242.
24. Benjamin, 'Franz Kafka', 795.
25. Ibid. 796.
26. Benjamin, 'Critique of Violence', 241.

27. Ibid. 242.
28. Ibid. 242.
29. Ibid. 250.
30. Ibid. 250.
31. Santner, *My Own Private Germany*, 10.
32. Recently Slavoj Žižek has done the most to develop the claim that law is constituted on a repressed 'obscene underside'. The idea runs through his work, but texts particularly relevant to my discussion include: *Gaze and Voice as Love Objects*, 98–103; 'Neighbors and Other Monsters: A Plea for Ethical Violence'; and 'Odradek as a Political Category'.
33. See Hanssen, *Walter Benjamin's Other History*, 150–62; and Lupton, 'Creature Caliban', 1–2.
34. Santner, *On Creaturely Life*, 28.
35. Ibid. 26.
36. Santner, *On the Psychotheology of Everyday Life*, 50.
37. Ibid. 41–2.
38. Agamben, *State of Exception*, 1.
39. From here we can understand the (trial and) tribulations of Joseph K. in a new light. The fundamental problem is not his infinite guiltiness before a transcendent Law; his mistake is to assume that his guilt actually *belongs to him*. This is because the guilt, in fact, is actually that of the law itself: it is the hidden by-product of the impossibility of its fully founded legitimation, the secret (or indeed secretion) of its oscillations between lawmaking and law-preserving violence. Joseph K. embarks on a process doomed to bad infinity, searching for 'the missing foundation of the institutional authority that issued the call' (Santner, *On the Psychotheology of Everyday Life*, 51). His shameful, doglike demise is the inevitable result of this mistake: he dies as mere life because, little did he know, it was precisely the foundation for which he was searching.
40. Derrida, 'Force of Law', 298.
41. Ibid. 298.
42. Ibid. 298.
43. Benjamin, 'Critique of Violence', 249.
44. Ibid. 249.
45. Hanssen writes, for example: 'The essay squarely fits in an antiliberal tradition that does not shun force to achieve its transformative sociopolitical agenda' (*Walter Benjamin's Other History*, 3).
46. Benjamin, 'Franz Kafka', 810.
47. Ibid. 810.
48. Ibid. 811.
49. Ibid. 811.
50. Nietzsche writes:

    They do not know what is meant by yesterday or today; they leap about, eat, rest, digest, leap about again, and so from morn till night and from day to day, fettered to the moment and its pleasure or displeasure, and thus neither melancholy nor bored . . . A human being may well ask an animal: 'Why do you not speak to me of your happiness but only stand and gaze at me?' The animal would like to answer and say: 'The reason is I always forget what I was going to say' – but then he forgot this answer too, and stayed silent: so that the human being was left wondering. ('On the Use and Disadvantages of History for Life', in *Untimely Meditations*, 60–1)

51. Kafka, 'The Burrow', 327.
52. Kafka, 'The Cares of a Family Man', 429.
53. Kafka, 'A Crossbreed', 426.
54. Ibid. 427.
55. Benjamin, 'Franz Kafka', 811.
56. See Santner, *On Creaturely Life*, 24–5.
57. Of course, if the animal is ultimately inassimilable, then the problem could not simply consist in a failure of reconciliation (which would simply be a basic axiom of human life). Rather, it would have to consist in a *denial of this failure*. The problem is not the human's inability to render the opaque transparent, but its refusal to maintain itself in relation to this fundamental opacity. So another way of framing the schema would be to say: *the creature is the result of the forgetting of the forgetting of the animal*. If the animal is the repository of the forgotten, then the creature is the form the animal takes when its forgetting is itself forgotten. I return to this problematic in the next chapter.
58. Benjamin, 'Franz Kafka', 812.
59. Ibid. 811.
60. Hanssen, *Walter Benjamin's Other History*, 165.
61. Agamben, *The Open*, 3. I return to this idea – and complicate it – in the next chapter.
62. Dickinson, *Agamben and Theology*, 130.
63. Kafka, 'The Coming of the Messiah', 81.
64. Agamben, *State of Exception*, 57.
65. It is possible to trace this commitment to materialism through all of Benjamin's works. Here one could cite his ambivalence to aura in his essay on the work of art, where the decline of art's connection to ritual in capitalism deprives it of its sacred character, and in so doing opens the potential for new possibilities for its appropriation and use by the proletariat. One could point as well to his piece on the storyteller, where he praises Leskov for interpreting the Resurrection 'less as a transfiguration than as a disenchantment' ('The Storyteller', 158), or to his description of his own project in terms of making 'arable' the fields of the irrational with the 'sharp axe of reason', of purifying the 'entire ground . . . from the jungle of delusion and myth' (quoted in Wolin, *Walter Benjamin*, xxiv). Benjamin's entire philosophy, despite its speculative nature, its richly imagistic style

and its deep engagement with theology and mysticism, is marked by an extreme and paradoxical sobriety. Even in his theory of divine violence, Benjamin remains a materialist.
66. Agamben, *The Coming Community*, 102. One also thinks of this text's opening image: the inhabitants of limbo who, lacking any vision of God, persist 'without pain in divine abandon'. These unbaptised beings are '[n]either blessed like the elected, nor hopeless like the damned'; instead, 'they are infused with a joy with no outlet' (6).
67. Agamben, *State of Exception*, 88.
68. Ibid. 53.

6. The Animal for which Animality is an Issue

Being – we have no idea of it apart from the idea of 'living.'[1]

It appears this theory of law and violence – and, in some respects, the concept of atheist redemption at work in political ontology – chimes with the diagnosis of modernity one finds in Nietzsche. For Nietzsche not only shares with political ontology a commitment to a certain this-worldliness, to the idea that modernity is the age in which the possibility of a purely profane existence arises. He also figures this in terms of the human relation to its animal life: for Nietzsche, the possibility of overcoming nihilism rests on whether and how the human animal could come to terms with – and learn to affirm – its animal instincts. In both Nietzsche's model and political ontology, then, the human animal possesses a divided relationship to its living. In both theories this division is taken to have a political aspect, such that membership in political community as we know it is conditional on the human animal's alienation from its biological being. Both models are concerned with the possibility of transformation and, because of the connection they establish between politics and animality, link this possibility to a change in the human relation to its being alive. Yet Nietzsche and political ontology end up with a very different understanding of the nature of this change, and an entirely different understanding of its potential scope. Nietzsche poses the problem in terms of affirmation, arguing that the task is one of establishing a non-resentful, welcoming relationship to one's biological being: an unconditional *yes* to life. In Agamben's work things are more ambiguous, and there is emphasis on the properly aporetic structure of the problem. Agamben does not quite figure it in terms of a demand for the affirmation of life, and does not follow Nietzsche in restricting the scope of redemption to those who possess the strength necessary to carry this out. Rather, his Pauline concept of redeemed humanity is resolutely non-hierarchical, turning on the possibility of a collective appropriation of our *common* consignment to unassumable animality. In this chapter, I clarify this disagreement between Nietzsche and Agamben, using it to come to a better understanding of political ontology. In particular, I return to Kafka in an attempt at complicating the problems of animal life and redemption raised in the previous chapter. As I will work to show, Agamben's concept of the anthropological machine challenges the Nietzschean programme of the affirmation of life as will to power.

In 'On Truth and Lie in an Extra-Moral Sense', Nietzsche experimented with the provocative understanding of the problem of human life for which he has since become infamous. 'What', Nietzsche asks, 'does man know of himself?' He goes on:

> Can he even once perceive himself completely, laid out as if in an illuminated glass case? Does not nature keep much the most from him, even about his body, to spellbind and confine him in a proud, deceptive consciousness, far from the coils of the intestines, the quick current of the blood stream, and the involved tremors of the fibres? She threw away the key; and woe to the calamitous curiosity which might peer just once through a crack in the chamber of consciousness and look down, and sense that man rests upon the merciless, the greedy, the insatiable, the murderous, in the indifference of his ignorance – hanging in dreams, as it were, upon the back of a tiger.[2]

According to this image, the human animal distinguishes itself from other animals not through its capacity for language or reason, but more fundamentally through its ability to horrify or sicken itself, and a subsequent compulsion to turn away from the fact of its being alive, to forget its own animality. Human animals, as Nietzsche will put it in the *Genealogy of Morals*, are like sea creatures compelled to live on land, animals that suddenly had to 'walk on their feet and "bear themselves" when hitherto they had been borne by the water: a dreadful heaviness [lies] upon them'.[3] The human animal, Nietzsche claims, is marked by a 'hatred of the human, and even more of the animal . . .'.[4] It is an animal with a peculiar burden: animality.

Importantly, however, Nietzsche does not understand this as a universal feature of human experience. Instead he sees it as the result of particular historical circumstances, a confluence of disparate historical forces that have led the human animal into a predicament. Life, for Nietzsche, is in itself profoundly innocent: naturally affirmative, it is a force that precedes all judgement, knows nothing of burden and takes a kind of joy in itself (or rather *is* itself a kind of joy). Natural life is happiness, and the instincts discharge themselves for the sake of the pleasure of expiation. Of course this discharge sometimes manifests itself in the form of extreme cruelty, of the infliction of suffering and/or death upon others, but life in its natural state knows nothing of the moral condemnation that usually accompanies wanton cruelty within the boundaries of civilisation. In his *Genealogy of Morals*, then, Nietzsche sets himself the task of explaining exactly what *has gone wrong* such that the human animal has come to develop an ambiguous relation to its own instinctual drives, such that life itself is taken as something evil, sinful or shameful. This is why he sets out to write a genealogical history of the moral systems of the human animal.

A key starting point in this genealogical history is a sweeping etymological claim: that 'designations for "good" coined in the various languages . . .'[5] had their origin in an aristocratic concept of nobility. Mastery, strength, joy, the exercise of power: in pre-historical humanity, all these were taken as self-evidentially good; on the other hand the common, the plebeian, the low were (literally) synonymous with the bad (which is importantly distinct from 'evil'). This original system of values, which is not the same thing as a moral system, then underwent a series of reversals. Nietzsche blames this change on the 'slave morality' that grew out of the resentment of the oppressed toward his oppressor, arguing that the noble value system was turned upside down by the envious rabble. In Ancient Greece, for instance, man first lived in a fatalistic and mythological world where misdeeds were simply taken to be the result of folly: '[T]his much even the Greeks of the strongest, bravest age conceded of themselves as the reason for much that was bad and calamitous – foolishness, not sin!'[6] Human folly, in turn, was itself understood in terms of the whims of the gods: noble Greeks, Nietzsche says, explained 'every incomprehensible atrocity or wantonness with which one of their kind polluted himself . . .' by saying '[h]e must have been deluded by a god'.[7] With the rise of Socratic reason, however, came concepts and values of truth and justice that were antithetical to this fateful and mythological world. The plays of Euripides are paradigmatic for Nietzsche here, for in these works 'noble actions are no longer simply any actions performed pre-reflectively by noble persons . . . but rather actions performed reflectively in accordance with noble principles'.[8] Thus in Euripides the tragic event is not the result of fate and godly whim but rather has a direct causal relationship to the premeditated actions of calculating, rational protagonists; his works 'represent the movement of Greek myth from the realm of the unquestioned to the world of the questionable and, thereby, set the scene for the displacement of myth by reason'.[9] Greek rationality as it emerged with the demise of Dionysian tragic theatre is therefore understood by

Nietzsche as a kind of subversive weapon constructed with the slave morals of the 'newborn demon'[10] Socrates.

Importantly, it is the very idea of 'evil' that marks the emergence of slave morality. In master morality there are good and bad actions leading fatefully to good or bad consequences, but no idea of an evil action (and still less an evil person). Master morality takes the oppressor's domination of his slaves as a natural fact stemming from his strength and position of power, and the practical capacity for instinctual expression that these entail. Slave morality, by contrast, takes this as a sign of the moral depravity of the master, his selfishness and lack of sympathy for others, his callous disregard for the rational principle of justice. This construction of an idea of evil, for Nietzsche, stems from the palpable hatred at the origin of slave morality; it is first and foremost an expression of malice toward the master, an act of 'imaginary revenge'.[11] After the rise of slave morality the natural drives become morally loaded, no longer understood as amoral natural facts but determined as evil and/or shameful.

As a result of this development, Nietzsche argues, the human experience of and relation to its instinctual life was transformed. It represented the beginnings of what he calls 'bad conscience', which is a kind of splitting within the self between instinctual life and a 'consciousness' that arises over and against it. This splitting represents the emergence of a new structure in subjectivity: the human animal, after the positing of bad conscience, loses a fundamental naivety and an original innocence, and starts to regard its instinctual nature from a moral and moralising position. This change, which produced '[t]he existence on earth of an animal soul turned against itself, taking sides against itself . . .', was so significant that 'the aspect of the earth was essentially altered . . .'.[12] It represented, after all, the beginnings of reflective consciousness: the very ability for the human being to have knowledge of itself (here we see why Nietzsche linked bad conscience and the Socratic imperative to know thyself).

It is notable that Nietzsche ends up with models of subjectivity and moral life that echo those of Kant. Kant posited a rift in the subject between the transcendental ego, which is a condition for the unity of experience, and the empirical ego, or the self that engages concretely in the phenomenal world. The transcendental ego is a contentless observer, whereas the empirical self has no form: it is 'in itself diverse and without relation to the [true] identity of the subject'.[13] Nietzsche and Kant thus end up with a similar structure in their understanding of moral life, where a detached observing self (identified with bad conscience in Nietzsche and with the transcendental subject of reason in Kant) arises over and above the flux of instinctual (Nietzsche) or empirical (Kant) subjectivity. The salient difference is that Kant takes this structure as universal, indeed as logically necessary, and locates the condition of the possibility of moral autonomy in the capacity for reason characteristic of the transcendental ego. Nietzsche, on the other hand, understands this splitting in subjectivity as a historical phenomenon (arising, as we have seen, as the result of a conjunction of historical forces), and sees in it a kind of masochism ('the categorical imperative smells of cruelty'[14]). Nietzsche took the historical results of this claim seriously: it would be no exaggeration to say that for him bad conscience – that ingenious construction of slave morality – set into motion a course of events that culminated in the modern ideals of equality and democracy, the victory of the weak over the strong.[15]

Clearly Nietzsche's narrative has a mythic element to it, and it would not be misguided to see in it a kind of bizarre reworking of the myth of the fall. Nietzsche's account, we might say, is structurally isomorphic with the account given in Genesis, in that it explains human sin in terms of a loss of an original innocence. The crucial difference is that Nietzsche regards the fall into sin not as a real fall but rather as a fall into a kind of deception: a fall into the idea of sin which nevertheless has the effect of a real fall. The difference is crucial because it transforms the concept of redemption for Nietzsche, which is no longer redemption from sin, but rather – as with the account of Benjamin given in the previous chapter – redemption from the very idea of sin, redemption from the desire for salvation. For Nietzsche this fall from innocence is inextricable from the development of civilisation, of the beginnings of human history and the emergence of the state. 'I regard the bad conscience', he says, 'as the serious illness that man was bound to contract under the stress of the most fundamental change he ever experienced – that change which occurred when he found himself enclosed within the walls of society and peace.'[16] This is why he can write that '[a]ll of life would be possible without ... seeing itself in a mirror'.[17] Bad conscience, the self-regard of the animal ashamed of its animality, was no naturally occurring phenomenon, but rather arose alongside the construction of the state and the development of civilisation. Nietzsche's narrative of the fall, in other words, is also intended to explain the origins of political life as we know it.

In the opening section of the second essay of the *Genealogy*, Nietzsche links this to a complex dialectic of forgetting and remembering. The human animal, he claims here, is the animal that remembers. Its ability to remember, which is linked with the experience of extreme forms of suffering, forms the condition for society, which is itself forged on the basis of the ability to make promises. What is particularly interesting about this claim from Nietzsche (which can be understood as a typically provocative version of a social contract theory) is that this ability to remember is itself predicated on a more original forgetfulness (Nietzsche calls it a 'positive' or 'active' forgetfulness). This is the forgetting that is 'responsible for the fact that what we experience and absorb enters our consciousness as little while we are digesting it . . . as does the thousandfold process, involved in physical nourishment . . .'.[18] Forgetting here is a condition for remembering; we selectively forget so as to be able to remember. Forgetfulness, as Nietzsche will put it, is 'like a doorkeeper, a preserver of psychic order, repose, and etiquette . . .'.[19] He thus understands the animal that makes promises – that is, the human animal – as the animal that emerges on the basis of a faculty of active forgetting, and in particular an active forgetting of the biological processes, of 'our underworld of utility organs working with and against one another . . .'.[20] The human is the animal that has to forget the animal, and Nietzsche understands the emergence of civilisation and the state as founded on the basis of an exclusion of the biological or animal substrate of the human. '[C]ivilisation', as Vanessa Lemm puts it, 'coincides with the forgetting of animality, the silencing of the animal within the human.'[21] The human animal for Nietzsche could become the social animal we know today only on the basis of a kind of blindness before – and evasion of – the fact of its being alive. It has a divided, opaque relationship to its own biological being: it has the ability, indeed needs the ability, to hide its own living from itself.[22]

Here the Nietzschean analysis converges in a fascinating way with Agamben's biopolitical schema. For in operation here is a version of what Agamben identifies as the 'inclusive exclusion', which, as we have seen, he understands as something like the defining paradox at the heart of the Western *polis*, and which produces the metaphysical image of bare life. Agamben's claim rests on a different genealogy (indeed a different methodology) to the one presented by Nietzsche, but he also traces this paradox as far back as the classical world. And like Nietzsche, Agamben finds that this exclusion can never quite reach completion, because it was always already an implication of biological life in political life. As such biological life, as the unthought presupposition of the *polis*, is never successfully banished and by the time of modernity reappears in a new form as the basic political object. He gives the name 'bare life' to this object to try and mark something of the change it undergoes as part of this process: what returns is not natural or animal life, but rather a metaphysical image of 'a life that is separated and excluded from itself'.[23] As with Nietzsche again, the idea is that the state is constituted on the basis of an exclusion of animality, and that this exclusion is one that always leaves an ambiguous remainder (think here of Nietzsche's many remarks on the savage beast or wild animal that remains alive within the human, despite the attempts by civilisation and its priests at taming it). In *The Open*, Agamben names this dialectic of human and animal 'the anthropological machine',[24] arguing that the attempt to create and police a border between the human and its animal life is haunted by the figure of a bare life that it must both banish and include. Agamben uses the refugee as one of his key contemporary examples, pointing out how this figure, which as the human being stripped of the predicates of nationality, represents a kind of blind spot in the functioning of modern liberal democracies, which have proved themselves 'absolutely incapable not only of resolving the problem but also simply of dealing with it adequately'.[25] The refugee is not literally reduced to bare life, but is rather an exemplary figure bringing to light the metaphysical remainder that is bare life. In modernity, the 'production of man'[26] carried out by the anthropological machine entails the production of the metaphysical image of bare life, which comes back to haunt the space from which natural life was originally expelled.

Here we see the glimmer of Agamben's debt to Heidegger, and *The Open* is perhaps the recent text by Agamben in which the influence of Heidegger's fundamental ontology on his thought is most obvious. For the whole analysis (here as in the *Homo Sacer* series) turns on that ingenious transposition of the ontological difference onto biological categories. This allows Agamben to crucially modify the Heideggerian understanding of the problem of human life: Dasein is not just the being for which being is an issue, but also the animal for which animality is an issue. The Heideggerian problematic of the 'forgetting of being' thus takes on a biopolitical character, such that what Western metaphysics tries to forget is not just the fact that beings are, but the fact of biological life itself.[27] In other words, Agamben draws up the problems of politics in terms of a Heideggerian understanding of the metaphysical tradition, finding that the Western political space is following a particular metaphysical logic when it works to forge the human through the exclusion of the animal (an exclusion that is always already an inclusion).[28] As he puts it: 'Ontology, or first philosophy, is not an innocuous academic discipline, but in every sense the fundamental operation in which anthropogenesis, the becoming human of the living being, is realized.'[29] Does the human forget the animal because it has already forgotten being? Or does the human forget being because it has already forgotten the animal? For Agamben, these two questions are actually equivalent, and the answer to both of them is yes. Instead of the forgetting of being or the forgetting of animality, what we find here is something like the forgetting of being (animal).[30]

The congruence is important: bringing Agamben and Nietzsche together in this way may provide an important supplement to the Heideggerian and post-Heideggerian project of the overcoming of metaphysics. Among other things, it may help fill an explanatory gap in this project, perhaps accounting for something of what motivates the forgetting of being in the first place: on a Nietzschean reading of Agamben's Heideggerian project, we might say, it emerges that the human animal forgets being because it can't bear its animality, turning away from the intensity of its attendant affects; that it feeds itself into the anthropological machine of sovereign power in an attempt at escaping the fact of animal life. Nietzsche's work, in other words, may help us map those psychic processes of resentment, bad conscience and active forgetting by which the inclusive exclusion of being (animal) is carried out, giving us a subjective description of the events and processes that Agamben describes in stricter political ontological terms. What Nietzsche can provide, then, are the means of concretely accounting for ontological forgetting: the problem, it emerges on a Nietzschean analysis, is not simply our way of thinking and speaking; or rather, that is precisely the problem, but our way of thinking and speaking is itself part of the history of the instinctual and social conflicts of the human creature, which is marked by its irreducibility to either 'nature' or 'culture'. To forget being is to forget living, and vice versa. The Heideggerian history of being can be *fleshed out* in a Nietzschean theory of human animality.[31]

Kafka can help us here. In particular his characteristically enigmatic (and allegedly unfinished) short story 'The Burrow' dramatises these problems in a particularly clear and compelling way. The piece, which is narrated by an animal of an unnamed burrowing species, is Kafka's second last story, which gives it a certain pathos, and opens the temptation to regard it as some kind of summation of his vision (it was written, after all, in the final stages of the author's illness[32]). The animal protagonist is, like so many of Kafka's animal protagonists, a complicated mixture of anxiety and beatitude, an obsessive and perhaps even delusionally paranoid figure which nevertheless takes an occasional pleasure in the simple fact of its being alive:

> [T]he most beautiful thing about my burrow is the stillness. Of course, that is deceptive. At any moment it may be shattered and then all will be over. For the time being, however, the silence is still with me . . . Sometimes I lie down and roll about in the passage with pure joy.[33]

The animal is obsessed with its burrow, having apparently spent a large portion of its life on the planning, construction, renovation and maintenance of the underground dwelling (most of the text is taken up with the animal's recounting of the various virtues and failings of its baroquely structured home). The narrative arc of the story is typical Kafka in that it is both simple in its basic structure yet strikingly opaque when it comes to issues of motivation and causal detail (what, exactly, is happening in the middle section, where our narrator inexplicably maroons himself outside his burrow? Why does the animal have to leave the burrow? Why does it wait so long to risk returning? If the danger is so great, why start and then abandon the second entrance?).

The pivotal moment in the story comes when an 'almost inaudible whistling noise'[34] arrives in the burrow and rouses the narrator from sleep. The animal immediately blames the 'small fry'[35] – the little creatures which populate the earth around it – which, it reasons, must have 'burrowed a new channel somewhere during my absence, this channel must have chanced to intersect an older one, the air was caught there, and that produced the whistling noise'.[36] Thus it begins searching for the origin of the sound, striking out with extreme haphazardness through the passages of the burrow, and digging 'at random'[37] to cut new trenches. The initial search turns up nothing, and the original explanation soon gives way as the animal comes to realise that the sound is actually present with the same volume at each point in the burrow: 'Had I rightly divined the cause of the noise, then it must have issued with greatest force from some given place, which it would be my task to discover . . .'[38] Here it entertains other hypotheses: that there are in fact two noises being produced at equal distances from the burrow, producing a relatively uniform sound throughout; that the sound could be coming from the burrowing sounds of 'a whole swarm of little creatures'[39] larger than the small fry; that it may instead be coming from another swarm 'far tinier'[40] than that. In a decision that is largely inexplicable given these premises, the animal then decides to 'dig a wide and carefully constructed trench in the direction of the noise and not cease from digging until, independent of all theories, I find the real cause of the noise'[41]; it concedes, however, that it does not really believe the plan will work, and decides to 'postpone the task for a little while'.[42] It then starts to consider strategies for the defence of the burrow, having become convinced that the sound is emanating from something or someone with malevolent intentions; it then abandons all its plans, in which it can now find 'no slightest trace of reason . . .'.[43] The whole progression reads like a bizarre parody of scientific method, where a hyper-rational desire for certainty, an obsession with empirical verification, is itself propelled onwards by a series of desperate and wildly irrational leaps in logic.

Finally the animal admits what has been haunting it all along: 'I have actually come to believe – it is useless to deny it to myself – that the whistling is made by some beast, and moreover not by a great many small ones, but by a single big one.'[44] Of course the facts contradict the hypothesis, but in true paranoid style the animal comes to believe that this is just further justification of its fears: that the beast is 'not so much impossible, as merely dangerous beyond all one's powers of conception'.[45] This new theory drives the animal to distraction over the final pages of the story, as it becomes mired more and more deeply in speculations regarding the powers of its new opponent, cursing itself for failing to prepare properly for the event: 'But apart altogether from the beast's peculiar characteristics, what is happening now is only something which I should really have feared all the time, something against which I should have been constantly prepared: the fact that someone would come.'[46] The story then abruptly ends, with the animal interrupting a series of speculations regarding whether or not the beast knows of the burrow to observe the fact that will have been obvious to the reader since the arrival of the noise on the scene: 'But all remained unchanged.'[47]

As Britta Maché points out,[48] any full interpretation of the story must include an explanation of the noise in the burrow. Is it, as Hermann Weigand argues, a 'psychotic hallucination'?[49] Or is the beast some kind of metaphor for Kafka's own encroaching illness, as Mark Boulby[50] and Maché herself have claimed? There is an interpretation of the story in which these two readings are both deepened and supported. Blanchot hints at it when he writes: 'What the beast senses in the distance – that monstrous thing which eternally approaches it and works eternally at coming closer – is itself.'[51] This is to say that what the animal hears is nothing other than the sound of its own being alive, the whistle of its own breath; that it is haunted not by a malevolent opponent (or swarm of them) but rather by itself, by its own status as an animal. This reading has the merit of explaining a key conundrum of the story: the uniformity of the noise at each point in the burrow, which is the very fact that drives the animal to the brink of insanity; the noise is uniform wherever the animal goes because it is the sound of the animal itself. It can also help account for passages like the following:

> Lying in my heap of earth I can naturally dream of all sorts of things, even of an understanding with the beast, though I know well enough that when we see each other, more, at the moment when we merely guess at each other's presence, we shall both blindly bare our claws and teeth, neither of us a

second before or after the other, both of us filled with a new and different hunger, even if we should already be gorged to bursting.⁵²

The simultaneity of the encounter here – 'neither of us a second before or after the other' – is telling: the animal seems to intuit in the form of an image what it could not consciously countenance; it is as though it possesses an obscure awareness of what is really driving his obsession, but that even obliquely accessing it entails setting off a violent fantasy of mutual/self destruction. In this sense it is very useful to know that Brod reports that many of the words in the text are ones that he and Kafka used together on a daily basis, pointing out that 'the animal = the hacking cough' (das Tier = der quälende Husten)⁵³ that dogged Kafka at the end of his life. Benjamin was aware of this connection as early as 1934, writing that 'because the most forgotten source of strangeness is our body – one's own body – one can understand why Kafka called the cough that erupted from within him "the animal." It was the vanguard of the great herd.'⁵⁴ It is not enough, then, to read the whistling noise as a hallucination, nor simply as a metaphor for Kafka's own impending death: rather it is the return of the forgotten fact of biological existence itself, a fear of mortality of sorts, but only insofar as the fear of death can be understood in a more original sense as an inability to accommodate the sheer fact of life itself in the face of one's certain biological demise. This can help shed some light on the problem of whether or not this story is in fact unfinished, lending weight to the claim from Blanchot that the idea that in the missing pages Kafka staged some final confrontation or fight to the death between the animal protagonist and the whistling beast is based on a 'rather poor reading'. After all, if the animal is hearing itself, then 'there could be no decisive combat'⁵⁵: rather what the story shows is that this very desire for a final showdown, this obsessive search for the beast, was always going to misfire before it really got started.

This problem of a final confrontation with the beast is one that is common to both Nietzsche and political ontology. It will also allow us to draw a distinction between them. Agamben's work should compel us to consider the extent to which this image of 'decisive combat' remains a kind of fantasy – in Nietzschean terms, this is the fantasy of a full affirmation of or reconciliation with the beast – which is not external to but actually conditions the whole failed process of exclusion. Kafka's story shows the paradoxes inherent in the problem of animal life; taking its claims seriously will lead us to complicate the Nietzschean programme of affirmation. The demand that we affirm the beast cedes too much to the anthropological machine. As Murray writes: 'It is not a matter of choosing animal life or human life, but of attempting to render the machine inoperative, to stop it from working.'[56] For this reason, the Nietzschean equation between redemption and the possibility of a renewal of or return to animal life is too quick, at least to the extent that it passes over the properly aporetic structure of the problem. The idea of the 'natural' (and any concept of the animal that is dependent on it) is a condition for the functioning of the anthropological machine, which must presuppose it in order to police the borderlines between these oppositions (nature/culture; animal/human; life/language). As such, the task is not simply to affirm what has been excluded via 'the return of humanity to its animal self',[57] but rather to undermine the very logic of (inclusive) exclusion. In that sense, political ontology may give us reason to be sceptical of a Nietzschean 'affirmative biopolitics'.[58]

As we saw, Nietzsche understands life as such as profoundly innocent: it is evaluative, in that it makes selections (as he asks in aphorism nine: '[I]s not living – estimating, preferring, being unjust, being limited, wanting to be different?'[59]), but is not itself beholden to moral principles, both pre-existing them historically and subsisting beneath them after the positing of civilisation. His theory of redemption, which is embodied in the figure of the overhuman, is a complex figure of both remembering and forgetting: the overhuman is the being that is able to forget resentment and live free from the poison of bad conscience, but this in turn means it is the being that is able to remember its animality, to retrieve its natural drives from the taming clutches of civilisation.[60] We might even say that things are more complex than this, because the animal, as the paradigm of another type of forgetfulness, may itself be the very resource that allows the forgetting of resentment: the overhuman, then, is the animal that can forget resentment of its animality through a kind of mobilisation of that animality. To quote from Lemm once again: '[T]he strength of the overhuman is reflected in its ability to contain within itself an increasing degree of struggle between the greatest plurality of animal passions.'[61] The double aspect of this process helps explain a key Nietzschean metaphor: that of the human animal as a 'rope' or 'bridge'[62] between the overhuman and the animal. Nietzsche's redemptive ideal does not ask the human animal to progress beyond its humanity in the way civilisation alleges the human progressed beyond animality, but rather asks the human animal to climb in both directions at once, moving through the overhuman to a new relation to its animality while simultaneously moving through the animal to an overcoming of an all too human version of humanity. If and when the human animal arrives at either end, then, it will have already found itself at the other.[63]

As with Nietzsche's, Agamben's political ontological approach to these problems is predicated upon the possibility of their transformation: the claim that human beings could experience a change in their relation to their animality. This proposition – which is phrased in *The Open* in terms of a demand that we 'render inoperative'[64] the anthropological machine of humanism – can be understood as a call to definitively abandon any idea of realising a human essence, whether it be through work, philosophy or revolutionary politics. I referred to the key image of the text in the last chapter: Agamben's description of an illustration from a thirteenth-century Hebrew Bible which depicts 'the messianic banquet of the righteous on the last day'.[65] This image is surprising, Agamben says, because the figures are depicted with animal heads, because 'the artist of the manuscript . . . intended to suggest that on the last day, the relations between animals and men will take on a new form, and . . . man himself will be reconciled with his animal nature.'[66] Despite (or perhaps because of) its reference to the Judeo-Christian tradition, Agamben's claim here seems very Nietzschean, especially if we understand the overhuman as the figure of remembered and affirmed animality. Yet we find this suggestion on the third page of the book. By the end of the text Agamben has developed his account in such a way that any idea of a 'reconciliation' between the human being and its animality appears impossible, and the desire for reconciliation even appears as a symptom of the very problem he wants to resolve. In the final chapter of *The Open*, then, we find him writing the following:

> And if one day, according to a now-classic image, the 'face in the sand' that the sciences of man have formed on the shore of our history should finally be erased, what will appear in its place will not be . . . a regained humanity or animality. The righteous with animal heads . . . do not represent a new declension of the man-animal relation so much as a figure of the 'great ignorance' which lets both of them be outside of being, saved precisely in their being unsavable . . .[67]

The problem is no longer being posed in terms of how to reconcile the human to its animal nature but in terms of 'an inquiry into the practico-political mystery of separation'.[68] What happens over the course of the text, which in this respect actually represents an important development from the *Homo Sacer* series, is a kind of deconstruction of the very terms of the problem of how the human could re-engage with or retrieve the animal life that was banished from the *polis*.[69]

The key difference between an Agambenian account and that of Nietzsche comes to light here. If in Nietzsche the task is to forget resentment and affirm life as will to power,[70] then in political ontology the desirability and indeed even the very possibility of such affirmation becomes questionable. We see this difference in Agamben's profound ambivalence regarding Nietzsche's eternal return, which is certainly the Nietzschean concept that he cites most regularly.[71] I want to argue, however, that this ambivalence is actually symptomatic of a deeper difference, and that when the works of these two thinkers are framed by the ontology of life at play in each we get to the heart of the disagreement from which Agamben's ambivalence stems. The eternal return, after all, is Nietzsche's great redeeming test, the ultimate ethical challenge whereby the all too human animal is given a chance to redeem itself through a primordial act of absolute affirmation. This redeeming test of Nietzsche's can be compared productively with the passage from Agamben's short essay 'On Potentiality':

> For everyone a moment comes in which he or she must utter this 'I can,' which does not refer to any certainty or specific capacity, but is, nevertheless, absolutely demanding. Beyond all faculties, this 'I can' does not mean anything – yet it marks what is, for each of us, the hardest and bitterest experience possible: the experience of potentiality.[72]

Once again this sounds very Nietzschean, but once again appearances deceive. The difference between the Nietzschean account of affirming the will to power in the potentially crushing experience of the eternal return and the Agambenian account of uttering the 'I can' in the experience of potentiality is that Agamben frames this experience in terms of an originary impotential or constitutive impotence. If for Nietzsche what is affirmed in the 'I can' of the redemptory response to the eternal return is the totality of life, the sum of all past and future events, then for political ontology what is affirmed is not existence as a whole in its actuality but rather potentiality, and so the 'potential not to' that subsists within every action as its original enabling condition. For political ontology every ability to be able is itself predicated on a more original inability, an 'I can't' that stems from the ontological nature of potential as something which can never fully discharge itself, as something that could always have been otherwise. This is how we should interpret Agamben's claim that '[b]eings that exist in the mode of potentiality *are capable of their own impotentiality*' or that '[e]very human power is *adynamia*, impotentiality; every human potentiality is in relation to its own privation'.[73] In Nietzsche, life is will to power, and the test posed by the eternal return is a test of affirming life as pure power. In Agamben, life is passivity and receptivity, a *potentia passiva*, and the ethical test of the experience of potentiality is not a test of strength but rather a test of the *ability to be unable*, the affirmation of a privation. If for Nietzsche the human animal flees from the affective intensity and sheer potency of life and makes itself anaemic, then for Agamben it flees from its original impotence and makes itself monstrous.

This is why Agamben and Nietzsche, despite the clear and fascinating similarities in their work, both end up with an entirely different understanding of the *scope* of redemption. For as Jacob Taubes points out, Nietzsche is in resolute agreement with the 'ancient type of philosophy' in which truth is 'difficult to attain, accessible only to a few'.[74] The affirmation of the will to power practised by the overhuman is only possible for those with a particular kind of strength, with the fortitude of a being that can face up to the unending repetition of life in the eternal return; Nietzsche, as is obvious from even the most cursory reading of his texts, saw self-overcoming as something available to a select and extremely small subset of human animals. Against Nietzsche, however, Agamben's Pauline concept of redemption is absolutely non-hierarchical. This is because it has its basis in an idea of the human being as living with and as a kind of original weakness, a passivity that human animals share in virtue of being what they are. Each one of us suffers; each singular human animal knows an experience of radical passivity. To paraphrase Heidegger, the question is not how to overcome it, but how to get into it in the right way. After all, what is so harrowing about Kafka's story is the profound sense of the animal's *isolation* as it fortifies itself in the bowels of the earth. Agamben's work indicates that if the animal is to present as something other than a beast that must be tamed or destroyed, it will be because it is able to appear as a sign of our being in common.

What does this indicate about the kind of political ontological change toward which Agamben's work gestures? The lesson here is not that there is something natural – a pure or innocent animal life, such as the one Nietzsche seemed to believe was expressed in pre-historical humanity – that we need to pry from the clutches of the state and affirm, but rather that the very opposition between the animal and the human, between nature and culture, is itself a fantasy constitutive of the state as we know it (and one that conditions the insanity of Kafka's animal, just as it conditions the real exclusions of today's states: refugee camps, 'detention centres', Guantanamo Bay, etc.). As Agamben writes of Kafka's story (which, he reports, is the work by Kafka that made the strongest impression on Heidegger):

> The nameless animal that is the protagonist of the story – mole, fox, or human being – is obsessively engaged in building an inexpugnable burrow that instead slowly reveals itself to be a trap with no way out. But isn't this precisely what has happened in the political space of Western nation-states? The homes – the 'fatherlands' – that these states endeavoured to build

revealed themselves in the end to be only lethal traps for the very 'peoples' that were supposed to inhabit them.[75]

The drive for security that plagues Kafka's animal protagonist, just like the drive for the same which plagues contemporary superpowers, is not only hopeless in a fundamental sense (in that the security sought could never be fully attained), but also bound up with the very problem it is ostensibly designed to solve: the animal needs the beast to justify the burrow; the beast responds by transforming the burrow into a trap. Kafka's animal experiences a kind of haunting. But it is a fantasmatic haunting: the animal convinces itself that it is being haunted by something radically other, but this is a defence against the intimacy of what is really bothering it. This is why the fantasy of final confrontation that arises in the closing pages of the story is crucially ambiguous: if the animal destroys the beast, it destroys itself; if the animal welcomes the beast, it will be destroyed (winning means losing, and vice versa). The fantasy of full affirmation, then, is just the flipside to the fantasy of total destruction. In Agamben's terms, one is a fantasy of exclusion without inclusion, the other a fantasy of inclusion without exclusion (importantly, these are both fantasies of totality[76]). What is needed, then, is not the affirmation of the beast as Nietzsche seems to demand, but the undoing of the metaphysical logic that posits it as such; what needs to be resisted is the idea of a return to – a final confrontation and/or reconciliation with – the beast in its natural form. This is because the beast, as Agamben says of bare life, 'is a product of the machine, and not something that pre-exists it'.[77] Kafka's animal digs its burrow in order to escape itself, in order to banish the fact of its own being alive; what it finds, of course, is that the object of its fear pursues it. One cannot make peace with the beast just as one cannot make peace with bare life, for they are not concrete opponents but rather the twin images of the return of a repressed metaphysical problem.

At this point, we can modify Nietzsche's image of the bridge between the animal and the overhuman by imagining instead that it reaches between the human and the animal, and insisting that the question is not whether we could one day make it across, but whether we can appropriate – indeed whether we can learn to collectively *use* – our basic inability to ever make that crossing. This would entail not the lauding of the singular individual who proves himself able to rise above the herd by affirming his own instinctual life, but rather a reorientation of the problem around being in common, a recognition of the fact that if the anthropological machine is to be stopped, it could only be via a collective appropriation of our shared consignment to *unassumable* animal life. This is not an ethic of reconciliation between the human and the animal in the human, but rather an ethic of attentiveness, an ethic that asks us to attend to animal life as something ungraspable. To the extent that the animal in me presents to my consciousness, it can only do so as an insoluble enigma.[78]

NOTES

1. Nietzsche, *The Will to Power*, 582; 312e.
2. Nietzsche, 'On Truth and Lie in an Extra-Moral Sense', 44.
3. Nietzsche, *On the Genealogy of Morals*, II, 16; 520e.
4. Ibid. III, 28; 598e.
5. Ibid. I, 4; 463e.
6. Ibid. II, 23; 530e.
7. Ibid. II, 23; 530e.
8. Owen, *Maturity and Modernity*, 49–50.
9. Ibid. 49–50.
10. Nietzsche, 'The Birth of Tragedy', 12; 82e.
11. Nietzsche, *On the Genealogy of Morals*, I, 10; 472e.
12. Ibid. II, 16; 521e.
13. Kant, *Critique of Pure Reason*, B133; 153e.
14. Nietzsche, *On the Genealogy of Morals*, II, 6; 501e.
15. This is not the place to go over Nietzsche's full historical argument, which is more complex than I have been able to indicate here. For a useful reconstruction, see Owen's *Maturity and Modernity*, 17–83.
16. Nietzsche, *On the Genealogy of Morals*, II, 16; 520e.
17. Nietzsche, *The Gay Science*, 354; 212e.
18. Nietzsche, *On the Genealogy of Morals*, II, 1; 411e.
19. Ibid. II, 1; 494e.
20. Ibid. II, 1; 493e.
21. Lemm, 'The Overhuman Animal', 222. Lemm's book-length study of these problems is also invaluable here (see *Nietzsche's Animal Philosophy*). This work, which is the 'first systematic treatment of the animal in Nietzsche's philosophy as a whole' (1), repeatedly insists on a fact that is pivotal for the argument in this chapter: the animal in Nietzsche is not (just) a metaphor, but rather a central figure of his philosophy. As well as this, Lemm returns repeatedly to the problem of forgetting as a condition of political life as we know it, arguing that '[c]ivilization and forgetfulness belong together insofar as it is only because of the forgetfulness of the human being's animal beginning (animal origin) that it can come to understand itself as a moral and rational being . . .' (17).
22. This can help explain the importance of art in Nietzsche's philosophy. An aesthetic experience, we might say, is an experience in which I am able to reconnect with the animal in me, an experience in which I am reminded of my own biological being in a way that produces pleasure instead of (or, as

Nietzsche would probably have insisted, as well as) horror. The 'buzz' we get from painting or music is not purely biological (in the sense of being simply stimulating). Nor is it purely intellectual (in the Kantian sense of being 'devoid of interest'). Rather in aesthetic experience this distinction breaks down. In buzzing before a painting, I am able to conceptualise my own animality: there is an invasion of the intellectual by the biological that does not simply represent the overriding of the former by the latter (as might take place, for instance, when I am exposed to actual physical danger). Aesthetic experience is the experience of a confluence between the biological and the conceptual; good art is intellectually enlivening. As Rampley puts it, 'Nietzsche forms a critique of the notion of disinterested aesthetic experience ... in the name of physiology. Deriving aesthetic judgment from the physiology of the human organism, Nietzsche's position is hostile to any theory that separates questions of beauty from those of desire' (*Nietzsche, Aesthetics and Modernity*, 176). Or to quote from Nietzsche himself:

> Art reminds us of states of animal vigor; it is, on the one hand, an excess and overflow of blooming physicality into the world of images and desires; on the other, an excitation of the animal functions through the images and desires of intensified life; that is, an enhancement of the feeling of life, a stimulant to it. (*The Will to Power*, 802; 422e)

23. Agamben, *The Open*, 38.
24. Ibid. 37.
25. Agamben, 'We Refugees'.
26. Agamben, *The Open*, 37.
27. Daniel McLoughlin writes in 'The Sacred and the Unspeakable':

> Agamben frequently intimates that there is a close relationship between ontology and politics, and his explicitly political texts draw on a range of concepts such as potentiality, play, and happy life, developed in his earlier first philosophical thought. Nonetheless, the nature of the relationship between the two remains indistinct, a difficulty that is particularly evident in the ambiguous role that 'bare life' plays in *Homo Sacer*.

Like McLoughlin's, the reading of Agamben I am presenting insists on the primacy of ontology in his thought. It not only has the merit of allowing us to explain these crucial passages in *Homo Sacer*; arguably it can help resolve the problem McLoughlin identifies here, and allow us to put Agamben's claims in their most compelling form.

28. Though it only refers to Agamben in passing (and does not even mention Nietzsche), Daniel Heller-Roazen's fascinating (and indeed deeply Agambenian) study of the philosophical history of the faculty by which 'the animal feels ... that it lives' (*The Inner Touch*, 63) is a useful reference point here. Particularly relevant for this book is the striking claim that this

faculty – which was crucial for Aristotle (as well as his stoic, scholastic and early modern interpreters) – undergoes a radical transformation in modernity. For Heller-Roazen, the development of the Cartesian philosophy of consciousness, with its emphasis on epistemology and obsession with cognition, effected a progressive elimination of the concept of the 'inner touch' from intellectual history. After this 'metaphysical determination of human nature . . .', Heller-Roazen argues in the penultimate chapter of the book, '[t]he animal vanishes from man: in a speaking being, thought and existence remain, at last absolved of the animal power that was the sense of life' (287). It is appropriate that Heller-Roazen returns in his final chapter to Aristotle's *Ethics*, for an ethics of potentiality is exactly where the history of being (animal) should return us in the end.

29. Agamben, *The Open*, 79.
30. Though he is right to emphasise the importance of Heidegger, Miguel Vatter may therefore have things backwards when he writes that Agamben 'map[s] the problem of Heideggerian facticity onto the space of modern biopower explored by Foucault' ('In Odradek's World', 47). If my reading is correct, then Agamben maps biopolitics onto fundamental ontology.
31. Eric Santner's recent study of the political theology of 'the flesh' is a useful point of reference and comparison here. *The Royal Remains* can be read as a kind of sequel to his 1996 study of Schreber (see *My Own Private Germany*) that incorporates the insights developed in two more recent works (see *On Creaturely Life* and *On the Psychotheology of Everyday Life*). In it Santner sets up a theory of 'the flesh' or the 'sublime substance' (ix) of the body of the King which, he argues, remains at work in the *polis* even after the deposition of monarchs at the beginnings of modernity. Though Nietzsche plays a relatively minor role in Santner's book (the methodology of which owes a much stronger debt to psychoanalysis), the work's insistence on relating the problems of sovereignty back to the nervous and affective symptoms of the human – the repeated demonstrations of how biological life and political power intertwine to produce creatures that are divided from themselves – could certainly be brought into a fruitful dialogue with the Nietzsche of the *Genealogy*. Particularly relevant to this study is the claim from Santner that Agamben's concept of 'bare life' 'needs to be understood as the spectral dimension of the flesh . . .' (76): the flesh is not identified with bare life, which (as I have indicated) is better understood as the return of a repressed metaphysical problem; rather, the flesh for Santner is the concrete, affective dimension of the metaphysical image that 'bare life' names. To put this in the terms of my argument, what Santner shows is how the question of being *materialises* in the vicissitudes of human animality: the flesh, we might say, is how and where the question of being (animal) haunts the human.
32. See Snyder, 'Kafka's "Burrow"', 113; see also Koelb, 'Kafka Imagines his Readers', 137.
33. Kafka, 'The Burrow', 327.

34. Ibid. 343.
35. Ibid. 343.
36. Ibid. 343.
37. Ibid. 343.
38. Ibid. 345.
39. Ibid. 347.
40. Ibid. 348.
41. Ibid. 348.
42. Ibid. 349.
43. Ibid. 352.
44. Ibid. 353.
45. Ibid. 353.
46. Ibid. 354.
47. Ibid. 359.
48. Maché, 'The Noise in the Burrow', 526–7.
49. Weigand, 'Franz Kafka's "The Burrow" ("Der Bau")', 155.
50. Boulby, 'Kafka's End', 175.
51. Blanchot, *The Space of Literature*, 169.
52. Kafka, 'The Burrow', 358.
53. Brod, 'Nachwort', 349–50.
54. Benjamin, 'Franz Kafka', 810.
55. Blanchot, *The Space of Literature*, 169.
56. Murray, *Giorgio Agamben*, 45.
57. Berkowitz, 'Liberating the Animal'.
58. Lemm, *Nietzsche's Animal Philosophy*, 152.
59. Nietzsche, *Beyond Good and Evil*, 9; 205e.
60. As this point indicates, reading Nietzsche in terms of the problematic of (the forgetting and remembering of) the animal implicitly supports the idea that the figure of the *Übermensch* remains at work in Nietzsche's 'mature' texts (of which his *Genealogy* is usually understood to be exemplary). This is because the concept of animality and its link to overcoming provides a clear basis for reading the *Genealogy* (which is replete with references to the human animal's divided relation to its instinctual drives) alongside *Zarathustra* (in which animals repeatedly play a role in the transformations of the protagonist). Thus it lends support to the claims of a small but growing body of scholars who are working to challenge the (until recently) consensual position in Nietzsche scholarship that in the *Genealogy* the older 'poetic' figure of the *Übermensch* gives way to the more historically specific (and, from the vantage point of Anglo-American philosophy, rather more palatable) figure of the sovereign individual (see Hatab, *Nietzsche's Life Sentence*, 42–52; Acampora, 'On Sovereignty and Overhumanity'; Loeb, 'Finding the Übermensch in Nietzsche's Genealogy of Morality'; see also Rainer Hanshe's fascinating esoteric reading of Nietzsche's use of dashes in 'Invisibly Revolving— —Inaudibly Revolving'). The continued importance of animality for the 'mature' Nietzsche is evidence of

the continued importance for him of an idea of radical overcoming; in the *Genealogy*, animality remains a figure of a possible *übermenschlich* redemption.
61. Lemm, *Nietzsche's Animal Philosophy*, 23.
62. Nietzsche, *Thus Spoke Zarathustra*, First Part, 4; 13e.
63. Of course, we need to qualify this in light of Nietzsche's pointing out that the overhuman is not a goal. This simultaneous movement, we have to recognise, is just that: a movement, a continual process of becoming.
64. Agamben, *The Open*, 92. Krzysztof Ziarek ('After Humanism') argues Agamben's demand contains a residual humanism.
65. Ibid. 1.
66. Ibid. 3.
67. Ibid. 92.
68. Ibid. 92.
69. It is worth pointing here to *The Beast and the Sovereign*, Jacques Derrida's recently published lecture series on these problems. In this work Derrida works to deconstruct some of Agamben's own concepts, including the very opposition between *zoē* and *bios* (see 408–43). While this is not the place for a proper engagement with Derrida's critique, I believe the reading of Agamben I present here – where the *zoē/bios* distinction is read in the terms of fundamental ontology – may provide grounds for defending Agamben, whose claims will no longer stand or fall on the basis of this linguistic distinction. On my reading of Agamben, the *zoē/bios* distinction is not as fundamental to his project as it may appear; rather, it is another version of the (more primordial) ontological difference. As such, the project is based on a properly *philosophical* (Heideggerian) distinction, rather than a conceptual divide with a (potentially spurious) basis in an ancient linguistic opposition.
70. 'A living thing', Nietzsche writes in aphorism thirteen of *Beyond Good and Evil*, 'seeks above all to *discharge* its strength – life itself is *will to power*...' (*Beyond Good and Evil*, 13; 211e).
71. See Durantaye, *Giorgio Agamben*, 314–23 for an excellent account of this.
72. Agamben, 'On Potentiality', 178.
73. Ibid. 182.
74. Taubes, *The Political Theology of Paul*, 80.
75. Agamben, 'In This Exile', 139–40.
76. I analyse this problem at length in the next three chapters.
77. Agamben, *State of Exception*, 87–8.
78. As Elizabeth Bishop writes in 'IV / O Breath':

> Equivocal, but what we have in common's   bound to be there,
> whatever we must own   equivalents for,
> something that maybe I   could bargain with
> and make a separate peace   beneath
> within   if never with.

7. Understanding the Happy

All of existence is squeezed into the philosopher's tomato when he rolls it towards his overwhelming question.[1]

All cognition of the Whole originates in death, in the fear of death.[2]

What are the consequences of our taking the world as a picture, of viewing it as though it were a picture, of *picturing* the world? This question, which is arguably at the heart of the problem of representation, is complicated by the depth at which the picture-concept – the idea of the world as a representable totality of facts – is embedded in our ways of speaking and writing. In everyday language we find 'points of view' and 'perspectives' (not to mention *Weltbilder* and *Weltanschauungen*); we say 'that's not how I see it', 'I see what you mean', or 'I get the picture' (presumably operating under a version of the idea that communication, at least in its deliberative modes, is a way of sharing these objects, of opening our own views of the world to the views of others). Similarly in philosophical language we often refer to the positions of various writers as 'pictures', and of philosophical debate in terms of arguments over differing 'views' of whatever matter is at hand. In other words, this metaphorical register – the language of pictures, views, frames, perspectives and so on – is highly intuitive for us, and even appears as a natural way of presenting and comparing claims and arguments. However as with many such intuitions – like for instance the intuition that the mind or soul is 'in' the body – what seems like a natural way of taking things can become insanely beguiling when held up for philosophical analysis. In this chapter, I am interested in how the (critique of the) picture-concept can provide a way of understanding the therapeutic goals of Wittgenstein's philosophy, clarification of the ethical stakes of the problem of representation, and a deepening of the question of life raised in the previous two chapters. Joining the 'resolute' readers of the *Tractatus* – which means abandoning the idea that Wittgenstein's text somehow hints at ('shows') the ineffable – I work to demonstrate how it sets up and then undermines a 'picture theory' of language. If successful, this undermining will make us wary of philosophical talk in which the existence of the world is passed over as a non-problem, or taken as a fact like other facts; it will shake us out of the philosophical commitments that prevent us from understanding the difference between the happy and the unhappy.[3] Above all, 'throwing away the ladder' in the way that Wittgenstein demands means letting go of the philosophical fantasies that allow us to imagine ourselves as viewers of the world.

Wittgenstein's *Tractatus* famously begins with the assertions that 'the world is all that is the case'; that it is the 'totality of facts, not of things'.[4] It would be hard to overestimate the importance of this deceptively subtle idea, which Max Black called 'the outstanding innovation of Wittgenstein's ontology'.[5] What is the nature of this (apparent) innovation? To invoke a familiar story: it reorients philosophy around language and its ability to represent facts, leaving behind more traditional concerns with the nature of reality itself. As such, it can be understood as inaugurating a profound shift in the nature of philosophical inquiry. The fact ontology is, after all, the basis of the highly influential 'picture theory' of language, which can be broken down in something like the following way: a picture is a model of states of affairs (2.12). It is made up of elementary propositions. Elementary propositions are logically simple statements; they have truth conditions that are contingent upon their correct representation of particular atomic states of affairs (4.21). A picture is an arrangement of elementary propositions; it makes assertions regarding the relations between them. Its truth conditions are contingent upon whether it shares its 'pictorial form' with the facts (2.17). All this would seem to result in two requirements: a correct picture must be (1) isomorphic with the logical structure of the world; and (2) correctly representative of one of the sets of logically complex states of affairs that make up the world. Both of these claims are quite intuitive: saying (1) is the same as saying that the elementary propositions collected in a picture must themselves have a sense for it to be able to 'depict . . . in any way at all' (2.18); that for a picture to be meaningful the propositions that make it up must *have* truth conditions; saying (2) is the same as saying that 'the picture agrees with reality . . .' (2.21); that a correct picture has truth conditions that *obtain*. Wittgenstein's thus looks like a particularly sophisticated version of the 'correspondence theory' of truth that has been at work in Western philosophy at least since Aquinas's *veritas est adaequatio rei et intellectus*: his innovation, we might say, was to metaphysically deflate the correspondence theory by substituting 'fact' for 'thing' and 'proposition' for 'intellect'.

As is well known, one of the troubling upshots of the picture theory is the effect it has on the claims we make about all those objects that are not reducible to 'facts' in any obvious way (such as moral value, aesthetic quality, religious experience and so on). It is no accident, for instance, that Ayer's emotivist theory of moral judgement arises as a direct result of the enthusiastic uptake of (a version of) the picture theory by him and other logical positivists. The problem is that claims about value do not have clear relations to states of affairs: that the apparently similar surface grammar of 'murder is wrong' and 'the cat is black' conceals the fact that the former statement does not have obvious truth conditions (we can investigate whether the cat is black by investigating the facts of the matter regarding the colour of the cat; but how can we investigate the facts of the matter regarding the wrongness of murder? Where would we start looking for such facts?). Ayer's response was to claim that 'murder is wrong' really means 'down with murder' or 'boo murder' or something to that effect:[6] that to make a moral claim is not to make a claim about mind-independent facts, but rather to express one's own feelings on a particular matter. As Ayer was happy to admit, however, this undermines the normative force of claims about value, because such 'pure expressions of feeling . . . do not come under the category of truth and falsehood. They are unverifiable for the same reason as a cry of pain or a word of command is unverifiable – because they do not express genuine propositions.'[7] It therefore seems that there is no way to meaningfully debate about normative issues, because there are no facts of the matter to debate about. Now Ayer's emotivism is only one (rather extreme) way of dealing with the problem of value after the advent of the fact ontology, but it demonstrates one of its basic tendencies: a problematisation of the very idea of 'value', which once categorically divorced from 'fact' starts to become difficult (if not impossible) to coherently account for.

Of course, Wittgenstein himself was acutely aware of these problems, and his way of dealing with them is more nuanced than the above may indicate. He seems to give a typical non-cognitivist argument when he writes in the *Tractatus* that '[i]n the world everything is as it is, and everything happens as it does happen: *in* it no value exists – and if it did exist, it would have no value' (6.3751). The world is the totality of facts, but none of these facts are values in the robust sense (there are facts relating to the values a person or community may hold: 'Alfred feels that charity is valuable' might picture certain facts about Alfred, but 'charity is valuable' does not picture facts). So it would seem that

Wittgenstein, like Ayer, consigns propositions about values to the realm of nonsense (*Unsinn*). Yet we would be mistaken to read Wittgenstein as a logical positivist in anything like the usual sense. This claim is supported by a series of factors: he was emphatic in his claims that the positivists had radically misunderstood his *Tractatus*;[8] he tells Ficker in a 1919 letter that the point of the book is 'an ethical one';[9] and as the autobiographical evidence shows, Wittgenstein was himself obsessed with how to live a good life (Ray Monk writes that 'spiritual and ethical preoccupations . . . dominate his life'[10]). The question is how to reconcile this evidence with the text: the fact that Wittgenstein seemingly relegates value to the realm of nonsense (in contemporary terms, putting forward a meta-ethical 'error theory' and espousing a radical kind of non-cognitivism) while nevertheless remaining convinced that the very heart of the *Tractatus* was 'ethical' in some sense of the word. As James Conant argues, the fact that Wittgenstein never puts forward anything resembling a 'moral philosophy' is not sufficient grounds for claiming that his philosophy has no ethical force, nor is the fact that the *Tractatus* is apparently a treatise on logic and language; as he puts it, 'ethical and logical concerns equally pervade the whole'[11] of the work. But what is the nature of this pervasion?

Here I want to turn to what I would argue is one of the most important sentences in the book (and one that, Agamben indicates, is important for *The Coming Community*[12]). I am referring to note 6.44: 'It is not *how* things are in the world that is mystical, but *that* it exists.' The mystical, Wittgenstein seems to be saying, consists not in the facts that make up the world, in how it is with the world, but in the plain fact of the world's existence. This is why he emphasises the word 'in' in the passage quoted above ('*in* [the world] no value exists'). Though I will complicate this below, it would seem that Wittgenstein is claiming that there is no value *in* the world, no fact in the world that would necessarily entail a value judgement or call for a judgement of value; rather it is the existence of the world itself that is valuable. Here we should emphasise the inextricability of all of Wittgenstein's claims about value, the mystical, aesthetics and so on. It would be a mistake to regard these as claims about disparate realms of inquiry, as though Wittgenstein were working under the kind of institutional and professional conditions that lead contemporary philosophers to specialise in various sub-fields (such that some philosophers 'do' ethics, others philosophy of language). It is not that there are separate spheres of philosophical inquiry in which philosophers have a tendency to start talking (different types of) nonsense; it is wrong to read Wittgenstein as claiming that there are *certain aspects* of human life that cannot be sensically described (as Cora Diamond says, we should not understand Wittgenstein to be claiming that there are certain 'features of reality'[13] that cannot be talked about). Or as she puts it in another essay:

> We think that one way of dividing philosophy into branches is to take there to be, for every kind of thing people talk and think about, philosophy of that subject matter ... We may then think that there is thought and talk that has as its subject matter what the good life is for human beings, or what principles of action we should accept; and then philosophical ethics will be the philosophy of that area of thought and talk. But you do not have to think that; and Wittgenstein rejects that conception of ethics.[14]

'Aesthetics and ethics are one,' Wittgenstein says in the *Tractatus*, or as he writes in a 1929 notebook, '[w]hat is good is also divine. Queer as it sounds, that sums up my ethics.'[15] Taken together, these remarks appear to result in a surprising erasure of the distinctions between a series of what are usually taken as disparate fields: aesthetics = ethics = theology. Queer as it may be, it shows how wrong we would be to apply our usual philosophical categories to Wittgenstein's ethical philosophy (if indeed we can meaningfully refer to such a thing).

One can find further evidence for these claims in the 1929 lecture on ethics, which turns on what Wittgenstein calls 'absolute or ethical value'.[16] As we have seen, Wittgenstein is not (does not present himself as) a moral realist, which means he does not believe that value is a property that inheres in certain objects, people or actions: this is why he says in this lecture (in a claim that mirrors the apparent non-cognitivism of the *Tractatus*) that if someone were to write a book consisting of perfectly accurate descriptions of all the states of affairs that make up the world, then this book would not contain a single fact of real ethical significance. This is because value is something that seems to exist outside this world of facts. That this is the case is shown in a certain experience, which Wittgenstein describes as follows: 'I believe the best way of describing it is to say that when I have it *I wonder at the existence of the world*. And I am then inclined to use such phrases as "how extraordinary that anything should exist" or "how extraordinary that the world should exist."'[17] To return once again to 6.44, the experience he is describing is not an experience of wonder at *how* the world is (at, for instance, the complexity of the human body, the size of the Sun, or the pyramids) but *that* it exists (which is not a fact in anything like the usual sense). Wittgenstein: 'If for instance I had this experience while looking into the blue sky, I could wonder at the sky being blue as opposed to the case when it's clouded. But that's not what I mean. I am wondering at the sky being *whatever it is*.'[18] One of the remarkable things about this lecture, however, is just how circumspect it is.

Throughout it, Wittgenstein's statements about value are always made with extreme caution, and often in the conditional mode (this is characteristic of the later Wittgenstein, who often employs clauses such as 'I want to say' or 'I am inclined to say'). Indeed, Wittgenstein makes a number of claims in the lecture that he quickly rejects, and even says that the experience of wonder he is describing is 'an entirely personal'[19] one. It seems, then, that Wittgenstein makes the claims he does about value despite himself, and despite his own sense of their questionable philosophical and semantic legitimacy. As the text goes on, the reader comes to understand the experience in question is one that calls philosophical language and even the possibility of 'expression' into question: '[T]he verbal expression which we give to these experiences is nonsense!'[20]

This should be taken alongside the concepts of nonsense at work in the *Tractatus*. Very much hangs on how we interpret the status of these claims, which are connected to the philosophical problems associated with the picture theory. The question is how seriously we should take them. According to what Conant calls the 'ineffability interpretations'[21] of the *Tractatus*, Wittgenstein would here be attempting to show something that cannot be said, to hint at a thought of value that is not expressible in language. Yet Conant, in his 'resolute' reading of the text, problematises such interpretations on the grounds that they (and in this sense they are just like the positivist readings of which they tend to be critical) employ an insufficiently clear (Conant uses the word 'austere') concept of nonsense. For Conant, who in this respect is a paradigmatic 'new reader' of the book, Wittgenstein's own instructions to the reader of his work should be taken at their word. The especially relevant note is 6.54:

> My propositions serve as elucidations in the following way: anyone who understands me eventually recognizes them as nonsensical, when he has used them – as steps – to climb out through them, on them, over them. (He must, so to speak, throw away the ladder after he has climbed up it.)

For Conant, the *Tractatus* has to be read as a very particular sort of text: one that is designed to undermine itself, as structurally ironic in a quasi-Kierkegaardian sense (one of the sections of his essay on Frege and Wittgenstein contains an epigraph in which the Danish philosopher speaks of 'a kind of deception in which one deceives a person for the truth's sake ...'[22]). According to his reading of the book, then, we have to take Wittgenstein seriously and literally when he says that his propositions must be recognised as nonsensical. To quote from Conant:

> [T]he elucidatory strategy of the *Tractatus* depends on the reader's provisionally taking himself to be participating in the traditional philosophical

> activity of establishing theses through a procedure of reasoned argument; but it only succeeds if the reader fully comes to understand what the work means to say about itself when it says that philosophy, as this work seeks to practice it, results not in doctrine but in elucidations ... [T]he attainment of this recognition depends upon the reader's actually undergoing a certain *experience* ...[23]

If the book succeeds in its goal, then, it will not be because it has managed to convey a new and more perspicuous theory of the logic of our language, nor because it has somehow been able to hint at ineffable truths that are not expressible in language (on resolute readings the *Tractatus*, if properly understood, conveys no truths at all, ineffable or otherwise), but rather because of a kind of philosophical confidence trick in which the reader begins by believing that she understands what Wittgenstein puts forward with the picture theory, yet ends with the realisation that it was always already a chimera. The text is therapeutic because in going through this process, the reader comes to understand something of herself: of what it was in her that led her to want to understand, and indeed believe she understood, the picture theory. This is why Conant distinguishes his own 'austere' concept of nonsense from the 'substantial' concepts that are characteristic of earlier readings of the *Tractatus*. On these latter, more traditional readings, there are 'two different kinds of nonsense: mere nonsense and substantial nonsense'. The former conveys no thought, but the latter 'is composed of intelligible ingredients combined in an illegitimate way'.[24] If we admit of such a distinction, then Wittgenstein's propositions about absolute value might appear as syntactically confused while nevertheless somehow working to hint at the ineffable, to show something that cannot be said. Yet Conant does not admit of such a distinction, and claims that Wittgenstein does not either.[25] This 'austere reading' has some difficult consequences, but it has a number of clear advantages: as we have seen, it allows us to take Wittgenstein at his word at certain key points in the text (and, I would add, at key points in his lecture on ethics); it can help make sense of what seems like the fundamental incoherence of a book that claims to make claims about logical form while simultaneously holding that logical form cannot be represented (i.e. that '[t]he picture cannot ... depict its pictorial form ...' (2.172)); it allows us to take the *Tractatus* as a non-thetical, therapeutic philosophical work; this means it lets us read it usefully alongside (as opposed to against) the *Investigations*; it helps explain why a thinker so obsessed with ethics might have come to write a book on logic. But what effect does such a reading have on the so-called 'picture theory' (which can no longer be regarded as a 'theory' in any of the usual senses)? What happens to

Wittgenstein's remarks about 'the mystical' on such a reading? And what is the relation between these two results?

Before answering these questions, let us first go a little deeper into Wittgenstein's confidence trick. Look again at Wittgenstein's claim about the mystical: that value is to be found not in the particular facts that make up the world, but rather in the fact that existence exists. Part of the problem, then, is that the claims Wittgenstein wants to make about value rest upon a tautology. After all, the clause 'existence exists' is not only tautological, but it is so in two senses: first, and perhaps most noticeably, its verb corresponds exactly to its noun (as in 'singers sing' or 'writers write'). The second tautology is deeper, as it relates to the nature of the 'object' in question, the fact that the mundane truth that existence exists would seem to be presupposed by every utterance, including of course the utterance that 'existence exists'. So this utterance is singular insofar as it does not appear to express a claim at all (because what could such a claim be *about*?). Indeed it does not seem to express a mental state at all (at least if we hold the position that mental states are always intentional, 'directed toward the world' in the form of a 'belief or judgment whose content ... is that things are thus and so'[26]). Wittgenstein will say that the difficulty consists in the fact that one can't express wonder before something one can't conceive of being otherwise. It may be perfectly legitimate, for instance, to 'wonder at the size of a dog which is bigger than any one I have ever seen before', but if I say that 'I wonder at the existence of the world' then 'I am misusing language',[27] engaging in a confused application of the concept of wonder. The problem stems from the Kantian result that has turned up repeatedly in this book: being is not a real predicate. Propositional language is always engaged in what we can follow Aristotle in calling a *saying something of something (legein ti kata tinos)*. As such, it cannot possibly express the fact of existence, because existence is not and cannot be a 'property' of existence. So it seems that according to Wittgenstein there is an important experience, but describing it means being confronted by the limits of propositional language: running, as he would put it, up against the walls of one's cage.

Another way of elucidating the problems with these statements is as follows. They seem to rely on a rather idiosyncratic conception of what 'the world' might mean, seemingly implying that it is a fact like other facts, even that it could somehow become an object of experience. If we take seriously the Tractarian assertion that the world is the totality of facts, then from what position or perspective could this totality be pictured? If such a position exists, it would have to be extraneous to the totality of facts that the world, on the Tractarian model, ostensibly is: we would have to be viewing the world from outside the world, picturing it in the way that we picture other facts. But such a position cannot possibly exist, because by definition every fact must be included in the set of all facts. As Mulhall says, such a viewpoint of the totality would really be a 'God's eye view on the world, a view from sideways on ...'.²⁸ Wondering at the existence of the world, at the *thatness* of existence, then, would require one '[t]o view [*Anschauung*] the world sub specie aeterni ...', 'to view it as a whole – a limited whole', the very concept of which is extremely problematic (Mulhall again: '[T]hat perspective is not open to mortal beings, ones whose existence is spatio-temporal ...'²⁹). As Jonathan Rée puts it: '[u]nlike the "facts" of which it is the "totality," *the world cannot be pictured*. All you can ever represent to yourself is discrete, determinate possibilities within the world. The world is not one of the things that you come across ...'³⁰

So how can we understand Wittgenstein when he makes claims that are nonsensical (claims, it is clear, he nevertheless found himself very inclined to make)? One cannot but agree with the resolute Conant when he says that there is only one type of nonsense: plain nonsense (*einfach Unsinn*); that it is wrong to believe a senseless statement could possibly express anything, or alternatively 'show' something that cannot be put into words. So what in the world do these statements *do*? Here it is worth turning to a distinction drawn by Diamond in her essay 'Ethics, Imagination and the Method of Wittgenstein's *Tractatus*'. In particular I want to pick out an important moment in the essay, where she draws our attention to the surprising phrasing of the book's penultimate note, and which is perspicuous enough to warrant quoting at length:

> Wittgenstein says: my propositions serve as elucidations in that whoever understands me will recognize them as nonsensical. It is very natural to misremember that sentence, to think that Wittgenstein said that his propositions serve as elucidations in that whoever understands them will recognize them as nonsensical. But the sentence is meant to strike the reader by its not being that. The sentence fails to be what we expect at just that point, and very deliberately. That is, at this significant point in the book, Wittgenstein chooses his words to draw attention to a contrast between understanding a person and understanding what the person says. If you recognize that Wittgenstein's propositions are nonsense, then you may earlier have thought that you understood them, but you did not. In recognizing that they are nonsense, you are giving up the idea that there is such a thing as understanding them. What Wittgenstein means by calling his propositions nonsense is not that they do not fit into some official category of his intelligible propositions but that there is at most the illusion of understanding them.³¹

One cannot understand what Wittgenstein is *saying* when he says he wonders at the existence of the world, but one may nevertheless come to understand *Wittgenstein* when he says he wonders at the existence of the world. Wittgenstein, unlike the metaphysician, is a 'self-aware user of nonsense';[32] he deliberately uses nonsense, and deliberately marks that fact by referring to his nonsense as such (or by employing rhetorical devices such as 'I am inclined to say' or 'I want to say'). Consider here the last sentence in note 6.43: 'The world of the happy is quite another than that of the unhappy.' Even if we grant that the idea that the happy and the unhappy live in 'different worlds' will lead us into confusion if given any metaphysical weight, we can still make a distinction between the happy and the unhappy. And it is worth trying to understand the happy (if not what they say). Wittgenstein speaks nonsense 'in order to make philosophically intelligible the delight with which the artist (happily) views the world. To make the artist's delight philosophically intelligible, we have to present it as rational; and to present it as rational, we have to present it as a rational response to a certain fact, a *that*.'[33] The delight that Wittgenstein presents is not philosophically intelligible, but it is *imaginatively* intelligible, in the sense that we can come to understand the *happiness of the man* who tries (and fails) to express it (Diamond: 'Although all nonsense is simply nonsense, there is an imaginative activity of understanding an utterer of nonsense, letting oneself be taken in by the appearance of sense that some nonsense presents to us'[34]). There is a difference, I want to suggest, between nonsensically presenting the world as a fact like other facts, as a fact that one could come to wonder at in the way that one wonders at other facts, and living what Wittgenstein called 'a wonderful life'.[35] The difficulty is that to express philosophically what it is like to live the latter, Wittgenstein has to resort to the former (and so produce statements that express no philosophical sense).

There is a problem with Morris and Dodd's language in the citation I employed in the above paragraph. It is their use of the three words 'view the world' (I leave open the question as to whether the authors can be regarded as employing these words in a 'self-aware' way). After all, it is the very idea of a *view of the world* that Wittgenstein wants to undermine. In fact this is a way of describing the distinction between the happy and the unhappy: part of the happiness of the happy consists in the fact that they are not confusedly attached to the idea of a view of the world, not philosophically beguiled by the picture-concept. It is not that the happy are happy because they are somehow able to see the world as wonderful (which would require exactly the kind of stepping out of the world that characterises the metaphysical conception), but because they are able to live non-metaphysically in the *midst* of it. Diamond: 'The attractiveness of the forms of words expressive of philosophical confusion arises out of the imagining of a *point of view* for philosophical investigation.'[36] Or again: 'There is an understanding of the would-be engager in ethics as someone who has what looks to him as if it is *a point of view* from which he speaks, an understanding that imaginatively enters into seeing from that *point of view* (which it nevertheless takes to be illusory) . . .'.[37] On the philosophical model, the happy are taken to be expressing a particular *point of view*: a point of view that turns out to be philosophically unintelligible. But what characterises the happy is their having been able to throw away this idea of an external standpoint. It seems the philosopher, in trying to understand the happy, has to translate their happiness into what appear to be philosophically intelligible terms – into an 'experience of P', or a 'knowing that P', where P is a particular object – but that doing so immediately undermines the specificity of what is being described. This is because the 'fact' in question is a special kind of fact: in particular, it is not the kind of fact that can be known, not the kind of fact that can be represented (the world is not a P). As Cavell puts it: '[S]ince we cannot know that the world exists, its presentness to us cannot be a function of knowing.'[38] This is part of why Wittgenstein wants to pull the rug from under the picture-concept: it makes it impossible to understand the happy.

At this point, it is useful to compare Wittgenstein with Franz Rosenzweig, the German Jewish theologian from whose *Star of Redemption* I quoted in the epigraph to this chapter (I will turn to the other quotation shortly). In his introduction to Rosenzweig's *Understanding the Sick and the Healthy*, Hilary Putnam writes (not without a certain rhetorical arrogance) of his 'enormous surprise' at finding that the book reminded him of Wittgenstein: '*Wittgenstein?* Rosenzweig and *Wittgenstein?*'[39] As he goes on to show, however, there are important affinities between the two authors: there is their shared debt to Kierkegaard; there is their understanding of philosophy as traditionally conceived as a kind of sickness; there is their therapeutic conception of a different kind of philosophical practice, in which a different kind of thinking is meant to act as a cure for that sickness (Putnam writes that 'I can very easily imagine [Wittgenstein] reading and enjoying Rosenzweig's "little book" . . .';[40] later, he compares Rosenzweig's excursus on the manifest absurdity of certain philosophical arguments about semantics with Wittgenstein's own critique of the same[41]). More specifically, I want to argue, what the two authors share is a philosophical concern with wonder, and the role it can play in leading us into (and out of) the kinds of confusion (the kinds of unhappiness) that characterise traditional or metaphysical philosophy. In the first chapter of his book, Rosenzweig distinguishes between the everyday wonder characteristic of 'the non-philosophizing half of mankind' and the wonder of the philosopher (it is a crude distinction, but this is a simple book). Everyday wonder, Rosenzweig claims, is characterised by its fleeting nature; all wonder 'requires that man pause', but the non-philosopher does not remain in that pausing for long: 'He merely drifts and goes on living, and then, at last, the numbness caused by his wonder passes.' The philosopher, however, 'is unwilling to accept the passing of the numbness wonder has brought'; he clings to his wonder and will not let it go. Rosenzweig goes on:

> He insists on a solution immediately – at the very instant of his being overcome – and at the very place wonder struck him . . . He separates his experience of wonder from the continuous stream of life, isolating it . . . He does not permit his wonder, stored as it is, to be released into the flow of life.[42]

What characterises the philosopher is that he wants to get out of life, out of the flow of it: he cannot follow his experience of wonder back into the world. This is what marks the philosopher and appears to separate him out from ordinary life, in which, as in the exemplary case of a couple in love, 'the solution and dissolution of their wonder is at hand – the love which has befallen them. They are no longer a wonder to each other; they are in the very heart of wonder.'[43] The philosopher's wonder sets off in him a kind of rage to know that prevents him from living with it. As Santner writes in his study of Rosenzweig and Freud: 'The philosopher appears to be in the thrall of a fantasy that the universal principle he seeks can be attained from a position outside the everyday activities that make up a human life . . .'[44] This is why the problems that face the philosopher cannot be solved by further clarification of the picture-concept: every picture is a (fantasy of a) way out.

Another important convergence between Wittgenstein and Rosenzweig arises here. Consider again the epigraph to this chapter, where Rosenzweig speaks about the fear of death. This is one way of understanding the lure of the picture-concept: in allowing us to believe that we can step outside the world (or language), and contemplate it (or language) as an object, it leads us to believe that we can deny our own being in the world, our finitude as biological creatures, our embedding in linguistic practices that cannot be founded on any ultimate metaphysical ground. As Cavell writes:

> That on the whole we [understand one another] is a matter of our sharing routes of interest and feeling, senses of humour and of significance and fulfilment, of what is outrageous, of what is similar to what else, what a rebuke,

what forgiveness, of when an utterance is an assertion, when an appeal, when an explanation – all the whirl of organism Wittgenstein calls 'forms of life.' Human speech and activity, sanity and community, rest upon nothing more, but nothing less, than this. It is a vision as simple as it is difficult, and as difficult as it is (and because it is) terrifying.[45]

This is an oft-quoted passage, but it sheds light on the relationship between the *Tractatus* and the *Investigations*: if we accept the resolute reading of the former, we can see how both books work from different directions toward a single (or similar) goal. Roughly, we might say that the former works to explode the picture-concept via a single trajectory or movement, while the latter chips away at it again and again from a series of different angles (there is, as Conant argues, 'significant discontinuity in the form of the investigation through which this aim is prosecuted . . .'[46]). In each case, however, there is an attempt at showing that the attempt to get outside of the world and view it is driven by a kind of sickness or mania, a kind of mad desire to know/escape that ends up only exacerbating the original problem. As Cavell puts it in *The Claim of Reason* (in a passage that is not 'oft-quoted'):

> [T]he reason that no basis is satisfactory is not that there isn't one where there ought to be, but that there is no claim which can provide the relevance of a basis. The reason we cannot know what the thing is in itself is not that there is something we do not in fact know, but that we have deprived ourselves of the conditions for saying anything in particular. There is nothing we cannot say. That doesn't mean we can say *everything*; there is no 'everything' to be said. There is nothing we cannot know. That doesn't mean that we can know everything; there is no everything, no totality of facts or things, to be known.[47]

As is his wont, Cavell is more concerned in *The Claim of Reason* with the later Wittgenstein, but as his telling use of 'totality of facts' indicates, the point is also directly relevant to the *Tractatus*. As we have seen, the picture-concept is characterised by the fantasy of a point of view, a fantasy of taking the world as an object. As the above quotations indicate, another way of describing this fantasy is in terms of a fantasy of conceiving of the world as a totality. Getting out of the picture-concept, then, actually requires that we *throw everything away*, where 'everything' is understood in the philosophical sense as the set of all possible facts (remember that the set theoretical solutions to Russell's paradox – via either the axiom of foundation/regularity or the axiom of separation – result in the methodological proviso that there can be no set of all sets). Like Eliot's Prufrock, in whom we can recognise some of his characteristics, the beguiled philosopher thinks he can squeeze the universe (or language) into a sphere and experience it as an object (he wants to master it, to roll it like a ball or Cavell's tomato), but thinking this is tantamount to taking himself to be a kind of Lazarus. This would be a way of schematising the difference between philosophy and poetry: philosophers think they can talk about 'the universe', 'totality' or 'the world as a whole' (when they wonder if 'this chair really exists outside of me' they aren't really talking about a specific chair, for any object would have done); the poet, on the other hand, makes something radically *particular* present to us (try to imagine Pablo Neruda writing an 'Ode to Everything'). The unhappy Prufrock allows himself to think he has conquered death and 'Come back to tell you all', but what he finds is 'not what I meant at all; / That is not it, at all'.[48] No one can tell everything, not at all. Yet this is precisely not a restriction or limit on what we can tell.

This can help elucidate what Wittgenstein wants to achieve in the *Investigations*, and why he wants to achieve it. A justly famous example is when he tries to shake us out of the commitment to the idea that we need to know, whether implicitly or explicitly, the necessary and sufficient conditions for something's being a game in order to talk meaningfully about games, or indeed to be able to say in good faith that we understand what a game is. Of course it is possible to draw boundaries around the concept 'game', saying for instance that to play a game is to involve oneself in a competitive activity with an opponent in which there will be (if the game is finished) a winner and a loser. In certain cases this and other definitions may be very useful. But counterexamples pop up: what about Solitaire? Let's then say that to play a game is to enter into a temporary situation structured by a set of rules, where deciding not to follow a particular rule is to decide to stop playing the game. But then what about relatively unstructured games like Ring a Ring o' Roses (Wittgenstein: 'here is the element of amusement, but how many other characteristic features have disappeared!'[49])? So perhaps a game is just an amusing pastime. Then what about Russian Roulette? As Wittgenstein says, 'the result of this examination is: we see a complicated network of similarities overlapping and criss-crossing: sometimes overall similarities, sometimes similarities of detail.'[50] Of course, the interlocutor is characteristically unimpressed with the implication: that we actually 'do not know the boundaries'[51] in this case: 'But if the concept "game" is uncircumscribed like that, you don't really know what you mean by a "game."'[52] Wittgenstein's point, however, is that even though there is no set of all the facts of the matter about what constitutes gamehood, no delimitable totality of necessary conditions for something's coming under the definition of 'game', this doesn't mean we don't understand what games are. After all, we know them when we see them, and we can play them (and if we don't, or can't, we can be taught to). Wittgenstein refers to Frege here (it is one of only a few explicit mentions of him in the *Investigations*): 'Frege compares a concept to an area and says that an area with vague boundaries cannot be called an area at all.'[53] To an adherent of Frege's principle of unrestricted comprehension, then, Wittgenstein's saying that the concept 'game' has 'blurred edges'[54] might seem like an admission of defeat, but as Wittgenstein asks rhetorically, 'is it senseless to say, "stand roughly there"?'[55] To undermine the attachment to totality in this way is not to undermine the possibility of a commitment to the fact that we are able to communicate (though it might make it surprising).

'What motivates Wittgenstein to philosophize, what surprises him', writes Cavell, 'is the plain fact that certain creatures have speech at all, that they can say things at all.' He goes on:

> No doubt it is not clear how one might go about becoming surprised by such a fact. It is like being surprised that there is such a thing as the world. But I do not say that Wittgenstein's thoughts demand that you grasp these surprises before you begin studying those thoughts. On the contrary, I believe that such experiences are part of the teaching which those thoughts are meant to produce.[56]

One of the lessons I take from Wittgenstein's work is that there are different kinds of wonder. Or rather, there are different ways of responding to it, some of which have a tendency to turn it into a kind of paralysed beguilement, and one of which allows for a certain happiness. The philosopher, who begins to reflect after (say) being struck by the fact that we are able to communicate, goes on from there to suppose that communication must take place on the foundation of certain rules or conditions. The philosopher's task then appears to be the clarification of those rules and conditions, to provide an *explanation* of what it is that makes communication possible. The problem lies in the way the first supposition – the idea that there *must* be basic rules and conditions – leads to a kind of paralysis once the philosopher finds that he cannot actually identify them (if communication requires rules and conditions, but there do not appear to be rules and conditions, then we can't really be communicating). And so, in the face of the apparent fact that we do communicate, the philosopher returns to his work.

The happy, on the other hand, do not let their surprise come between them and what surprises. The happy get amongst it. They do not let it (seem to) take them out of the world and language, to (seem to) offer up the world and language as an object for their view. In this sense, it is possible to characterise the happy as those for whom the fact/value distinction has dissolved: no longer is there a world of fact and a (perhaps subjectively 'projected') realm of value, such that the philosophical task is to show if and how the latter connects with (or supervenes upon, or whatever) the former. Rather, the happy are able to comport themselves in such a way that one very particular fact is lived as valuable. That is an *ongoing* task: because it is about attending to something rather than learning or coming to know it, responding rightly means finding – again and again, though each time differently – the right way of living. As Agamben writes in the line from *Infancy and History* I quoted earlier in this book, the proper response to the question of being as raised in the *experimentum linguae* is not to be found in philosophy as such (or as we know it) but in 'human life, as *ethos*, as ethical way'.[57] This is how we should understand him when he writes of 'form-of-life' as a life for which 'what is at stake in its way of living is living itself'.[58] The concept form-of-life, which Agamben uses interchangeably with 'happy life',[59] designates a life that encounters the fact of being not as a void to be evaded, nor as a brute fact to be confronted, but rather as an ethical problem and potential that unfolds in and as its very way of life. As the young Wittgenstein put it – in a notebook entry written during brutal fighting against the Brusilov Offensive, when his thinking appears to have undergone a fundamental change[60] – 'It seems one can't say anything more than: Live happy!'[61]

NOTES

1. Cavell, *The Claim of Reason*, 236.
2. Rosenzweig, *The Star of Redemption*, 3.
3. I translate *Glücklichen* as 'the happy' to avoid the gender bias evident in the 'happy man' of Pears and McGuiness.
4. Wittgenstein, *Tractatus Logico-Philosophicus*, notes 1 and 1.1; citations henceforth given in the text.
5. Black, *A Companion to Wittgenstein's* Tractatus, 2.
6. Ayer, *Language, Truth and Logic*, 106–7.
7. Ibid. 107.
8. See James Conant, 'Two Conceptions of Die Überwindung der Metaphysik', 54.
9. Wittgenstein, quoted in Monk, *Ludwig Wittgenstein*, 178.
10. Monk, *Ludwig Wittgenstein*, xviii.
11. Conant, 'What "Ethics" in the *Tractatus* is Not', 43.
12. Agamben writes that the appendix to the book – which deals with the concept of the irreparable – can be understood as an extended commentary on note 6.44. The appendix also contains an allusion to Wittgenstein's remarks on happiness (which I treat in detail below):

> The world of the happy and that of the unhappy, the world of the good and that of the evil contain the same states of things; with respect to

their being-thus they are perfectly identical. The just person does not reside in another world. The one who is saved and the one who is lost have the same arms and legs. The glorious body cannot but be the mortal body itself. What changes are not the things but their limits. It is as if there hovered over them something like a halo, a glory. (*The Coming Community*, 92)

13. Diamond, 'Throwing Away the Ladder', 181.
14. Diamond, 'Ethics, Imagination and the Method of Wittgenstein's *Tractatus*', 153.
15. Wittgenstein, quoted in Monk, *Ludwig Wittgenstein*, 278.
16. Wittgenstein, 'Ethics, Life and Faith', 254.
17. Ibid. 254.
18. Ibid. 255.
19. Ibid. 254.
20. Ibid. 255.
21. Conant, 'Elucidation and Nonsense in Frege and Early Wittgenstein', 177.
22. Kierkegaard, quoted in Conant, 'Elucidation and Nonsense in Frege and Early Wittgenstein', 195.
23. Conant, 'Elucidation and Nonsense in Frege and Early Wittgenstein', 196–7.
24. Ibid. 176.
25. Ibid. 176–7.
26. McDowell, *Mind and World*, xi.
27. Wittgenstein, 'Ethics, Life and Faith', 255.
28. Mulhall, 'Words, Waxing and Waning', 239.
29. Ibid. 239.
30. Rée, 'Subjectivity in the Twentieth Century', 210.
31. Diamond, 'Ethics, Imagination and the Method of Wittgenstein's *Tractatus*', 150.
32. Ibid. 162.
33. Morris and Dodd, 'Mysticism and Nonsense in the *Tractatus*', 271.
34. Diamond, 'Ethics, Imagination and the Method of Wittgenstein's *Tractatus*', 165.
35. Wittgenstein, quoted in Malcolm, *Ludwig Wittgenstein*, 81.
36. Diamond, 'Ethics, Imagination and the Method of Wittgenstein's *Tractatus*', 159 (my emphasis).
37. Ibid. 160–1 (my emphasis).
38. Cavell, 'The Avoidance of Love', 324.
39. Putnam, Introduction to Rosenzweig, *Understanding the Sick and the Healthy*, 2.
40. Ibid. 2.
41. Ibid. 4–6.
42. Rosenzweig, *Understanding the Sick and the Healthy*, 40.
43. Ibid. 40.

44. Santner, *On the Psychotheology of Everyday Life*, 14. In a sense this chapter could be understood as following up on a footnote to this page in Santner's text. He writes:

> It would, of course, be worthwhile to expand the present study to include Wittgenstein who, at some level, also understood his project as that of working through the metaphysical fantasies that distort our sense of what it means to be in the midst of life.

Though it is beyond the scope of this study, a psychoanalytic account of the problems of representation and fantasy as I have been presenting them would be extremely valuable. While psychoanalysis turns up only sporadically in Agamben's 'mature' works, his early book *Stanzas* is profoundly influenced by Freud. Colby Dickinson's book *Agamben and Theology* contains some fascinating reflections on Agamben and psychoanalysis (see in particular 107–41), as does Justin Clemens's paper 'The Abandonment of Sex', which makes the striking unorthodox claim that Agamben's mature work is 'formed as a result of a crucial encounter with psychoanalysis'. Perhaps the best place to start in such an endeavour, however, would be with Kenneth Reinhard's 'Toward a Political Theology of the Neighbor', which develops a brilliant Lacanian critique of political theology.

45. Cavell, 'The Availability of Wittgenstein's Later Philosophy', 52.
46. Conant, 'Putting Two and Two Together', 249.
47. Cavell, *The Claim of Reason*, 239.
48. Eliot, 'The Love Song of J. Alfred Prufrock', 14.
49. Wittgenstein, *Philosophical Investigations*, §66; 27e.
50. Ibid. §66; 27e.
51. Ibid. §68; 28e.
52. Ibid. §71; 29e.
53. Ibid. §71; 29e.
54. Ibid. §71; 29e.
55. Ibid. §71; 29e.
56. Cavell, *The Claim of Reason*, 15.
57. Agamben, *Infancy and History*, 10.
58. Agamben, 'Form-of-Life', 4.
59. See Mills, 'Agamben's Messianic Politics', 48–50.
60. See Monk, *Ludwig Wittgenstein*, 140–3.
61. Wittgenstein, *Notebooks*, 78 (translation slightly modified).

8. *The Picture and its Captives*

> *And we could not get outside it, because it lay in our language and language seemed to repeat it to us inexorably.*[1]

It is characteristic of Wittgenstein's work that the picture-concept and the philosophical problems associated with it appear as if they have sprung up from nowhere. What I mean is that Wittgenstein's analyses can give the impression of dealing with issues that are secure in their status as internal to philosophy, as having no obvious relation to the wider historical milieu in which we work on them. Connected to this is the sense that Wittgenstein's therapeutic approach to philosophy is relevant only *to philosophers*, only to the kinds of people who, whether because of temperament, intellectual propensity, economic capacity or whatever, have a tendency to embark on philosophical inquiries (such that the philosophical questions he tries to deflate have no real bearing on everyday or 'non-philosophical' life). For instance when Wittgenstein writes in the *Investigations* that he will have succeeded as a thinker if and when he finds himself 'capable of stopping doing philosophy when I want to',[2] one might be forgiven for thinking that his therapeutic methods are aimed at a relatively small subset of the human population: those, like himself, who can't stop doing philosophy. It is worth clarifying the relation between these two issues – the apparent absence of any historical element to Wittgenstein's work, and the fact that Wittgenstein's therapeutic method seems relevant only to those involved in philosophical practice – which stem from attributing to him a reified conception of philosophy as an autonomous sphere of inquiry. Debunking them would mean showing that we are not compelled to read him in this way, opposing an insufficiently thick conception of what it would mean to find oneself caught in philosophical unhappiness in Wittgenstein's sense. This, in turn, would mean showing the extent to which the problems associated with the picture-concept arise in (what we call) ordinary life, emphasising the fact that overturning it would require not only philosophical therapy, but perhaps also a change in the conditions that have produced us as forms of life that find themselves beguiled by it.

In this chapter I want to accomplish this by setting Wittgenstein's analyses against the arguments Heidegger makes about modernity in 'The Age of the World Picture'. For if Heidegger and Wittgenstein could be said to be dealing with a similar problem – the nihilism or scientism characteristic of the picture-concept – and indeed to be working toward a similar goal – to loosen our attachment to certain concepts of representation – it remains the case that both thinkers approach this in very different ways. After all, part of what Heidegger wants to achieve requires his showing that the picture-concept – or what he calls the world picture (*Weltbild*) – is historically contingent: that the intuitive and even apparently natural metaphorical register of picturing the world has actually had a long and complex genesis which, he argues, is intimately bound up with the 'essence of modern science'[3] as the metaphysical scheme of modernity. Working through Heidegger's world picture can help clarify these problems about the relationship between philosophy and the ordinary – problems that will, as I show in the next and final chapter, become crucial in understanding Agamben's positive political ontology.

In the opening paragraphs of 'The Age of the World Picture' Heidegger lists five phenomena as representative of modernity: science, machine technology, art considered as an expression of human life, the idea of culture and the departure of the gods.[4] All these phenomena are presented as 'equally essential',[5] but Heidegger's primary concern in this essay is science. His discussion of it begins with a comparative move, as he gets us to consider the difference between the modern use of the word and the medieval (*doctrina* and *scientia*) and ancient Greek (*episteme*) versions of it. Greek science, Heidegger says, 'was never exact',[6] but this is not because of a deficit in the Greek way of revealing; rather, Greek science 'could not be exact and did not need to be exact'.[7] To say that the exactitude of modern science makes it more rigorous than the science of antiquity depends for Heidegger on a category mistake: it would mean importing a modern concept of exactitude into a context in which it would have made no sense. Similarly, it would be wrong to say that 'the Galilean doctrine of freely falling bodies is true and that Aristotle's teaching, that light bodies strive upward, is false . . .'.[8] Much depends on how we take these claims (and especially the latter with its seemingly cavalier use of 'true' and 'false'), which appear to invite strongly anti-realist readings. Yet it is possible to read Heidegger here not as espousing the kind of relativism or irrationalism which holds that all claims are equally valid, but as making a more subtle point about historicity (it is one that is implied by the temporality of discourse as presented in *Being and Time*, and which I analysed in Chapter 2). To say that the Aristotelian view of bodies is 'false' is to misunderstand the extent to which our statements are embedded in historical context: it is to import a particular historical way of revealing being into another historical system, ending up with claims that would have to deny their own embedding for us to regard them as binding. Of course, claims within a particular historical system – such as our own, modern, Galilean, mathematical one – can certainly be set against one another: some will be correct within that system, others will not. The problem begins when we try to think and talk as though we are not always already presupposing a certain way of revealing things (this leaves room for a Heidegger that is broadly pragmatist regarding science: he can allow that modern science 'works' in a historically unprecedented way while cautioning us against the idea that this is because it is somehow more 'truthful' than pre-modern systems). In this sense, it is possible to regard Heidegger as anticipating Thomas Kuhn's *The Structure of Scientific Revolutions*, one of the upshots of which is the claim that competing scientific paradigms are in certain essential senses incomparable and indeed incommensurable with one another (remember that for Kuhn, 'the incommensurability of competing paradigms' entails that 'the proponents of competing paradigms practice their trades in different worlds'[9]).

Having (all too) briefly touched on these issues, Heidegger turns to the concept of 'research', which he says is '[t]he essence of what we today call science'.[10] The fundamental feature of research, Heidegger says, consists '[i]n the fact that knowing establishes itself as a procedure within some realm of what is, in nature or in history'.[11] What does Heidegger mean when he speaks of 'some realm of what is'? '[E]very procedure', Heidegger writes, 'already requires an open sphere in which it moves. And it is precisely the opening up of such a sphere that is the fundamental event in research.'[12] By 'open sphere' Heidegger means a particular discursive and methodological field, characterised by a certain set of basic presuppositions regarding its objects and methods of inquiry; later, he uses the term 'object sphere' in the same way. Trish Glazebrook, who uses the (less loaded) term 'research area' here, puts it like this: 'A research area is defined – that is, both opened up and delimited – by such projection of the "what" of an area of study.'[13] An 'object sphere' or 'research area' is a field, and a field is defined by what it studies: biology (life), physics (matter) and anthropology (the human) are all obvious examples. 'The projection', Heidegger says, 'sketches out in advance the manner in which the knowing procedure must bind itself and adhere to the sphere opened up.'[14] Different scientific fields require different methods, and what characterises modern science is not 'the scientific method' as such, but rather the very plurality of methods operative in separate fields, each of which has its own particular style and standards of rigour, its own characteristic procedures (this is not the same thing as specialisation, which is another important feature of modern science, but which happens *within* a particular object sphere). All are governed by a broad ideal of rigour, but different object spheres require different kinds of rigour. In Heidegger's example, the rigour required of a physicist is not of the same kind as that which is required of the historian: '[T]he humanistic sciences ... must necessarily be inexact just in order to remain rigorous.'[15] Thus Glazebrook appears to confuse things when she writes that '[o]n the basis of its rigor, science can be contrasted with historiography'.[16] For Heidegger, it is not that the physical sciences are necessarily more rigorous than the human sciences, but rather that the rigour proper to the latter precludes their adopting the standards of quantificational exactitude characteristic of the natural sciences (this fits with the German term *Wissenschaft*, which includes in its scope both the natural and the human sciences).

Of course, Heidegger is less concerned with providing a philosophy of science in this essay than with bringing out the historical significance of modern science as representative of the modern epoch itself. What unites the sciences in their disparity, for Heidegger, and what forms their condition of possibility is the 'objectifying of whatever is',[17] which we can characterise in terms of a *setting up of the world as representable*. 'We first arrive at science as research', Heidegger says, 'when and only when truth has been transformed into the certainty of representation.'[18] Heidegger provides what is perhaps his clearest definition of what he means by representation (*vorstellen*) in one of the appendices to the essay: 'To represent means ... to set something before oneself and to make secure what has been set in place, as something set in place.'[19] Heidegger is playing on the literal meaning of the German *vorstellen* here: *stellen* is a verb meaning 'to place' or 'to set'; *vor* means 'before' or 'in front of'. For Heidegger, these connotations of activity are basic to the verb *vorstellen*: to represent, for him, is not just to present a fact about the world, but also connotes a certain idea or image of subjective will; representing is not just a reporting, it is a *putting into place* of something, and in particular it is a setting of something *before oneself*. For Heidegger, to represent is to place something at one's disposal: representation 'aims at bringing each particular being before it in such a way that man who calculates can be sure, and that means be certain, of that being'.[20] Representing is 'a laying hold and grasping of . . .'.[21] Or again: 'Representing is making-stand-over-against, an objectifying that goes forward and masters.'[22] For Heidegger, the opening of object spheres characteristic of modern science clearly indicates this dual nature of representation: modern science, unlike its Aristotelian counterpart, is not based on a receptive description of the world (as Glazebrook says, it is 'not phenomenological'[23]), but rather an active *projection* of a certain way of revealing things onto nature. This is what Heidegger means when he writes that in modern science, nature is 'calculated in advance':[24] the fundamental event of scientific research – the opening of an object sphere – is a set up.

For Heidegger, the setting up of things that takes place in the projection of representation is not a neutral reporting back on the world, but is rather bound up with a certain unacknowledged desire for control (Heidegger: 'What presences does not hold sway, but rather assault rules'[25]). This is why the Lovitt translation of Heidegger's essay is perhaps infelicitous in its rendering of *griechischen Vernehmen* as 'Greek apprehending'.[26] The English 'apprehending' has connotations of 'taking hold' and 'grasping', coming as it does from the Latin *prehendere* meaning 'to seize' and even 'to detain' (this is why the tongue of a giraffe is called 'prehensile': it literally grasps the leaves), all of which are foreign, indeed diametrically opposed, to Heidegger's understanding of the Greek way of revealing. The German *vernehmen*, in contrast, has connotations of 'listening' and 'receiving', which chime with Heidegger's setting of Greek culture against our own technological epoch. Similarly, to translate 'Der griechische Mensch *ist* als der Vernehmer des Seienden ...'[27] as 'Greek man *is* as the one who apprehends that which is . . .'[28] risks missing Heidegger's point. It is the *receptivity* of the Greek way of revealing that distinguishes it from our own more active 'apprehending'. As Frederick Dolan puts it, the representative mode of taking things (taking things: seizing them, grasping them) 'is dedicated to getting a grip on the world by simplifying it, in the form of a clear and distinct representation that can be composed and handled according to codifiable and transmissible rules. Such a world, in other words, is under the sway of a *subject*.'[29]

As this citation from Dolan indicates, Heidegger links representation and its desire for control with the Cartesian metaphysics of subjectivity of which he was always so critical. The *objectification* of the world that takes place in the modern period, in which the world is set up as a totality of facts, corresponds to a *subjectification* of human being:

there is for Heidegger a 'reciprocal conditioning'[30] at work here. When the world is set up as representable, the nature of the human is transformed, and 'the very essence of man itself changes, in that man becomes subject'.[31] The argument here anticipates the claims Heidegger will make in 'The Question Concerning Technology', where he tries to unearth the mode of revealing that is characteristic of the modern epoch (which is 'nothing technological', but is rather the metaphysical essence of technology). The technological mode of revealing, just like the mode of revealing characteristic of modern science, effects an objectification of the world (in this essay, Heidegger will say that it enframes it (*Gestell*) as 'standing-reserve'[32] (*Bestand*)) that is also always already a subjectification of the human: when the earth is set up as raw material for exploitation, the human is set up as the exploiter (and then, of course, the exploiting human himself becomes an exploitable 'human resource'). 'To be subject', as Heidegger puts it, 'now becomes the distinction of man as the thinking-representing being.'[33] As is already clear, these claims have historical stakes:

> In the planetary imperialism of technologically organized man, the subjectivism of man attains its acme, from which point it will descend to the level of organized uniformity and there firmly establish itself. This uniformity becomes the surest instrument of total, i.e., technological, rule over the earth. The modern freedom of subjectivity vanishes totally in the objectivity commensurate with it.[34]

What distinguishes this essay from the essay on technology, and which in many ways makes it more philosophically interesting, is how these claims find their centre of gravity in the concept of the world picture (*Weltbild*). Heidegger, who introduces it directly after making the link between the objectification of the world and the subjectification of human being, understands it in a way that is both more literal and more deep than our usual concepts of 'worldview' might indicate. The difference is that our 'world picture' is not one particular way of looking at things, one particular image of the world that could be contrasted with the ancient and medieval world pictures; rather, what is decisive for the modern age is that the world is taken as *something to be pictured* in the first place (I hope the problem comes to light in the turn of phrase 'one particular way of *looking at things*'). As Heidegger writes: '[W]orld picture ... does not mean a picture of the world, but the world conceived and grasped as picture.'[35] As such he is emphatically *not* defending what we might call a 'relativism of worldviews' here, such that different historical epochs are characterised by different images of the world, or indeed that different peoples or even individuals have different views of the world. Rather, these ideas are themselves the result of our particular way of revealing being: they seem intuitive or natural because of the depth at which the world picture operates in us. This is why Heidegger cautions against the use of phrases such as 'modern world picture' or 'world picture of the modern age' (a more natural English equivalent might be 'modern worldview'): they assume the idea that different epochs produce different pictures, and so do not get at the essential point that the modern age is the one in which the world *becomes a picture* (Heidegger says that such phrases 'assume something that never could have been before, namely, a medieval and an ancient world picture'[36]).

Just like Wittgenstein's picture theory of language, then, the concept of the world picture exhibits a beguiling self-referentiality. We imagine ourselves as operating within a particular picture of things, and so envision epochal change in terms of the possibility of a new picture of the world. But such imagining remains beholden to the *Weltbild* because it has always already presupposed it. What is needed is not a new picture, but rather a release from our captivation by pictures. The same problem arises in relation to Wittgenstein: what would it mean, for example, to speak of the picture theory of language as a particular 'picture' of language? Similarly, to say that we represent the world as representable – speaking for instance of a 'representational picture'[37] – is to fall back into the linguistic trap. In such moments we end up in a kind of tautological meta-confusion (just the kind of thing that Wittgenstein's own picture theory of language was ostensibly designed to solve), falsely imagining that a change in 'worldview' would mean anything more than an ontic modification. Consider for instance Wittgenstein's claim in the *Tractatus* that '[t]he picture . . . cannot represent its form of representation . . .' (2.172). As Proust and Buroker point out,[38] this claim is itself entailed by the way the text appears to take the logical structuring of the world as a transcendental condition of the possibility of representation. 'Logic is not a body of doctrine, but a mirror-image of the world,' says Wittgenstein. 'Logic is transcendental' (6.13). The sheer *representability* of the world, given through logic, is transcendental; as such representability is not itself a representable fact. Another way of saying this is the following: the picture can picture the world, but it cannot picture the fact of its picturing; the picture cannot picture itself. It is 'like a pair of glasses on our nose through which we see whatever we look at'.[39] This formulation is particularly useful insofar as it immediately invites the very response I have in mind. If the picture is like a pair of glasses, then couldn't we take them off and view things differently? Are there other 'pairs of glasses' we could use instead? The problem, however, is that these metaphors are characteristic of what captured us in the first place. As Wittgenstein puts it: 'The problems arising through a misinterpretation of our forms of language have the character of *depth*. They are deep disquietudes; their roots are as deep in us as the forms of our language and their significance is as great as the importance of our language.'[40] It is not that the therapeutic task is to change our view of things. Rather, it is to work our way out of our philosophical captivation by the metaphorical register of views, pictures and frames. We have to learn to 'see the frame' as it presents itself in that very turn of phrase.

There is another point of convergence between the Heideggerian and the Wittgensteinian analyses of the problem of the picture. It is that Wittgenstein's analysis also turns upon a problem of will. 'The world', Wittgenstein asserts in the *Tractatus*, 'is independent of my will' (6.373). This comes directly after a series of apparently Humean attacks on the idea of causal necessity: 'There is no compulsion making one thing happen because another has happened' (6.37); 'This procedure [of induction] . . . has no logical justification but only a psychological one' (6.3631); 'The whole modern conception of the world is founded on the illusion that the so-called laws of nature are the explanations of natural phenomena' (6.371). Wittgenstein appears to argue that this Humeanism is implied by the fact ontology that underlies the *Tractatus*, and which can account for composites of atomic facts (logical complexes) existing at particular points in space and time, but not for causal relations between them. The argument would seem to go something like this: 'I am planning on going to the movies tonight' pictures a fact about my intention to go to the movies, but not about my actually going or having gone; 'I went to the movies tonight' pictures a fact about my having gone, but not about my having intended to – for the picture-concept, there is no way of establishing a necessary connection between these facts. On the fact ontology that underlies the picture-concept, in other words, it seems that there is no *necessary* causal relation between any two sets of states of affairs: there are only the occurrences of states of affairs, which arise in succession but which cannot be shown to be causally linked to one another. As Wittgenstein puts it: 'Even if all that we wish for were to happen, still this would only be a favour granted by fate, so to speak: for there is no *logical* connexion between the will and the world . . .' (6.374).

Whether we accept that Wittgenstein's fact ontology really precludes the possibility of logically accounting for agency or indeed causality as such is relatively unimportant, because the more relevant claims for our purposes relate to the deeper, transcendental problematic of the text. Take for instance Wittgenstein's claim that '[i]f the good or bad exercise of the will does alter the world, it can alter only the limits of the world, not the facts – not what can be expressed by means of language' (6.43). It is clear enough that on the Tractarian model the good or evil will cannot affect what happens *in* the world (just as *in* it there is no value), because there is no logical necessity linking events together. What can we imagine Wittgenstein means, though, when he implies that it *can* alter the limits of the world? Here we should put the remark in its context: it is the opening sentence of proposition 6.43, which ends with the assertion I examined in the last chapter ('[t]he world of the happy is quite another than that of the unhappy'). The will has no logically necessary connection to particular events, but it does have a connection to the distinction between the happy and the unhappy. The difference between the good and the evil will is not that the good will wills good events while the evil will wills evil events; rather (as with the distinction between happiness and unhappiness) the good will is the will that has been able to reorient itself in relation to one very particular event: the 'event' of the world itself. For what characterises this event – this fact that is unlike other facts – is not only that it is unknowable, but also that the self can only relate to it in terms of an *absolute* passivity. After all, how could I even entertain the idea of having power over the fact of the world's existence? I might be able to convince myself that I have power over facts *in* the world, but I cannot even dream of having power over existence *as such*. Of course, I can entertain the idea of ending *my own* existence, but this just underlines the special nature of the fact in question, because '[i]f anything is not allowed, it is suicide that is not allowed'.[41] As Diamond argues, Wittgenstein sees suicide as an ultimate wrong because it involves a rejection of 'the powerlessness that belongs to life . . .'.[42] Thus it is not that the act of suicide is itself morally wrong (as Diamond aptly puts it, '[f]or Hume and Wittgenstein, there is nothing, no facts in the world and no facts beyond it, on which a prohibition on suicide can rest'[43]), but rather that it is itself expressive of an attitude in which one *rails against* the very fact of one's own being, impotently acting out against the fact of existing. It is a particularly clear example of the evil will.

It is worth following Michael Hodges in the distinction he makes between empirical happiness and transcendental happiness. For Wittgenstein it is entirely possible to operate under a certain illusion of agency, believing that one's willing certain events actually plays a role in their occurrence. Happiness will then come about if and only if the events that occur are the events one has willed (Hodges calls this 'the satisfaction of our desires in the world'[44]). What Hodges calls 'transcendental or ethical happiness', however, 'must be a feature of the ethical subject itself'.⁴⁵ In his notebooks, Wittgenstein characterises this in terms of living in a kind of 'agreement' with the world, writing that 'in order to live happily *I* must be in agreement with the world. And that is what "being happy" means.'⁴⁶ The ethical or happy will – they are the same – is the will that has been able to accept the world, the will that has been able to relate to the fact of the world without fear or horror. The world thus becomes 'an altogether different world' (6.43); my attitude to it changes. As Hodges writes, '[t]his transformation does not alter the facts; it alters the meaning, value, or significance of the facts.'⁴⁷ This is why characterising Wittgenstein as espousing some kind of neo-stoicism with regard to will is a little misleading: it is not that he is advocating a stoic resignation to the ways of the world (the way things are *in* it), but rather a ground-level acceptance of the very fact of the world itself in its ultimate inexplicability.

This can help shed some light on a familiar question: if we accept Heidegger's historical diagnosis of modernity, in which the world picture is symptomatic of a desperate and indeed violent unacknowledged need for control, then how can we imagine or account for the possibility of change? More specifically, if our ways of revealing being are determined in their ground by deep and usually hidden metaphysical conditions, appearing as a historical destiny into which human beings are thrown, then how could we ever neutralise the kind of violence that Heidegger finds at the heart of our epoch? This is made more pressing by the fact that Heidegger's diagnosis is, as we have seen, concerned not only with objectification but also with a simultaneous rise in a metaphysics of will and control, meaning that any idea of *deliberately* working toward a different mode of revealing would appear to lead us right back into that metaphysics. Here is Heidegger:

> Man cannot, of himself, abandon this destining of his modern essence or abolish it by fiat. But man can, as he thinks ahead, ponder this: Being subject as humanity has not always been the sole possibility belonging to the essence of historical man . . . nor will it always be.⁴⁸

There is no possibility of change through will, but this is not to say that change is impossible: as is demonstrated by the fact that the metaphysics of objectivity and subjectivity are only a few hundred years old, the metaphysical conditions of the modern epoch are by no means permanent. Heidegger goes on:

> A fleeting cloud shadow over a concealed land, such is the darkening which that truth as the certainty of subjectivity – once prepared by Christendom's certainty of salvation – lays over a disclosing event [*Ereignis*] that it remains denied to subjectivity itself to experience.⁴⁹

This shadow, here described in an appendix, also turns up in the concluding paragraphs to Heidegger's essay, where he presents it as a kind of residue of the mode of being characteristic of the age of the world picture, writing of an 'invisible shadow that is cast around all things everywhere when man has been transformed into *subiectum* and the world into picture'.[50] What is this shadow? In the main body of the text it arises in the context of the predominance of calculation, or the 'extended emptiness of the purely quantitative'[51] – features of the age of the world picture in which everything is set up as an object that would in principle be calculable by a subject. And this becoming calculable of things brings with it the shadow of a 'becoming incalculable'.[52] What is it that becomes incalculable? What is denied to subjectivity to experience? By now, the answer should be obvious enough: the fact of being itself, which is the one fact that cannot be represented, the one fact that cannot be pictured. The world, as I put in the last chapter, is not a P: we cannot represent its being; it cannot be apprehended in the way a leaf is grabbed by a giraffe's tongue; it is ungraspable. Heidegger: '[W]e experience the incalculable as that which, withdrawn from representation, is nevertheless manifest in whatever is . . .'[53] The world picture is constituted on the basis of a passing over of the fact of being, which is *included in it in the form of an exclusion*. Heidegger's shadow is thus just like Agamben's bare life or Levinas's *il y a*: it is the return of a repressed metaphysical problem. It must be included for the *Weltbild* to maintain its claim to totality, but it cannot be.

Here we can explain Heidegger's remarks about Dasein's 'powerlessness' in *The Metaphysical Foundations of Logic* (remarks which, again, should be read alongside Wittgenstein's own remarks about the impotence of the will): '[Dasein's] powerlessness is metaphysical, i.e., to be understood as essential; it cannot be removed by reference to the conquest of nature, to technology, which rages about in the "world" today like an unshackled beast; for this domination of nature is the real proof for the metaphysical powerlessness of Dasein . . .'[54] The technological domination of nature, which might appear to demonstrate human power and ingenuity, is a response to the fundamental passivity of the human before something it cannot take hold of. The Cartesian subject is for Heidegger wrought by a certain metaphysical *desperation*: it presents itself as mastering the world in order to hide its metaphysical impotence. This is the real crux of the problem of will as I have presented it in this chapter: the metaphysics of subjectivity that Heidegger decries, and the will of the unhappy as Wittgenstein describes it, are not the simple results of Promethean hubris; rather, they are the effect of an evasion. This is why Cavell, in an essay on the uncanny in Heidegger and Wittgenstein, writes of a 'growing violence in our demand to grasp or explain the world'.[55] The desire for ultimate explanations is a violent kind of railing against our passivity before the ungraspable fact of being, an attempt at denying our powerlessness that itself sparks a certain delusion of absolute power. This may help explain what Wittgenstein means when, in the preface to the *Investigations*, he wonders whether his book will have any impact on 'the darkness of this time'.[56] This darkness, we might say, is the shadow of the failed exclusion of a fact from the represented totality.

This citation from Wittgenstein indicates that even as he avoids explicitly embracing a version of Heidegger's hyperbolic and rather pathos-laden epochal discourse of the history of being, he nevertheless did understand his work in a certain historical spirit. As Diamond puts it: '[W]e do not read the *Tractatus* well unless we see how its temper is opposed to the spirit of the times, and how it understands that spirit expressed in connected ways in the idea of *natural laws always as explanatory of phenomena*, in philosophy, and in relation to what Wittgenstein thinks of as ethics.'[57] The *Tractatus*, with its attempt at undermining the picture-concept from within, is opposed to what Wittgenstein saw as the scientism characteristic of his age, and in particular the fact/value distinction that is so pivotal for it.[58] As he wrote in a draft of the preface to his *Philosophical Remarks*: '[T]he disappearance of a culture does not signify the disappearance of human value, but simply of certain means of expressing this value . . .'.[59] In claiming, for instance, that there is no value *in* the world, there is an important sense in which Wittgenstein is actually trying to *save* value: it is just that he knows that the best way to carry this out is by *following through* on the picture-concept, albeit with a rigour that in the end should lead it to destroy itself. As such, it is certainly worth reading Heidegger and Wittgenstein together on the problem of the picture, for it is not only the case that there are important parallels in their diagnosis of the problem, but also that we can learn very much from the resonances and divergences between their approaches to resolving it. Most obviously, what they share is the sense that working our way out of the metaphorical register of picturing is formidably difficult: for Heidegger this is because of the deep historical/metaphysical structures that lead us into it; for Wittgenstein this is the result of the arduousness of evading the urge to start doing philosophy in the traditional, explanatory sense. This sense of the difficulty of escaping the philosophical dilemmas internal to the picture-concept is evident in the extreme caution with which both Wittgenstein and Heidegger approach language: for each thinker, language has a way of ensnaring us without our realising it, of mutely dictating the very possibilities of thought through grammar, vocabulary and metaphor; the picture-concept subsists beneath our cognitions while simultaneously conditioning them. This is why both philosophers take style to be of key importance, as more than merely 'decorative'. Heidegger's infamous stylistic contortions are the result of hard and constant *work* on his part: a sort of linguistic twisting that is bent on escaping the traps set by the traditional metaphorical register of philosophy; Wittgenstein's own ordinary, conversational style in the *Investigations* is designed to make us more wary of *philosophical* language as traditionally conceived. The difference in their approach to these problems, one might say, is that Wittgenstein takes them somewhat more seriously, attempting as it were to undo them 'from the inside'; Heidegger, on the other hand, is more dismissive, and is content to show their status as historically contingent, and to work toward a mode of thought that is designed to open the possibility of another mode of revealing. Typical of the picture-concept is a sense of *necessity*: we think things simply *must* be this way (Frege's commitment to the principle of unrestricted comprehension was deep seated in just this way – or it was, of course, until he encountered Russell's paradox). What this means is that the contradictions and confusions that arise regarding the picture-concept will seem like problems to be solved; they will seem like problems that *must* have a solution, if only we could find it. For Heidegger and Wittgenstein, it is this sense of necessity that we need to be shaken out of.

This can help resolve the other problem relating to Wittgenstein's work that I flagged in the opening paragraph of this chapter: the sense that his attempt to undermine the picture-concept seems relevant only to philosophers, only to those who find themselves *philosophically* (indeed perhaps professionally) beguiled by it. For if we read Heidegger and Wittgenstein together on this, taking heed of the fact that they both understood their work as opposing the times in which they produced it, we can see that the beguilement characteristic of the picture-concept is perhaps more insidious and problematic than its apparent status as internal to philosophy might indicate. Here I want to acknowledge – indeed emphasise – the fact that Wittgenstein took the ordinary to be a key therapeutic reference point, such that the philosophical method employed in the *Investigations* often consists in showing how philosophical beguilement begins when we extract words from ordinary usage and employ them in ways that would never make sense in their everyday context (in Wittgenstein's words, philosophical language is language that 'goes on holiday'[60]). The obvious example here is the opening of the *Investigations*, where Wittgenstein evokes the Augustinian understanding of language in the context of how it is transmitted from adults to children as they grow up and learn to speak (the idea, as Wittgenstein summarises it, is the following: 'individual words in language name objects – sentences are combinations of such names ... Every word has a meaning. This meaning is correlated with the word. It is the object for which the word stands'[61]). Now there is a certain sense in which the Augustinian model is basically unproblematic: of course words name objects, and sentences are combinations of names; of course every word has a meaning correlated with it. This is all perfectly workable on the level of ordinary language and practice (where we might encourage a child to understand the word 'dog' by pointing at a dog, getting her to grasp that the word refers to that particular kind of thing: that this, in other words, is the meaning of 'dog'). Problems begin, however, when these words ('meaning', 'refers', 'thing') are given *philosophical* weight, such that meaning then appears as some kind of intentional object 'in' the mind, and which we use language to 'express' to other subjects. Problems begin, in other words, when we try to build a theory with them (for instance as when Locke argues that words are 'signs' that human beings use to express 'internal conceptions', that they are 'marks for the *ideas* within [one's] own mind ...'[62]). This is what Cavell means when he writes that Wittgenstein's invocation of the Augustinian model is one of 'countless moments in the book in which we are made uncertain whether an expression is remarkable or casual, where this turns out to be a function of whether we leave the expression ordinary or elevate it into philosophy ...':[63] this way of taking meaning works well enough in ordinary language, but when we try to take it further and build metaphysical theories on its basis we start to confuse ourselves. (Wittgenstein: 'The more narrowly we examine actual language, the sharper becomes the conflict between it and our [philosophical] requirement ... The conflict becomes intolerable; the requirement is now in danger of becoming empty. – We have got on to slippery ice where there is no friction and so in a certain sense the conditions are ideal, but also, just because of that, we are unable to walk. We want to walk: so we need *friction*. Back to the rough ground!'[64])

What reading Wittgenstein with Heidegger should force us to register, however, is just how unstable this dichotomy between the ordinary and the philosophical can be. To speak of one's 'getting the picture' or of someone's having a particular 'point of view' in ordinary language is perhaps unproblematic, but ordinary language can quickly become metaphysically inflated to the point of resembling philosophical language in such cases (as when, for instance, someone cancels an argument by declaring that his own claims are merely the result of his particular 'perspective', and that if others 'see things differently' then that is their prerogative). Heidegger, we might say, focuses on the historical and so fails to take the picture-concept quite as seriously as Wittgenstein (we see this attitude at work in the occasionally dismissive talk about the 'everyday' in the passages in *Being and Time* on inauthenticity); Wittgenstein bypasses the historical in any explicit sense and so misses the extent to which the problems associated with the picture-concept are contingent on a certain historically conditioned way of revealing (there might be a general lesson in this about the difference between the 'analytic' and 'continental' traditions in philosophy). If we read the two together, though, we get the sense that philosophical beguilement can come (has come) to penetrate everyday life.

In the section from *The Claim of Reason* that directly follows the statement about the philosopher's tomato that turned up in the last chapter, Cavell describes an experience he has 'found to be fundamental in classical epistemology':

> The experience is one I might now describe as one of looking at the world as though it were another *object*, on a par with particular envelopes, tomatoes, pieces of wax, bells, tables, etc. If this is craven, it is not a craving for generality (if that means for *generalization*) but for *totality*. It is an expression of what I meant when I said we want to know the world as we imagine God knows it. And that will be as easy to rid us of as it is to rid us of the prideful craving to be God – I mean to *rid* us of it, not to replace it with a despair at our finitude.[65]

As we have seen, the picture-concept does not only set up the world as representable: it also sets up the world as a representable *totality*. '[T]he modern system', Wittgenstein says in the *Tractatus*, 'tries to make it look as if *everything* [*alles*] were explained' (6.372). Or as Dreyfus writes of Heidegger's *Weltbild*: '[R]ationality consists in human beings imposing a *total*, systematic order on all that is. Heidegger calls this *totalizing* understanding of being, technological.'[66] And as Cavell puts it here, this setting up of the world as a totality is *craven* in a certain fundamental sense (this is, once again, a problem of will). The picture-concept, in setting up the world as a totality of representable facts, purports to grasp the whole; yet it is constituted on the basis of the passing over of a fact. And this passing over has consequences: it leads us onto shaky philosophical ground in which we are caught trying to explain (away) something inexplicable, or trying to get at something that we feel we cannot properly express (running against the walls of our cage). The fact of the world is not a part of the world; it is not something *in* it; it is subtracted from it. It is what makes every picture of the world

The Picture and its Captives   177

necessarily incomplete in its craving for totality. Here (the reader will recognise the logic at work here from earlier chapters) the condition of the impossibility of the success of the *Weltbild* is what drives and exacerbates the whole process. The question remains: what would it mean to rid ourselves of this craving?

NOTES

1. Wittgenstein, *Philosophical Investigations*, §115; 41e.
2. Ibid. §133; 44e.
3. Heidegger, 'The Age of the World Picture', 127.
4. Ibid. 116.
5. Ibid. 116.
6. Ibid. 117.
7. Ibid. 117.
8. Ibid. 117.
9. Kuhn, *The Structure of Scientific Revolutions*, 150.
10. Heidegger, 'The Age of the World Picture', 118.
11. Ibid. 118.
12. Ibid. 118.
13. Glazebrook, *Heidegger's Philosophy of Science*, 110.
14. Heidegger, 'The Age of the World Picture', 118.
15. Ibid. 120.
16. Glazebrook, *Heidegger's Philosophy of Science*, 110.
17. Heidegger, 'The Age of the World Picture', 127.
18. Ibid. 127.
19. Ibid. 149.
20. Ibid. 127.
21. Ibid. 149.
22. Ibid. 150.
23. Glazebrook, *Heidegger's Philosophy of Science*, 112.
24. Heidegger, 'The Age of the World Picture', 127.
25. Ibid. 149.
26. Ibid. 131.
27. Heidegger, 'Die Zeit des Weltbildes', 91.
28. Heidegger, 'The Age of the World Picture', 131.
29. Dolan, 'Representing the Political System', 94.
30. Heidegger, 'The Age of the World Picture', 128.
31. Ibid. 128.
32. Heidegger, 'The Question Concerning Technology', 17.
33. Heidegger, 'The Age of the World Picture', 151.
34. Ibid. 152–3.
35. Ibid. 129.
36. Ibid. 130.
37. Guignon, 'Philosophy after Heidegger and Wittgenstein', 668.

38. They write:

> We have seen that for Wittgenstein logical form functions as a condition of the possibility of representing the world. Logic is a transcendental condition in the sense that without it, the thought of any state of affairs whatever would be impossible. The logical form of the representation corresponds to the logical form of the state of affairs represented. But the correspondence is not itself representable ... ('Formal Logic as Transcendental in Wittgenstein and Carnap', 507)

39. Wittgenstein, *Philosophical Investigations*, §103; 39e.
40. Ibid. §111; 41e.
41. Wittgenstein, *Notebooks*, 91.
42. Diamond, 'Ethics, Imagination and the Method of Wittgenstein's *Tractatus*', 154.
43. Ibid. 154.
44. Hodges, *Transcendence and Wittgenstein's* Tractatus, 122.
45. Ibid. 122.
46. Wittgenstein, *Notebooks*, 75.
47. Hodges, *Transcendence and Wittgenstein's* Tractatus, 122.
48. Heidegger, 'The Age of the World Picture', 153.
49. Ibid. 153.
50. Ibid. 135.
51. Ibid. 135.
52. Ibid. 135.
53. Ibid. 154.
54. Heidegger, *The Metaphysical Foundations of Logic*, 215.
55. Cavell, 'The Uncanniness of the Ordinary', 159.
56. Wittgenstein, *Philosophical Investigations*, x.
57. Diamond, 'Ethics, Imagination and the Method of Wittgenstein's *Tractatus*', 171 (my emphasis).
58. For a book-length study of how Wittgenstein took his work to be opposed to the dominant culture, see DeAngelis's *Ludwig Wittgenstein*. As DeAngelis describes it, his book is an 'attempt to come to terms with Wittgenstein's assessment of his time, some of the unexpressed, underlying purposes of his philosophical writings, and the connections between them' (2).
59. Wittgenstein, *Culture and Value*, 6e.
60. Wittgenstein, *Philosophical Investigations*, §38; 16e.
61. Ibid. §1; 2e.
62. Locke, *An Essay Concerning Human Understanding*, III, I, 2; 176.
63. Cavell, 'The Uncanniness of the Ordinary', 166.
64. Wittgenstein, *Philosophical Investigations*, §107; 40e.
65. Cavell, *The Claim of Reason*, 237.
66. Dreyfus, 'Being and Power', 7 (my emphasis).

9. The Passing of the Figure of This World

Nothing could be more remarkable than seeing someone who thinks himself unobserved engaged in some quite simple everyday activity. Let's imagine a theatre, the curtain goes up and we see someone alone in his room walking up and down, lighting a cigarette, seating himself etc. so that suddenly we are observing a human being from outside in a way that ordinarily we can never observe ourselves; as if we were watching a chapter from a biography with our own eyes, – surely this would be at once uncanny and wonderful. More wonderful than anything that a playwright could cause to be acted or spoken on the stage. We should be seeing life itself. – But then we do see this every day and it makes not the slightest impression on us! True enough, but we do not see it from that point of view.[1]

In his brilliant study of what he calls 'the politics of logic', Paul Livingston investigates the relations between the linguistic and logical paradoxes that arose in the twentieth century and recent European political thought. In particular Livingston shows the paradigmatic status of the Russell set which, as the set of all sets that are not members of themselves, appears to both include and exclude itself. To quote from him:

> The paradoxical structure of sovereignty, upon which is founded its power to determine the distinction between the normal and the exceptional, law and fact, is ... formally identical to the Russell paradox. The sovereign, on Schmitt's analysis, is that which must be able to decide, in each possible case of fact or action, on the normalcy or exceptionality of the particular case. But in reserving to itself the power to declare a state of exception, and thus to suspend the entirety of this order, the sovereign demonstrates its exceptional position with respect to the ... ordinary distinction between normalcy and exceptionality itself. The very power to choose is neither normal nor exceptional; like the Russell set, it both includes and does not include itself.[2]

As the reader will have gleaned, Livingston works to make explicit the metalogical problematic implicit in Agamben's critical political ontology. In the terms of the last two chapters, he shows that the problems associated with the picture-concept – which take on a paradoxical status because of its self-referential structure, and its apparently simultaneous inclusion and exclusion of a certain fact from the totality it pictures – are themselves versions of the problems that have worried philosophy since 1901, when Russell wrote to Frege to share his discovery of the paradox of set-membership (as Arthur Sullivan says, it was something from which the German logician 'never recovered'[3]). Crucial for Livingston's project is Agamben's work on the paradox of sovereignty, especially as presented in the *Homo Sacer* series. Consider (Agamben's own quotations here are from Schmitt):

> The paradox of sovereignty consists in the fact that the sovereign is, at the same time, inside and outside the juridical order. If the sovereign is truly the one to whom the juridical order grants the power of proclaiming a state of exception and, therefore, of suspending the order's own validity, then 'the sovereign stands outside the juridical order and, nevertheless, belongs to it, since it is up to him to decide if the constitution is to be defended *in toto*.' The specification that the sovereign is '*at the same time* outside and inside the juridical order' is not insignificant: the sovereign, having the legal power to suspend the validity of the law, legally places himself outside the law. This means that the paradox can also be formulated this way: 'the law is outside itself,' or: 'I, the sovereign, who am outside the law, declare that there is nothing outside the law.'[4]

As Livingston shows, this is a version of Russell's paradox, here transposed onto the terrain of law: for the sovereign to take on the power to suspend the legal order in the state of exception, he must claim to stand in a position outside of it; and yet in order for the law to claim legitimacy, the sovereign must maintain that it applies to the totality of the legal order itself (the sovereign is thus paradoxically both included within and excluded from that totality). Or as Russell and Whitehead put it: 'In each contradiction something is said about *all* cases of some kind, and from what is said a new case seems to be generated, which both is and is not of the same kind as the cases of which all were concerned in what was said.'[5] It is clear how this arises in relation to the picture-concept which, as we have seen, can make its claim to totality only on the basis of the inclusive exclusion of a fact, which then returns (like a shadow) to haunt it, threatening to render it incomplete. Problems of self-reference are at work here too: remember how thinking our way out of the *Weltbild* so often seems to lead us right back into it; how the picture can picture everything save the fact of its picturing. As I discussed in Chapter 1, this is the return of the repressed metaphysical problem of the miracle: the picture-concept passes over the originary miraculousness of the world – the fact that its existence depends on no foundation, no *arche* – only to have the problem of the miracle return to haunt it in the form of an exceptional residue. The picture-concept, in other words, is constituted on the basis of a denial of the absolute exceptionality of the world itself, a denial which then sees the exception return at particular points in time to threaten it with rupture. The legal order, in order to maintain its claim to legitimacy, has to deny the self-referential paradoxicality inherent in that claim to legitimacy; the state of exception is the ontic moment in which the ontological paradoxes inherent in the picture-concept reveal themselves. This is the source of its potentially devastating power (as unleashed in the camp, which is the ontic site that opens up when the exception begins to become the rule): it is the space in which the sovereign works to stabilise the legal order by working to take hold of its basic instability, the extra-legal space in which the paradoxicality of the picture-concept arises to be captured. And what the sovereign tries to capture there is pure being (bare life): the very fact of existence, which within metaphysics can only emerge as a horrifying negativity. The legal order needs these spaces of capture because, in order to maintain the claim to legitimacy, it has to hide the radically anomic and indeed anarchic force of the exceptionality of existence as such.

Here it is worth turning to the extremely useful and perspicuous quadrilateral structure Livingston sets up in his book, in which thinkers are differentiated along two axes according to their 'attitudes towards the totality of language, the thinkable, or being'.[6] The four attitudes in play are: the ontotheological orientation, which includes Aquinas and Aristotle, and in which totality is simply posited as complete and consistent in itself (and yet as existing beyond the grasp of finite human cognition); the constructivist orientation, which includes Russell, Carnap and Rorty, and which involves an attempt at controlling the paradoxicality of totality via strategies of delimitation (the paradigmatic examples here would be Russell's theory of types, the logical positivist doctrine of meaning and the prohibitions on set construction operative in ZFC's axioms of foundation and separation); the generic orientation, which Livingston identifies with Badiou, and which is founded on the axiomatic decision against totality (Badiou: '[T]here is no universe'[7]); and the paradoxico-critical orientation, which is committed to emphasising the radical inconsistency of being and/or language, and which includes Derrida, Deleuze, Lacan, Wittgenstein and, most importantly for our purposes, Agamben. The generic and the paradoxico-critical orientations are united for Livingston in taking seriously the implications of the metalogical findings of the twentieth century, especially as manifest in the work of Kurt Gödel (though not usually explicitly, nor with formal rigour). Gödel's metalogical investigations, the reader will recall, produced the following results: no consistent formal system powerful enough to axiomatise arithmetic can ever be complete; and no complete formal system powerful enough to axiomatise arithmetic can ever be consistent.[8] For Livingston, the key innovation of the generic and the paradoxico-critical orientations over the constructivists and the ontotheologians is that they produce ontologies that deal with the problems Gödel and Russell unearthed. Badiou accepts the impossibility of totality, developing a mathematical ontology founded on the decision that 'the one *is not*';[9] Agamben accepts the impossibility of consistency (or, at least, its paradoxical status in relation to certain spheres, particularly the legal), and develops a critical political ontology designed to emphasise and indeed exploit the metaphysical paradoxes that inhere in the picture-concept of sovereignty. Agamben's approach, as Livingston puts it, 'leads to a rigorous and transformative articulation of the constitutive status of paradox and antinomy for the very structures of political life'.[10]

Yet Livingston's account leaves out an aspect of Agamben's project. The very term 'paradoxico-critical' makes it clear: what gets left out is how Agamben's philosophy is geared not only toward showing up the ontological paradoxes of modernity, but also toward opening the possibility of a different political logic. Take the following from Schmitt (who, perhaps more than anyone, mercilessly insists on the paradoxical metaphysical structure of modernity):

> The norm requires a homogenous medium. This effective normal situation is not a mere superficial presupposition that a jurist can ignore; that situation belongs precisely to its immanent validity. There exists no norm that is applicable to chaos. For a legal order to make sense, a normal situation must exist, and he is sovereign who definitely decides whether this normal situation actually exists.[11]

Yet being *as such* is without law; it is exceptional all the way down (and, one wants to say, it keeps going down: there is no foundation at the bottom). The state of exception is the space in which the sovereign tries to take hold of this fact, which *from the 'point of view' of metaphysics*, can only appear in the form of pure chaos. This, in other words, is where we have to depart from Schmitt: it is only because of the craven nature of the metaphysics of will driving the picture-concept that the fact of being appears as something chaotic, unspeakable or horrifying. Or to put this in terms of the problem of passivity: it is true that it reveals our powerlessness, but it is only within metaphysics that this powerlessness appears as a thought of the absolute *destitution* of the subject (think here again of Levinas's *il y a* as analysed in Chapter 4: this is the shadow of pure being appearing as an unspeakable *factum brutum* or, in Agamben's register, the pure subsistence of bare life). As Heidegger's point about the historical contingency of world picture should make clear, there is no absolute necessity behind this sense of horror.

There is a sense in which Livingston, with his emphasis on Agamben's attempts at bringing to light the paradoxical logic of sovereignty, ends up with an account of the Italian philosopher's thought that closely resembles Agamben's own (somewhat caricatured) version of Derrida. For Agamben, Derrida remains trapped in metaphysics precisely insofar as he understands his work in primarily 'critical' terms: he works to show the extent to which its claims to consistency are always already marred by paradox, but does not quite follow through on 'the aporias of self reference' that plague it;[12] he mistakes critique for overcoming. As Agamben puts it in *Language and Death*, in a backhanded compliment that is characteristic of his invocations of Derrida: 'Although we must certainly honor Derrida as the thinker who has identified with the greatest rigor ... the original status of the *gramma* and of meaning in our culture, it is also true that he believed he had opened a way to surpassing metaphysics, while in truth he merely brought the fundamental problem of metaphysics to light.'[13] As we saw in Chapter 4, for Agamben the critique of the metaphysics of presence remains insufficient because, in its insistence on the ungroundedness of being, it fails to take account of the haunting of metaphysics by absence and negativity. As such, the overcoming of metaphysics for Agamben requires not just the bringing to light of its aporias, but also the attempt to *resolve* them: to transform them, as he puts it, into *'euporias'*.[14] It is not enough, in other words, to insist on the abyssal ground of being and language: in its positive moment the critique of metaphysics should also work for the *solution* of this negative ground. Livingston, then, is right to emphasise how Agamben works to upset the pretence of consistency that sovereignty as we know it requires by emphasising the paradoxical nature of the very claim to legitimacy. Indeed his analysis of this is quite unprecedented in its clarity and rigour. But it is only half the story. Livingston, in claiming Agamben as a key representative of the paradoxico-critical orientation, argues that he responds to the Gödelian problematic by deciding to 'choose the All of totality and sacrifice the One of consistency'.[15] But arguably Agamben's understanding of totality is more ambiguous than this; arguably his positive political ontology challenges the concept of the 'All'.

This is what Agamben tries to formulate with his concept of the messianic. In *The Time That Remains*, which is Agamben's most systematic treatment of the thought he finds in Paul, Benjamin, Kafka and others, he defines it as 'the ungraspable quality of the "now"'.[16] This formulation should be set against the idea of the unrepresentability of the fact of being as presented in the last chapter (and throughout this book): this event is one in which we are placed in relation to something we cannot take hold of (something we cannot *apprehend*). It is an event of 'being seized',[17] the emergence of something absolutely inappropriable. And it calls for a certain response. This is why Agamben defines this event in terms of an *exigency*: it involves a demand that we maintain ourselves in relation to what is 'unforgettable'[18] insofar as it is impossible to properly remember. Refusing this demand by forgoing 'each and every relation to the mass of the forgotten that accompanies us like a silent *golem*'[19] – which in Wittgenstein's terms would represent the desire of the evil will – sees it 'reappear within us in a destructive and perverse way, in the form Freud called the return of the repressed . . .'.[20] Properly owning up to this demand, on the other hand, requires that the human being 'seize hold of his own being seized':[21] not to seize hold of the fact of being (which is impossible), but rather to seize hold of the fact he cannot seize hold of being (this is another version of the appropriation of inappropriability that I discussed in Chapter 4; in the terms of Chapter 6 it is the demand that we collectively appropriate the fact of our consignment to an *unassumable* animal life). What needs to be emphasised in relation to Livingston's understanding of the paradoxico-critical orientation is how Agamben sets this up in terms of a reconfiguration of the usual (metaphysical) understanding of the part in relation to the whole. Indeed Agamben puts this elsewhere in *The Time That Remains* – in a section on the political stakes of this event – in terms of the possibility of a people situating itself as a *remnant*. He describes this as follows:

> [T]he remnant is . . . a consistency or figure that Israel assumes in relation to election or to the messianic event. It is therefore neither the all, nor a part of the all, but the impossibility for the part and the all to coincide with themselves or with each other. *At a decisive moment, the elected people, every people, will necessarily situate itself as a remnant, as not-all.*[22]

This is the meaning of the messianic for Agamben: it is the event which, if properly responded to, would entail the *resolution* of the aporias of totality that characterise the age of the world picture. More accurately, it would entail their transformation into *euporias*.

Agamben's logic is, as we should expect from its basis in metaphysical paradox, anything but simple (if we were to formalise it – assuming this would be possible – we would probably end up with a paraconsistent dialetheist logic[23]). From here, however, it should be possible to explain what he means when he writes that for the messianic community 'that which was fulfilled becomes unfulfilled and the unfulfilled becomes fulfilled'.[24] This claim, which turns up in a paragraph comparing the messianic event with the 'panoramic vision that the dying supposedly have of their lives, when the whole of their existence passes before their eyes in a flash',[25] elegantly illustrates the ontological meaning of the messianic for Agamben. The unfulfilled, in this formulation, is what cries out for redemption: the suffering of the creaturely world, and the sum of the injustices of history (it is, in short, all that has been written out of the 'document of barbarism'[26] that is civilisation). However, the fulfilment of the unfulfilled – this recapitulation in which justice is done to the forgotten – would coincide with an unfulfilment of the fulfilled: a rendering *incomplete* of the claim to totality that characterises the non-messianic world. The remnant – this image of that which is passed over and forgotten – emerges out of the cracks in the whole to render it *not-all*. In this sense, Dickinson obscures the logic at work here when he writes that the call of the remnant is 'a radical universal vocation for all of humanity':[27] while it is indeed right to call it 'universal', this call also resists the image of the whole evoked by Dickinson's use of the word 'all'. Part of what is philosophically compelling about Agamben's thought of community is how he works to think universality without recourse to the category of totality.

This is why he emphasises the importance of happiness in Benjamin's understanding of the messianic. Benjamin refers to happiness in a number of places in his writings, but there are two occasions that are especially important. The first comes in his 'Theologico-Political Fragment':

> The order of the profane should be erected on the idea of happiness. The relation of this order to the messianic is one of the essential teachings of the philosophy of history. It is the precondition of a mystical conception of history, encompassing a problem that can be represented figuratively. If one arrow points to the goal toward which the profane dynamic acts, and another marks the direction of messianic intensity, then certainly the quest of free humanity for happiness runs counter to the Messianic direction; but just as a force, by virtue of the path it is moving along, can augment another force on the opposite path, so the profane order – because of its nature as profane – promotes the coming of the Messianic Kingdom. The profane, therefore, though not itself a category of this kingdom, is a decisive category of its most unobtrusive approach. For in happiness all that is earthly seeks its downfall, and only in happiness is its downfall destined to find it.[28]

As Durantaye acknowledges, what is important for Agamben here is the radical this-worldliness of Benjamin's concept of the messianic. 'The extraordinary nature of Benjamin's conception', as he puts it, 'lies in his effort to locate happiness not in a transcendent realm lying elsewhere, but instead here and now in this, and only this, world; in this, and only this, life.'[29] Benjamin, then, is inverting the usual Christian understanding according to which 'our idea of happiness should be shaped and our acts guided by a transcendental realm':[30] this is the event of *this* world. The second important reference to happiness comes in his second thesis on the philosophy of history:

> There is happiness – such as could arouse envy in us – only in the air we have breathed, among people we could have talked to, women who could have given themselves to us. In other words, the idea of happiness is indissolubly bound up with the idea of redemption. The same applies to the idea of the past, which is the concern of history. The past carries with it a secret index by which it is referred to redemption. Doesn't a breath of the air that pervaded earlier days caress us as well? In the voices we hear, isn't there an echo of now silent ones? Don't the women we court have sisters they no longer recognize? If so, then there is a secret agreement between the past generations and the present one. Then our coming was expected on earth. Then, like every generation that preceded us, we have been endowed with a *weak* messianic power, a power on which the past has a claim. Such a claim cannot be settled cheaply. The historical materialist is aware of this.[31]

Crucial in this passage is the linking of happiness with contingency: what one 'envies' in looking back over one's life are the events that never were but might have been. Happiness is bound up with the idea of redemption because, in yearning for that which never was, we are also yearning for a kind of worldly *restitution*. At work in both these passages, then, is a complex concept of completion. Happiness is what could have been, and what demands realisation. This is to say that happiness yearns to be completed: its exigency calls for its completion. But this completion of happiness would represent the *incompletion* of the totality of the world as we know it, of the world constituted on the basis of forgetting.

The etymological root of the English 'happiness' is the Middle English 'hap', which means luck, fortune or chance (the German *glücklich*, which in contemporary usage can also simply mean 'lucky', demonstrates this even more clearly). As we saw in relation to Wittgenstein's idea of happiness, a happy mode of being is one in which I am able to receive the fact of the world – its *happening* – in the right way: the happy are those who *live* this fact as something lucky or fortuitous, as something that could have been otherwise, but (happily) was not. 'Hap' can also mean 'absence of design or intent in relation to a particular event': what haps does so *for no reason*; it is literally graceful. The happiness in question is the happiness of living the fact that existence is unnecessary or gratuitous: not (empirical) happiness at the occurrence of this or that thing, but (transcendental) happiness at their happening. Lyn Hejinian describes this quite beautifully in an essay on Gertrude Stein's *Stanzas in Meditation* which, she says, 'begin in wonder at mere existence':[32] '[Stein's *Stanzas*] inhabit the astonishing and sometimes terrifying situation of improbability; the improbability of anything in particular's existing at all. It is against all odds that existence comes to any specific thing, idea, person, event and against all odds that they should come into the purview of one's life.'[33] Hejinian quotes Stein's grammatically challenging 'Portraits and Reception' – 'No matter how often what happened had happened any time any one told anything there was no repetition. This is what William James calls the Will to Live'[34] – and goes on to say that 'it is this that I am going to risk calling happiness'.[35] The demand of transcendental happiness, then, is the demand that the world be accepted in its absolute contingency. But this means it is simultaneously a demand for the *not-all*, for the rendering incomplete of the world picture that denies this anomic gratuity.

This can help explain what Benjamin means when he writes that 'the messianic world is the world of total and integral actuality' (*allseitige und integrale Aktualität*).[36] The completion at stake here – in which the world *as such* would be *actualised*, that is, made real to us – would come as the flipside to the rendering incomplete of the *Weltbild*. It is a completion that takes the form of an incompletion: it is, we might say, the completeness the world attains when all possible reference to another world has been erased. Remember Cavell in the last chapter ('I mean to *rid* us of it, not to replace it with a despair at our finitude'): this world is complete because it is *absolutely* incomplete. It is arguably this that Nancy describes in the following passage: 'That which, for itself, depends on nothing is an *absolute*. That which nothing completes in itself is a *fragment*. Being or existence is an absolute fragment. To exist: the *happenstance* of an absolute fragment.'[37] This world is a fragment that no longer refers back to a whole: it is more complete than any part; it undoes the logic of the part and the whole; it is a happenstance. In *The Arcades Project*, Benjamin sums this up in one sentence that perfectly capitulates the claims about happiness that he makes in the above two, better-known passages: 'Remembrance can make the incomplete (happiness) complete, and the complete (pain) incomplete.'[38] This happiness requires the incompletion of what pretends to be complete, and the completion of what is *absolutely* incomplete. In Nancy's terms, it requires the world become 'infinitely finite'.[39]

This may save our account from some of the serious criticisms one can make of the Heideggerian project of the overcoming of metaphysics. These relate to the familiar questions I raised in the last chapter, and to the whole problematic of the relation between theory and practice at work in this book: how can Heidegger, with his epochal understanding of the history of being as destiny, ever explain how we might find our way into another mode of revealing? What, in short, are we to *do* given Heidegger's diagnosis of modernity? His answer, basically, is very little: all we can do is work to think non-metaphysically in the hope that it might open the possibility of another beginning (something that would in an essential sense *not* depend on us, and especially not on any kind of *action*). Of course, this can itself be understood as a form of messianism; take for instance Heidegger's final interview with Der Spiegel, where he infamously pronounced that 'only a god can save us'.[40] Agamben, as we have seen, is very heavily indebted to the Heideggerian problematic, but there is a fundamental difference here: his Benjaminian version of this allows for a kind of 'two-way traffic' between the ontic and the ontological. What I mean here is indicated in the passages on happiness I cited earlier: we have been endowed with a *weak* power because, in the political struggle for happiness, we are hastening the quiet approach of the Kingdom. As Jessica Whyte aptly puts it: 'By deriving our vision of happiness from the world in which we find ourselves, it becomes possible to eschew a model of redemption based on divine intervention and to imagine a form of immanent social transformation, indeed, a form of politics.'[41] This may explain Agamben's repeatedly stating that Benjamin, for him, was a kind of antidote to Heidegger.[42] His philosophy allows us to link the ontological project of the overcoming of the picture-concept with ontic political struggle.

None of this is to say that political ontology can or should provide any kind of blueprint for political action. As the last chapter should have made clear, such a thing would be problematic enough on Heideggerian grounds. But arguably this is also just the nature of political ontology itself which, as we have seen, is concerned with the metaphysical structure of modernity before it is concerned with its ontic institutions. Perhaps more importantly it is also implied by the claim about the inextricability of theory and practice (thought and politics) running through this book: the task for thought is not to prescribe action, but to practise a thinking that tracks the conditions of the possibility of radical change; the political task is not to put theoretical or philosophical ideas 'into practice' but to think practically by experimenting with new political forms.[43] What emerges on our analysis are these two points: (1) there are ontic conditions for ontological change;

(2) many of the conditions for the overcoming of the picture-concept have been met.

Indeed this is how Agamben, in quasi-Marxist fashion, understands the historically unprecedented effects of capitalism.[44] Agamben makes this claim via a reading of Debord who, along with Lukács and Benjamin, made key contributions to the particular Western Marxist tradition from which he primarily draws (crudely, this is the tradition of Marxism which emphasises the concepts of commodification, alienation and experience in Marx's works). In *Society of the Spectacle*, for instance, Debord sets out to make a devastating critique of the way experience itself has been colonised and commodified by capital. The basic thesis of the book is summarised in its first two sentences: 'The whole life of those societies in which modern conditions of production prevail presents itself as an immense accumulation of *spectacles*. All that once was directly lived has become mere representation.'[45] Debord is extending the critique of reification that Lukács set up in 'Reification and the Consciousness of the Proletariat' (an essay that is all the more remarkable for having being published in 1923, nine years before the release of Marx's 1844 manuscripts). For Lukács, the rationalisation of labour that capitalism requires in order to function has important *experiential* effects: reification (the German is *verdinglichung*, which literally means 'to make into a thing') sees the human being's labour become 'something objective and independent of him, something that controls him by virtue of an autonomy alien to man'.[46] Capitalism turns the worker into a commodity, which is to say that it makes her and her work *exchangeable*: it uproots work from the qualitative embedding in life that is characteristic of it in pre-capitalist society; it abstracts it by transforming into something quantifiable. This changes the human being, which becomes 'less and less active and more and more *contemplative*':[47] viewing its life, world and the products of its labour from an alienated perspective.

As with Heidegger, this is more interesting than the bald claim that, in modernity, we have come to view the world from a *distorted* perspective, somehow misrepresenting to ourselves the way things are (this is one key difference between Lukács's critique of alienated thought and the vulgar Marxisms of which he was – at least in his better moments – so brilliantly critical). It is not simply that capitalism, with its powers of mystification, creates a 'false consciousness' in which the true nature of social reality is obfuscated. Rather, it is that the objectification and abstraction of social reality that takes place under capitalist social relations leads us into a theoretical, political and indeed philosophical impasse in which 'external' reality is set up as a brute objectivity, as an autonomous totality best describable in terms of the laws discovered by the natural sciences (and positivistic political economy), but in which the human role in the constitution of that reality becomes unintelligible. As a result of this objectification of the world, knowledge is transformed 'more and more into the systematic and conscious contemplation of those purely formal connections, those 'laws' which function in – objective – reality *without the intervention of a subject*'.[48] Part of what is lost in this process of objectification is any idea of how social change could be possible, any notion of how humanity might transform the conditions of its existence. Lukács finds the paradigm case of this in Kant's inability to deal coherently with the problem of freedom, which cuts through his concepts of both pure and practical reason, leading him into a position of necessary contradiction: 'The "eternal, iron" regularity of the processes of nature and the purely inward freedom of individual moral practice appear at the end of the *Critique of Practical Reason* as wholly irreconcilable and at the same time as the unalterable foundations of human existence.'[49] Thanks to the emergence of the commodity form and the abstraction of human reality that it requires, the contemplative mode – which had its beginnings in Ancient Greece with the Aristotelian concept of *theoria* – returns in capitalist modernity with a new sort of power and destructiveness: subjects now begin to look upon reality as something autonomous and objective, as brutely given like Levinas's *il y a*; the world, and the way things are in it, attain the semblance of inevitability and inexorability.

Debord extends these claims to argue that reification as Lukács described it has, with the development of mass media and communication technologies, morphed into imagistic form: that whereas in the nineteenth and early twentieth centuries modern subjects were objectified by capital, in late modernity capital turned the world into an image, such that 'reality unfolds in a new generality as a pseudo-world apart, solely as an object of contemplation'.[50] What characterises spectacular societies is that the process of abstraction has proceeded to such a degree that all that was once directly lived is now experienced as representation. So for Debord contemplative attitude is no longer simply an *effect* of the preponderance of the commodity form under capitalist social relations: rather it becomes the basic experiential and political form of capitalist society itself. What is so fascinating for our purposes, then, is how the work of Lukács and Debord chimes with the critique of the picture-concept as I have been presenting it. The spectacle, as Debord says, should be understood as a '*Weltanschauung* that has been actualized, translated into the material realm – a *world view* transformed into an objective force'.[51] It is very important that Debord's analysis in *Society of the Spectacle* relies so heavily on the metaphorical register of vision and images: the spectacle is a regime of spectation – of *theoria* divorced from praxis.

It would be a mistake, however, to simply assimilate these claims from Lukács and Debord to the critique of metaphysics as I have been presenting it. Capitalism is not just the expression of a certain metaphysical structure, but also a unique historical and material formation that needs to be theorised and critiqued in ontic political and economic terms. The point I want to make is more subtle: it is that capital, in its rapacious abstraction of life, its undermining of the qualitative experience of work, its objectification of human relations and its commodification of experience, has *exacerbated* the problems inherent in the picture-concept to such an extent that it has opened up the possibility of their resolution. Agamben describes the spectacle in *The Coming Community* in the following terms:

> When the real world is transformed into an image and images become real, the practical power of humans is separated from itself and presented as a world unto itself. In the figure of this world separated and organized by the media, in which the forms of the State and the economy are interwoven, the mercantile economy attains the absolute and irresponsible sovereignty over all of social life. After having falsified all of production, it can now manipulate collective perception and take control of social memory and social communication, transforming them into a single spectacular commodity where everything can be called into question except the spectacle itself, which, as such, says nothing but, 'What appears is good, what is good appears.'[52]

He goes on to argue that the 'spectacle is language, the very communicativity or linguistic being of humans . . .'[53] and compares its expropriation of human linguistic being with the cabalistic story of the 'isolation of the Shekinah' (in which the Rabbi Aher ends up in spiritual exile because he separates language from what it reveals). That he understands this destructive power of the spectacle in the dialectical sense I have been describing is made clear when he writes that 'the spectacle retains something like a positive possibility that can be used against it'.[54] He goes on:

> [T]he era in which we live is also that in which for the first time it is possible for humans to experience their own linguistic being – not this or that content of language, but language *itself*, not this or that proposition, but the very fact that one speaks. Contemporary politics is this devastating *experimentum linguae* that all over the planet unhinges and empties traditions and beliefs, ideologies and religions, identities and communities. Only those who succeed in carrying it to completion – without allowing what reveals to remain veiled in the nothingness that reveals, but bringing language

itself to language – will be the first citizens of a community with neither presuppositions nor a State . . .[55]

To put this in the terms I have been developing: capital has exacerbated the problems contained in the picture-concept to such an extent that the nihilism – the denial of the world, its consignment to a kind of nothingness – that was always already latent in it has revealed itself. We now *know* that there is no value in the world (or rather, that the only value in it is exchange value, which amounts to the same thing), but for that very reason we have been given the chance to live the good in the happening of the world itself. The world is what can never be exchanged, measured or placed into relation to anything else; it is incalculable and unquantifiable in an *absolute* sense. That Agamben puts this in terms of language should make this clear: what is at stake, after all, is language in its capacity (or otherwise) to reveal the world, and in its tendency in certain circumstances to fall into paradox when it refers to itself. The *experimentum linguae* of which Agamben writes is what happens when the picture-concept is pushed to its limit. As such, however, it opens the possibility of its resolution via a different experience of the word/world, indeed via the possibility of what Agamben, in both a Pauline and a Marxist sense, calls its 'use'.[56] This is to say that capitalism, as the system in which 'all that is solid melts into air',[57] has opened up an unprecedented opportunity for human beings to face up to – and perhaps appropriate – their own groundlessness.

In the final chapter of *The Time That Remains*, Agamben identifies a secret influence on Benjamin's philosophy by Saint Paul. He first establishes this striking philological claim by pointing to Benjamin's emphasis (via the insertion of spaces between the letters) on the word s c h w a c h e when he writes of a *weak* messianic power, arguing that it is a 'citation without citation marks' of 2 Corinthians 12:9–10.[58] As he goes on to reveal a series of textual correspondences between Benjamin and Paul, he evokes the Benjaminian idea of the *Bild* or image, which 'encompasses, for Benjamin, all things (meaning all objects, works of art, texts, records, or documents) wherein an instant of the past and an instant of the present are united in a constellation where the present is able to recognize the meaning of the past and the past therein finds meaning and fulfillment'.[59] He draws attention to a passage from Benjamin's fifth thesis on the philosophy of history (and which has already turned up in this chapter) – '[t]he true image of the past *flees* by' (*das wahre Bild der Vergangenheit h u s c h t vorbei*)[60] – and speculates that the emphasis here is another veiled citation, this time of 1 Corinthians 7:31; Benjamin, Agamben says, may have taken from this passage 'the idea that the image of the past runs the risk of disappearing completely if the present fails to recognize itself in it'.[61] All of this culminates in what is perhaps the key philological idea of the book: that 'these two fundamental messianic texts of our tradition [the Pauline corpus and Benjamin's theses], separated by almost two thousand years, both written in a situation of radical crisis, form a constellation whose time of legibility has finally come today . . .'.[62] This theory of reading and citation implies that Paul's corpus has only now 'come forth to full legibility . . .'.[63]

Yet a version of this idea has been at work in Agamben at least since *The Coming Community*. Consider the phrasing employed by Agamben in the citation above, where he describes *the figure of this world* separated and organised by the media. This is itself a 'citation without citation marks' of the very same passage from I Corinthians 7:31 that Agamben links with Benjamin, and which he invokes on a number of other occasions in *The Time That Remains*.[64] It contains the key to Agamben's political ontology: it links the overcoming of spectacular capitalism with a fulfilment of the problems of representation inherent in the Western metaphysical tradition. This is why it is wrong to regard Agamben's discourse as 'apocalyptic':[65] his ontology of the remnant is not concerned with the 'end of the world', but rather with thinking what it would mean to live and think beyond the picture of the world, of the world set up as a representable totality of facts. This is how we should read his repeated invocations of this passage which speaks of the passing away of the *figure of this world* (the word 'figure' here translates Paul's *skhēma*, which in Greek could also mean 'shape', 'form', 'plan' and 'diagram', and which in the various English translations of the New Testament has often become 'fashion', 'way' and 'form'; think here of the English idioms 'the way of the world' or 'the present *scheme* of things'). The time that remains is not the time before the end of the world, but something more subtle and far more interesting. It is the time that remains before the end of the picture-concept, before the passing of the *skhēma* of this world.

Part of what would characterise this dialectical change occasioned by the passing of the picture-concept is a demonstration of the *commonality* of life, language and the world itself. After all, what the ideology of capital (and this has proved to be particularly the case in its spectacular form) shares with the picture-concept is the image of an isolated subject, trapped in the privacy of his own experience (think here of the term 'Cartesian theatre',[66] which Dennett uses to ridicule traditional models in the philosophy of mind, but which could just as easily apply to the consumer in his home entertainment centre). Here I want to turn to the epigraph to this chapter, in which Wittgenstein speaks of how we are in a kind of ignorance of the uncanny and wonderful nature of our lives. It should be set against one of the key ideological fantasies of our time: the possibility, apparently made real by the advent of so-called 'reality television', of viewing *oneself* on screen ('We should be seeing life itself. – But then we do see this every day and it makes not the slightest impression on us! True enough, but we do not see it from that *point of view*'[67]). There is a kind of utopian demand at work in our desire to view ourselves in this way.[68] But what paralyses that utopian demand is the fantasy of the 'point of view' at work in it: it is a desire to *view* one's ordinary life as exceptional, which is a kind of distorted parody of the truly utopian desire to *live* it as such. Reality television, then, *screens us* from the ordinary even as it holds it up for our view. This may explain the extent of its obsession with the idea of competition – as we know, reality television shows are almost always structured in the form of a contest between participants, with all the game theoretical strategising that this entails – which perhaps arises as a kind of defence against the very commonality of the experience in question. As a *privatisation* of it. Consider here the kind of language we find ourselves falling into when under the sway of the (spectacular) picture-concept: it is a language of perspectives, viewpoints and worldviews, a language in which it seems entirely natural to claim that someone's view of things is different from the view of another, and hence perhaps that two people, whether literally or figuratively, can somehow 'see the world' differently, or perhaps even that they live in different worlds, alone in their own particular ways of framing things. Operative here is an idea of the self as something that *looks out at* the world, as something that views the world from an isolated position: I can debate with somebody about a particular issue, but in the end it might all come down to irresolvable differences of *perspective*, which seems to set us up as profoundly separated, private beings (it is no accident that significant portions of Wittgenstein's *Investigations* is concerned with problems of mental privacy[69]). And capital, of course, promotes just these kinds of fantasies of privacy, allowing and indeed encouraging us to think of ourselves as 'atomized individuals, individuals who imagined their commodity dream-world to be uniquely personal'.[70] This is why Agamben also defines the spectacle as 'the extreme form of [the] expropriation of the Common':[71] what is expropriated when our linguistic being is separated from us is the very commonality of the *logos* itself (Agamben refers here to Heraclitus's second fragment: '[A]lthough the *Logos* is common, most people live as if they had their own private understanding'[72]).

The change we are seeking, in which the event of the world is responded to in the right way, would therefore involve a basic insistence on the commonality of this experience, an insistence that we are exposed together to the *same* world, to the same *fact* of it. Of course there is a basic sense in which the exposure to being *as such* singularises the self – nobody is more singularly themselves than when alive to this fact – but this is also to say that we *share* this very singularity. This supports but in a deeper sense runs counter to Levinas's claim about the privacy of being:

> It is . . . the being in me, the fact that I exist, my existing, that constitutes the absolutely intransitive element, something without intentionality or relationship. One can exchange everything between beings except existing. In this sense, to be is to be isolated by existing. Inasmuch as I am, I am a monad. It is by existing that I am without windows and doors . . . [M]y relationship with existing . . . [is] the interior relationship par excellence.[73]

My existing, my absolutely particular response to the groundlessness of existence, *cannot be exchanged*. It is non-relational and therefore in a sense it is entirely private, unique to me alone. Yet so is yours, and that of any other living being. What is common, in other words, is our singularity in the face of the fact of the world; we are absolutely substitutable right where and when we are most unique. This is another way of understanding this idea of happiness: it is a happiness that singularises the self, but that does not exist except in common; it is the happiness, then, of the *sharing of singularity*, the happiness of our common exposure to the grace of the world. This is what cannot be exchanged; it undoes the very logic of exchange. After all, if being is not a property, then it cannot be *owned*: it is that which is subtracted from the logic of property, ownership and exchange. Living in proper response to it would involve the common appropriation of belonging itself: not any particular condition of belonging, but the fact of our being in common.

'Common' is a synonym for 'ordinary'. And as should be becoming clear, appropriating the commonality of our exposure to the fact of the world would mean a reconfiguration of the relation between the ordinary and the exceptional. Consider, again, Benjamin's eighth thesis on the philosophy of history:

> The tradition of the oppressed teaches us that the 'state of exception' [*Ausnahmezustand*] in which we live is the rule. We must attain a conception of history that accords with this insight. Then we will clearly see that it is our task to bring about a *real* state of exception, and this will improve our position in the struggle against fascism. One reason fascism has a chance is that, in the name of progress, its opponents treat it as a historical norm. The astonishment [*Das Staunen darüber*] that the things we are experiencing are 'still' possible in the twentieth century is *not* philosophical. This

astonishment is not the beginning of knowledge — unless it is the knowledge that the view of history which gives rise to it is untenable.[74]

As I have argued throughout this book, in the *'real'* state of exception everyday life enters a zone in which the difference between the ordinary and the exceptional becomes indiscernible. What should now be clearer, however, is what it would mean to own up to the fact that being *as such* is essentially exceptional. Indeed, there is another telling 'citation without citation marks' in this extract, as Benjamin implicitly refers to *thaumazein*, or the wonder in which Plato claimed philosophy begins.[75] This is fitting, for what is being raised here is the possibility of a new relation to the question of being. The state of exception as we know it (and the concept of history it gives rise to) is the site of a failed response to this question; a *real* state of exception would be one in which *thaumazein* is actualised in the form of a common experience of happiness. Thus the euphoric transformation of the paradoxes of the picture-concept would have to take place not only in philosophy as traditionally understood, but also on the terrain of politics (Marx: 'Philosophy cannot be actualised without the abolition [*Aufheben*] of the proletariat; the proletariat cannot be abolished without the actualisation of philosophy'[76]). A political movement dedicated to this would be one that insists on the *absolute exceptionality of the ordinary*, on the fact that nothing is more exceptional than the common fact of being itself, and nothing more common than exceptionality.[77] Benjamin gave us an image of this in his essay on the surrealists when he described the demand of communism in terms of 'an alarm clock that in each minute rings for sixty seconds'.[78]

The ordinary, if thought in the right way, is not the normal. Rather, it is something we might achieve, a notion of redemption. Yet Agamben's '*Aufhebung* of the state of exception'[79] will not require any redeeming event or new epochal sending of being. Instead it requires our attending to the fact that there will not be one: that being has no figure and imparts no destiny for humanity. No life is bare because being is already unveiled such as it is (in its concealment). There are no exceptions because being *as such* is exceptional (in its ordinariness). What remains after the passing of the figure of the world is just: the world.

NOTES

1. Wittgenstein, *Culture and Value*, 4e.
2. Livingston, *The Politics of Logic*, 49.
3. Sullivan, *Logicism and the Philosophy of Language*, 84.
4. Agamben, *Homo Sacer*, 15.

5. Russell and Whitehead, *Principia Mathematica*, 62.
 6. Livingston, *The Politics of Logic*, 68.
 7. Badiou, 'Notes Toward Thinking Appearance', 183.
 8. See Livingston, *The Politics of Logic*, 27–8.
 9. Badiou, *Being and Event*, 23.
10. Livingston, *The Politics of Logic*, 12. This is another way of understanding the issue of hyperbole that I dealt with in the opening chapter: Agamben's work is characterised on the one hand by undeniable critical power yet on the other by a lack of socio-historical nuance because he is first and foremost working to criticise the *logic* of modernity.
11. Schmitt, *Political Theology*, 13.
12. Agamben, 'Pardes', 219.
13. Agamben, *Language and Death*, 39.
14. Agamben, 'Pardes', 219.
15. Agamben, *The Time That Remains*, 100.
16. Ibid. 100.
17. Ibid. 78.
18. Ibid. 39.
19. Ibid. 40–1.
20. Ibid. 41.
21. Ibid. 78.
22. Ibid. 55.
23. See Livingston, *The Politics of Logic*, 39n.
24. Agamben, *The Time That Remains*, 77.
25. Ibid. 77.
26. Benjamin, 'On the Concept of History', 392.
27. Dickinson, *Agamben and Theology*, 95.
28. Benjamin, 'Theologico-Political Fragment', 305 (translation modified).
29. Durantaye, *Giorgio Agamben*, 375.
30. Ibid. 376.
31. Benjamin, 'On the Concept of History', 389–90.
32. Hejinian, 'A Common Sense', 362.
33. Ibid. 362.
34. Stein, quoted in Hejinian, 'A Common Sense', 361.
35. Hejinian, 'A Common Sense', 361.
36. Benjamin, 'Paralipomena to "On the Concept of History"', 405.
37. Nancy, *The Sense of the World*, 152.
38. This translation quoted in Agamben, 'Bartleby, or On Contingency', 267. The passage is from *The Arcades Project*, N8, 1; 571e.
39. See Nancy, *The Sense of the World*, 29–33.
40. Heidegger, 'Only a God Can Save Us', 57. He goes on: 'The only possibility available to us is that by thinking and poeticizing we prepare a readiness for the appearance of a god, or for the absence of a god in [our] decline, insofar as in view of the absent god we are in a state of decline.'

41. Whyte, 'A New Use of the Self', 2.
42. Durantaye discusses Agamben's repeated statements to this effect (see *Giorgio Agamben*, 53–4 and 303–13). I would argue that, while Agamben's philosophy is fundamentally post-Heideggerian, the influence of Benjamin is nonetheless pivotal: Benjamin's work, we might say, makes for Agamben that 'slight adjustment' (see *The Time That Remains*, 69) which transforms everything. This is why Benjamin so often turns up at the end of the analysis in Agamben. As Mills writes:

    > While Heidegger's work is palpable throughout Agamben's work . . . more often than not Benjamin provides Agamben with the conceptual tools for the *euporic* overcoming of the *aporias* that he diagnoses as underpinning the violence of modern democracy and consumer capital. (*The Philosophy of Agamben*, 6)

43. As Thanos Zartaloudis writes:

    > If there is no metaphysical vantage point from which to observe the form and decision-making of the law and the life of social praxis . . . a genuine realignment of thought and praxis is at stake – a realignment that does not succumb to the pseudo-dialectics between first principles and action, theory and praxis, truth and thought . . . (*Giorgio Agamben*, xiv)

44. Agamben's *The Kingdom and the Glory* may be his most consistent treatment of capitalism published to date. It is an attempt on his part at dealing in depth with something that his work had previously only touched upon: the question of economy. This is not the place to carry out an analysis of this dense and fascinating work, which has taken political ontology in a new direction, moving it from the critique of sovereignty and state violence toward a critique of government and bureaucracy. Zartaloudis makes the difference clear:

    > The target of proper critique has to be, then, directed, in this sense, not any longer at the mythological foundations and discourses of sovereign law and power, but, after their exposition, towards the messengers or functionaries who economically (functionally) administer, execute and police the laws and policies authorized by what they presuppose (but conceal) as an empty throne of sovereign or transcendental power and law. (*Giorgio Agamben*, xv)

    Despite this change of direction, it is worth noting that the work concludes by turning to the idea of spectacle (255–9), here understood as the modern form of 'glory' and 'acclamation' (concepts he traces back to their beginnings in early Trinitarian theology).

45. Debord, *Society of the Spectacle*, 12.
46. Lukács, 'Reification and the Consciousness of the Proletariat', 87.
47. Ibid. 89.

48. Ibid. 128.
49. Ibid. 134.
50. Debord, *Society of the Spectacle*, 12.
51. Ibid. 14 (my emphasis).
52. Agamben, *The Coming Community*, 80.
53. Ibid. 80.
54. Ibid. 80.
55. Ibid. 83.
56. Whyte provides an excellent account of Agamben's concept of use in 'A New Use of the Self'.
57. Marx and Engels, *The Communist Manifesto*, 38.
58. Agamben, *The Time That Remains*, 139–40.
59. Ibid. 142.
60. Benjamin, quoted in Agamben, *The Time That Remains*, 142.
61. Agamben, *The Time That Remains*, 142.
62. Ibid. 145.
63. Ibid. 145.
64. Ibid. 23, 24, 25, 142, 143.
65. See LaCapra's 'Approaching Limit Events', which describes Agamben's discourse in (post) apocalyptic terms.
66. See Dennett, *Consciousness Explained*, 101–11.
67. Wittgenstein, *Culture and Value*, 6e (my emphasis).
68. In the terms I will define shortly, it is a desire for the ordinary in its exceptionality.
69. Perhaps this can help explain the difference between the Wittgenstein of the *Tractatus* and that of the *Investigations* (something that is both necessary and difficult for any resolute reading of the former – why, the 'irresolute' reader asks, does Wittgenstein present the *Investigations* as a correction to the *Tractatus* if it had already undermined itself?). In the *Investigations* Wittgenstein is concerned with the *communal* nature of our linguistic practices; as such, he can be understood as working to escape the idea, which is perhaps implicitly promoted in the *Tractatus*, that the happy can be happy by themselves. The kind of surprise at language that runs through the later text is always already a surprise at the fact, given the absence of ground for our practices, we are intelligible to each other at all. In other words, the surprise that Cavell says Wittgenstein's work promotes (*The Claim of Reason*, 15) is surprise at the *commonality* of our linguistic practices in the absence of a foundation for them.
70. Buck-Morss, *The Dialectics of Seeing*, 260.
71. Agamben, *The Coming Community*, 80.
72. Translation in McKirahan, *Philosophy Before Socrates*, 112. This fragment also serves as one of the epigraphs to Livingston's book.
73. Levinas, *Time and the Other*, 42.
74. Benjamin, 'On the Concept of History', 392 (translation modified).
75. Socrates says: '... this is an experience which is characteristic of a

philosopher, this wondering: this is where philosophy begins and nowhere else' (Plato, *Theaetetus*, 155d; 173e).
76. Marx, introduction to the 'Critique of Hegel's Philosophy of Right', 70.
77. Dickinson gives this idea a rather beautiful theological spin:

> What once appeared so far away is now so close, and what was once unfamiliar is now familiar. The glorious divine presence and its joy unending are not something far away and unobtainable – they are right here, right now, if we could only see beyond the divisions we have arbitrarily created. (*Agamben and Theology*, 81–2)

78. Benjamin, 'Surrealism', 218.
79. Agamben, *The Time That Remains*, 108.

Bibliography

Acampora, Christa. 'On Sovereignty and Overhumanity: Why It Matters How We Read Nietzsche's Genealogy II: 2', in Christa Acampora (ed.), *Critical Essays on the Classics: Nietzsche's* On the Genealogy of Morals (Lanham: Rowman and Littlefield, 2006), 147–62.

Adorno, Theodore. *Minima Moralia*, trans. New Left Books (London: Verso, 2005).

Agamben, Giorgio. 'Bartleby, or On Contingency', in *Potentialities*, trans. Daniel Heller-Roazen (Stanford: Stanford University Press, 1999), 243–71.

Agamben, Giorgio. *The Coming Community*, trans. Michael Hardt (Minneapolis: University of Minnesota Press, 1993).

Agamben, Giorgio. 'Form-of-Life', in *Means Without End*, trans. Vincenzo Binetti and Cesare Casarino (Minneapolis: University of Minnesota Press, 2000), 3–12.

Agamben, Giorgio. *Homo Sacer*, trans. Daniel Heller-Roazen (Stanford: Stanford University Press, 1998).

Agamben, Giorgio. 'I am sure you are more pessimistic than I am', interview with J. Smith in *Rethinking Marxism* 16: 2 (2004), 115–24.

Agamben, Giorgio. 'The Idea of Language', in *Potentialities*, trans. Daniel Heller-Roazen (Stanford: Stanford University Press, 1999), 39–47.

Agamben, Giorgio. *Infancy and History*, trans. Liz Heron (London: Verso, 2007).

Agamben, Giorgio. 'In This Exile', in *Means Without End*, trans. Vincenzo Binetti and Cesare Casarino (Minneapolis: University of Minnesota Press, 2000), 121–42.

Agamben, Giorgio. *The Kingdom and the Glory*, trans. Lorenzo Chiesa (Stanford: Stanford University Press, 2011).

Agamben, Giorgio. *Language and Death*, trans. Karen Pinkus (Minneapolis: University of Minnesota Press, 1991).

Agamben, Giorgio. 'The Messiah and the Sovereign', in *Potentialities*, trans. Daniel Heller-Roazen (Stanford: Stanford University Press, 1999), 160–74.

Agamben, Giorgio. 'On Potentiality', in *Potentialities*, trans. Daniel Heller-Roazen (Stanford: Stanford University Press, 1999), 177–84.

Agamben, Giorgio. *The Open: Man and Animal*, trans. Kevin Attell (Stanford: Stanford University Press, 2004).
Agamben, Giorgio. '*Pardes*: The Writing of Potentiality', in *Potentialities*, trans. Daniel Heller-Roazen (Stanford: Stanford University Press, 1999), 205–19.
Agamben, Giorgio. 'The Passion of Facticity', in *Potentialities*, trans. Daniel Heller-Roazen (Stanford: Stanford University Press, 1999), 185–204.
Agamben, Giorgio. *Remnants of Auschwitz*, trans. Daniel Heller-Roazen (New York: Zone Books, 1999).
Agamben, Giorgio. *The Sacrament of Language: An Archaeology of the Oath*, trans. Adam Kotsko (Stanford: Stanford University Press, 2011).
Agamben, Giorgio. '**Se*: Hegel's Absolute and Heidegger's *Ereignis*', in *Potentialities*, trans. Daniel Heller-Roazen (Stanford: Stanford University Press, 1999), 116–37.
Agamben, Giorgio. *State of Exception*, trans. Kevin Attell (Chicago: University of Chicago Press, 2005).
Agamben, Giorgio. *The Time That Remains*, trans. Patricia Dailey (Stanford: Stanford University Press, 2005).
Agamben, Giorgio. 'We Refugees', on website for the European Graduate School, available at <http://www.egs.edu/faculty/agamben/agamben-we-refugees.html> (last accessed 21 May 2013).
Agamben, Giorgio. 'What is a Paradigm?', in *The Signature of All Things*, trans. Luca D'Isanto with Kevin Attell (New York: Zone Books, 2009), 9–32.
Agamben, Giorgio. 'The Work of Man', trans. Kevin Attell, in Matthew Calarco and Steven DeCaroli (eds), *Giorgio Agamben: Sovereignty and Life* (Stanford: Stanford University Press, 2007), 1–10.
Aristotle. *Nicomachean Ethics*, trans. J. E. C. Welldon (New York: Prometheus Books, 1987).
Ayer, A. J. *Language, Truth and Logic* (New York: Dover, 1952).
Badiou, Alain. *Being and Event*, trans. Oliver Feltham (London: Continuum, 2005).
Badiou, Alain. *Handbook of Inaesthetics*, trans. Alberto Toscano (Stanford: Stanford University Press, 2005).
Badiou, Alain. *Manifesto for Philosophy*, trans. Norman Madarasz (Albany: State University of New York Press, 1999).
Badiou, Alain. 'Notes Toward Thinking Appearance', trans. Ray Brassier and Alberto Toscano, in *Theoretical Writings* (London: Continuum, 2004), 182–93.
Bambach, Charles. *Heidegger's Roots* (Ithaca: Cornell University Press, 2003).
Benjamin, Andrew. 'Spacing as the Shared: Heraclitus, Pindar, Agamben', in Andrew Norris (ed.), *Politics, Metaphysics, and Death* (Durham, NC: Duke University Press, 2005), 145–72.
Benjamin, Walter. *The Arcades Project*, trans. Howard Eiland and Kevin McLaughlin (Cambridge, MA: Harvard University Press, 1999).

Benjamin, Walter. 'Critique of Violence', trans. Edmund Jephcott, in *Selected Writings Volume 1: 1913–1926*, ed. Howard Eiland and Michael W. Jennings (Cambridge, MA: Harvard University Press, 1999), 236–52.
Benjamin, Walter. 'Franz Kafka', trans. Harry Zohn, in *Selected Writings Volume 2: 1927–1934*, ed. Howard Eiland and Michael W. Jennings (Cambridge, MA: Harvard University Press, 1999), 714–818.
Benjamin, Walter. 'On the Concept of History', trans. Harry Zohn, in *Selected Writings Volume 4: 1938–1940*, ed. Howard Eiland and Michael W. Jennings (Cambridge, MA: Harvard University Press, 2003), 389–400.
Benjamin, Walter. 'Paralipomena to "On the Concept of History"', trans. Edmund Jephcott and Howard Eiland, in *Selected Writings Volume 4: 1938–1940*, ed. Howard Eiland and Michael W. Jennings (Cambridge, MA: Harvard University Press, 2003), 401–11.
Benjamin, Walter. 'The Storyteller: Observations on the Works of Nikolai Leskov', trans. Harry Zohn, in *Selected Writings Volume 3: 1935–1938*, ed. Howard Eiland and Michael W. Jennings (Cambridge, MA: Harvard University Press, 2002), 143–66.
Benjamin, Walter. 'Surrealism', trans. Edmund Jephcott, in *Selected Writings Volume 2: 1927–1934*, ed. Howard Eiland and Michael W. Jennings (Cambridge, MA: Harvard University Press, 1999), 207–21.
Benjamin, Walter. 'Theologico-Political Fragment', trans. Edmund Jephcott, in *Selected Writings Volume 3: 1935–1938*, ed. Howard Eiland and Michael W. Jennings (Cambridge, MA: Harvard University Press, 2002), 305–6.
Berkowitz, Roger. 'Liberating the Animal: The False Promise of Nietzsche's Anti-Human Philosophy', *Theory & Event* 13: 2 (2010).
Bernstein, J. M. 'Bare Life, Bearing Witness: Auschwitz and the Pornography of Horror', *Parallax* 10: 1 (2004), 2–16.
Bishop, Elizabeth. 'IV / O Breath', in *The Complete Poems of Elizabeth Bishop* (New York: Farrar, Straus and Giroux, 1984), 79.
Black, Max. *A Companion to Wittgenstein's Tractatus* (Cambridge: Cambridge University Press, 1971).
Blanchot, Maurice. *The Infinite Conversation*, trans. Susan Hanson (Minneapolis: University of Minnesota Press, 1993).
Blanchot, Maurice. 'Literature and the Right to Death', trans. Lydia Davis, in *The Station Hill Blanchot Reader* (New York: Station Hill Press, 1999), 359–99.
Blanchot, Maurice. *The Space of Literature*, trans. Ann Smock (Lincoln: University of Nebraska Press, 1989).
Blanchot, Maurice. 'Thomas the Obscure', trans. Robert Lamberton, in *The Station Hill Blanchot Reader* (New York: Station Hill Press, 1999), 55–128.
Boulby, Mark. 'Kafka's End: A Reassessment of the Burrow', *The German Quarterly* 55: 2 (1982), 175–85.
Brassier, Ray. 'I am a nihilist because I still believe in truth', interview with Marcin Rychter available at <http://kronos.org.pl/index.php?23151,896> (last accessed 21 May 2013).

Braver, Lee. *A Thing of This World* (Evanston: Northwestern University Press, 2007).
Brod, Max. 'Nachwort', in *Beschreibung eines Kampfes: Novellen, Skizzen, Aphorismen aus dem Nachlass* (Frankfurt: S. Fischer, 1954), 341–54.
Bruns, Gerald. *The Material of Poetry* (Athens, GA: University of Georgia Press, 2005).
Buck-Morss, Susan. *The Dialectics of Seeing: Walter Benjamin and the Arcades Project* (Cambridge, MA: MIT Press, 1990).
Calarco, Matthew, and Steven DeCaroli (eds). *Giorgio Agamben: Sovereignty and Life* (Stanford: Stanford University Press, 2007).
Cavell, Stanley. 'The Availability of Wittgenstein's Later Philosophy', in *Must We Mean What We Say?* (Cambridge: Cambridge University Press, 2002), 44–72.
Cavell, Stanley. 'The Avoidance of Love', in *Must We Mean What We Say?* (Cambridge: Cambridge University Press, 2002), 267–356.
Cavell, Stanley. *The Claim of Reason* (Oxford: Oxford University Press, 1999).
Cavell, Stanley. 'The Uncanniness of the Ordinary', in *In Quest of the Ordinary* (Chicago: University of Chicago Press, 1998), 153–78.
Clemens, Justin. 'The Abandonment of Sex: Giorgio Agamben, Psychoanalysis and Melancholia', *Theory & Event* 13: 1 (2010).
Clemens, Justin. 'The Role of the Shifter and the Problem of Reference', in Justin Clemens, Nicholas Heron and Alex Murray (eds), *The Work of Giorgio Agamben: Law, Literature, Life* (Edinburgh: Edinburgh University Press, 2008), 43–64.
Conant, James. 'Elucidation and Nonsense in Frege and Early Wittgenstein', in Alice Crary and Rupert Read (eds), *The New Wittgenstein* (London: Routledge, 2001), 174–217.
Conant, James. 'Putting Two and Two Together: Kierkegaard, Wittgenstein and the Point of View for their Work as Authors', in T. Tessin and M. Von der Ruhr (eds), *Philosophy and the Grammar of Religious Belief* (Basingstoke: Macmillan, 1995), 248–331.
Conant, James. 'Two Conceptions of Die Überwindung der Metaphysik: Carnap and the Early Wittgenstein', in Timothy McCarthy and Sean Stidd (eds), *Wittgenstein in America* (New York: Oxford University Press, 2001), 13–61.
Conant, James. 'What "Ethics" in the *Tractatus* is Not', in D. Z. Phillips and Mario von der Ruhr (eds), *Religion and Wittgenstein's Legacy* (Aldershot: Ashgate Publishing, 2005), 39–88.
Critchley, Simon. *Very Little . . . Almost Nothing* (London: Routledge, 2004).
Crowell, Steven, and Jeff Malpas (eds). *Transcendental Heidegger* (Stanford: Stanford University Press, 2007).
DeAngelis, William James. *Ludwig Wittgenstein: A Cultural Point of View* (Aldershot: Ashgate Publishing, 2007).
Debord, Guy. *Society of the Spectacle*, trans. Ken Knabb (New York: Zone Books, 1995).

Dennett, Daniel. *Consciousness Explained* (New York: Hachette Book Group, 1991).
Deranty, Jean-Philippe. 'Rancière and Contemporary Political Ontology', *Theory & Event* 6: 4 (2003).
Derrida, Jacques. *The Beast and the Sovereign*, trans. Geoffrey Bennington (Chicago: Chicago University Press, 2009).
Derrida, Jacques. 'Force of Law: The Mystical Foundation of Authority', trans. Mary Quaintance, in *Acts of Religion* (London: Routledge, 2002), 228–98.
Diamond, Cora. 'Ethics, Imagination and the Method of Wittgenstein's *Tractatus*', in Alice Crary and Rupert Read (eds), *The New Wittgenstein* (London: Routledge, 2000), 149–73.
Diamond, Cora. 'Throwing Away the Ladder', in *The Realistic Spirit* (Cambridge, MA: MIT Press, 1991), 179–204.
Dickinson, Colby. *Agamben and Theology* (London: T&T Clark, 2011).
Dolan, Frederick. 'Representing the Political System: American Political Science in the Age of the World Picture', *Diacritics* 20: 2 (1990), 93–108.
Dreyfus, Hubert. 'Being and Power: Heidegger and Foucault', *International Journal of Philosophical Studies* 4: 1 (1996), 1–16.
Dreyfus, Hubert. *Being in the World* (Cambridge, MA: MIT Press, 1991).
Dreyfus, Hubert. 'Heidegger's Critique of the Husserl/Searle Account of Intentionality', in Hubert Dreyfus and Mark Wrathall (eds), *Heidegger Reexamined*, vol. 1 (New York: Routledge, 2002), 135–56.
Dreyfus, Hubert. 'How Heidegger defends the possibility of a correspondence theory of truth with respect to the entities of natural science', in Theodore R. Schatzki, Karin Knorr Cetina and Eike von Savigny (eds), *The Practice Turn in Contemporary Theory* (New York: Routledge, 2000), 151–62.
Dreyfus, Hubert. 'Responses', in Jeff Malpas and Mark Wrathall (eds), *Heidegger, Coping, and Cognitive Science* (Cambridge, MA: MIT Press, 2000), 313–50.
Durantaye, Leland de la. *Giorgio Agamben: A Critical Introduction* (Stanford: Stanford University Press, 2009).
Eliot, T. S. 'The Love Song of J. Alfred Prufrock', in *Selected Poems* (London: Faber and Faber, 1961), 11–16.
Emerson, Ralph Waldo. 'New England, Lecture III: "New England: Genius, Manners, and Customs"', in *The Later Lectures of Ralph Waldo Emerson, 1843–1871*, vol. 1 (Athens, GA: University of Georgia Press, 2010), 39–56.
Faye, Emmanuel. *Heidegger: The Introduction of Nazism into Philosophy in Light of the Unpublished Seminars*, trans. Michael Smith (London: Yale University Press, 2009).
Fitzpatrick, Peter. 'Bare Sovereignty: *Homo Sacer* and the Insistence of Law', in Andrew Norris (ed.), *Politics, Metaphysics, and Death* (Durham, NC: Duke University Press, 2005), 49–73.
Foti, Veronique. 'Representation and the Image: Between Heidegger, Derrida and Plato', *Man and World* 18 (1985), 65–78.

Foucault, Michel. *The History of Sexuality*, vol. 1, trans. Robert Hurley (New York: Vintage, 1980).
Frege, Gottlob. *The Foundations of Arithmetic: A Logico-Mathematical Enquiry into the Concept of Number*, trans. John Austin (Evanston: Northwestern University Press, 1980).
Friedlander, Saul. *Reflections of Nazism: An Essay on Kitsch and Death*, trans. Thomas Weyr (Bloomington: Indiana University Press, 1993).
Glazebrook, Trish. *Heidegger's Philosophy of Science* (New York: Fordham University Press, 2000).
Guignon, Charles. 'Philosophy after Heidegger and Wittgenstein', *Philosophy and Phenomenological Research* 50: 4 (1990), 649–72.
Hallward, Peter. 'A Politics of Prescription', *South Atlantic Quarterly* 104: 4 (2005), 769–89.
Hamacher, Werner. 'Afformative, Strike: Benjamin's "Critique of Violence"', in Andrew Benjamin and Peter Osborne (eds), *Walter Benjamin's Philosophy: Destruction and Experience* (London: Routledge, 1994), 110–38.
Hanshe, Rainer J. 'Invisibly Revolving——Inaudibly Revolving: The Riddle of the Double *Gedankenstrich*', *The Agonist* 3: 1 (2010), 7–26.
Hanssen, Beatrice. *Walter Benjamin's Other History: Of Stones, Animals, Human Beings, and Angels* (Berkeley: University of California Press, 1998).
Harman, Graham. *Tool Being* (Chicago: Open Court, 2002).
Hatab, Lawrence J. *Nietzsche's Life Sentence: Coming to Terms with Eternal Recurrence* (New York: Routledge, 2005).
Heidegger, Martin. 'The Age of the World Picture', trans. William Lovitt, in *The Question Concerning Technology and Other Essays* (New York: Garland Publishing, 1977), 115–54.
Heidegger, Martin. *The Basic Problems of Phenomenology*, trans. Albert Hofstadter (Bloomington: Indiana University Press, 1988).
Heidegger, Martin. *Being and Time*, trans. Joan Stambaugh (Albany: State University of New York Press, 1996).
Heidegger, Martin. *Elucidations of Hölderlin's Poetry*, trans. Keith Hoeller (New York: Humanity Press, 2000).
Heidegger, Martin. *History of the Concept of Time*, trans. Theodore Kisiel (Bloomington: Indiana University Press, 1992).
Heidegger, Martin. *Introduction to Metaphysics*, trans. Gregory Fried and Richard Polt (New Haven: Yale University Press, 2000).
Heidegger, Martin. 'Introduction to *What is Metaphysics*', trans. Walter Kaufmann, in *Pathmarks*, ed. William McNeil (Cambridge: Cambridge University Press, 1998), 277–90.
Heidegger, Martin. 'Language', in *Poetry, Language, Thought*, trans. Albert Hofstadter (New York: Harper & Row, 1971), 187–208.
Heidegger, Martin. 'Letter on Humanism', trans. Frank Capuzzi, in *Basic Writings*, ed. David Farrell Krell (San Francisco: HarperCollins, 1993), 213–65.

Heidegger, Martin. *The Metaphysical Foundations of Logic*, trans. Michael Heim (Bloomington: Indiana University Press, 1992).
Heidegger, Martin. 'The Nature of Language', in *On the Way to Language*, trans. Peter Hertz (San Francisco: Harper & Row, 1971), 57–110.
Heidegger, Martin. *Nietzsche*, vol. 3, trans. David Farrell Krell (San Francisco: Harper & Row, 1991).
Heidegger, Martin. 'Only a God Can Save Us', interview with *Der Spiegel*, trans. Thomas Sheehan and included in his *Heidegger: The Man and Thinker* (New Brunswick, NJ: Transaction Publishers, 2010), 45–68.
Heidegger, Martin. *On Time and Being*, trans. Joan Stambaugh (New York: Harper & Row, 1972).
Heidegger, Martin. 'The Origin of the Work of Art', trans. Albert Hofstadter, in *Basic Writings*, ed. David Farrell Krell (San Francisco: HarperCollins, 1993), 143–212.
Heidegger, Martin. 'The Question Concerning Technology', trans. William Lovitt, in *The Question Concerning Technology and Other Essays* (New York: Garland Publishing, 1977), 3–35.
Heidegger, Martin. 'Seminar in Zähringen 1973', in *Four Seminars*, trans. Andrew Mitchell and François Raffoul (Bloomington: Indiana University Press, 2003), 64–81.
Heidegger, Martin. 'Die Zeit des Weltbildes', in *Holzwege* (Frankfurt: Vittorio Klostermann, 2003), 75–113.
Hejinian, Lyn. 'A Common Sense', in *The Language of Inquiry* (Berkeley: University of California Press, 2000), 355–82.
Heller-Roazen, Daniel. 'Editor's Introduction to *Potentialities*', in Giorgio Agamben, *Potentialities* (Stanford: Stanford University Press, 1999).
Heller-Roazen, Daniel. *The Inner Touch: Archaeology of a Sensation* (New York: Zone Books, 2007).
Hodges, Michael. *Transcendence and Wittgenstein's* Tractatus (Philadelphia: Temple University Press, 1990).
Jacobson, Eric. *Metaphysics of the Profane* (New York: Columbia University Press, 2003).
Kafka, Franz. 'The Burrow', trans. Willa and Edwin Muir, in *The Penguin Complete Short Stories of Franz Kafka*, ed. Nahum N. Glatzer (Harmondsworth: Penguin Books, 1983), 325–59.
Kafka, Franz. 'The Cares of a Family Man', trans. Willa and Edwin Muir, in *The Penguin Complete Short Stories of Franz Kafka*, ed. Nahum N. Glatzer (Harmondsworth: Penguin Books, 1983), 427–9.
Kafka, Franz. 'The Coming of the Messiah', in *Parables and Paradoxes* (New York: Shocken Books, 1962), 81e.
Kafka, Franz. 'A Crossbreed', trans. Willa and Edwin Muir, in *The Penguin Complete Short Stories of Franz Kafka*, ed. Nahum N. Glatzer (Harmondsworth: Penguin Books, 1983), 426–7.
Kafka, Franz. 'Leopards in the Temple', in *Parables and Paradoxes* (New York: Shocken Books, 1962), 93e.

Kant, Immanuel. *Critique of Pure Reason*, trans. Norman Kemp Smith (New York: Palgrave Macmillan, 2003).
Kishik, David. *The Power of Life: Agamben and the Coming Politics* (Stanford: Stanford University Press, 2012).
Koelb, Clayton. 'Kafka Imagines his Readers: The Rhetoric of "Josefine die Sängerin" and "Der Bau"', in Harold Bloom (ed.), *Franz Kafka* (New York: Infobase Publishing, 2010), 135–47.
Kuhn, Thomas. *The Structure of Scientific Revolutions* (Chicago: Chicago University Press, 1996).
LaCapra, Dominick. 'Approaching Limit Events', in Matthew Calarco and Steven DeCaroli (eds), *Giorgio Agamben: Sovereignty and Life* (Stanford: Stanford University Press, 2007), 126–62.
Laclau, Ernesto. 'Bare Life or Social Indeterminacy?', in Matthew Calarco and Steven DeCaroli (eds), *Giorgio Agamben: Sovereignty and Life* (Stanford: Stanford University Press, 2007), 11–22.
Lacoue-Labarthe, Philippe. *Heidegger and the Politics of Poetry*, trans. Jeff Fort (Illinois: University of Illinois Press, 2007).
Lafont, Cristina. 'Heidegger and the Synthetic A Priori', in Steven Crowell and Jeff Malpas (eds), *Transcendental Heidegger* (Stanford: Stanford University Press, 2007), 104–18.
Lafont, Cristina. *Heidegger, Language, and World-Disclosure*, trans. Graham Harman (Cambridge: Cambridge University Press, 2000).
Lemm, Vanessa. *Nietzsche's Animal Philosophy* (New York: Fordham University Press, 2009).
Lemm, Vanessa. 'The Overhuman Animal', in Christa Acampora and Ralph Acampora (eds), *A Nietzschean Bestiary* (Maryland: Rowman and Littlefield, 2004), 220–39.
Levinas, Emmanuel. 'Ethics as First Philosophy', trans. Seán Hand, in *The Levinas Reader* (Oxford: Blackwell, 1989), 75–87.
Levinas, Emmanuel. *Existence and Existents*, trans. Alphonso Lingis (Pittsburgh: Duquesne University Press, 1978).
Levinas, Emmanuel. *On Escape*, trans. Bettina Bergo (Stanford: Stanford University Press, 2003).
Levinas, Emmanuel. *Otherwise than Being or Beyond Essence*, trans. Alphonso Lingis (Pittsburgh: Duquesne University Press, 1998).
Levinas, Emmanuel. 'Signature', trans. Seán Hand, in *Difficult Freedom* (Baltimore: Johns Hopkins University Press, 1990), 291–5.
Levinas, Emmanuel. *Time and the Other*, trans. Richard Cohen (Pittsburgh: Duquesne University Press, 1987).
Levinas, Emmanuel. *Totality and Infinity*, trans. Alphonso Lingis (Pittsburgh: Duquesne University Press, 1969).
Librett, Jeffrey. 'From the Sacrifice of the Letter to the Voice of Testimony: Giorgio Agamben's Fulfilment of Metaphysics', *Diacritics* 37: 2–3 (2008), 11–33.
Littell, Jonathan. *The Kindly Ones*, trans. Charlotte Mandell (London: Chatto & Windus, 2009).

Livingston, Paul. *The Politics of Logic: Badiou, Wittgenstein, and the Consequences of Formalism* (London: Routledge, 2011).
Locke, John. *An Essay Concerning Human Understanding*, ed. Kenneth Winkler (Indianapolis: Hackett Publishing Company, 1996).
Loeb, Paul. 'Finding the Übermensch in Nietzsche's Genealogy of Morality', *The Journal of Nietzsche Studies* 30 (2005), 70–101.
Lukács, György. 'Reification and the Consciousness of the Proletariat', trans. Rodney Livingstone, in *History and Class Consciousness* (London: Merlin Press, 1971), 82–222.
Lupton, Julia. 'Creature Caliban', *Shakespeare Quarterly* 51: 1 (2000), 1–23.
McDowell, John. *Mind and World* (Cambridge, MA: Harvard University Press, 1996).
Maché, Britta. 'The Noise in the Burrow: Kafka's Final Dilemma', *The German Quarterly* 55: 4 (1982), 526–40.
McKirahan, Richard D. *Philosophy Before Socrates: An Introduction with Texts and Commentary* (Indianapolis: Hackett Publishing Company, 2011).
McLoughlin, Daniel. 'The Sacred and the Unspeakable: Giorgio Agamben's Ontological Politics', *Theory & Event* 13: 1 (2010).
Malcolm, Norman. *Ludwig Wittgenstein: A Memoir* (Oxford: Oxford University Press, 2001).
Marchart, Oliver. *Post-Foundational Political Thought: Political Difference in Nancy, Lefort, Badiou and Laclau* (Edinburgh: Edinburgh University Press, 2007).
Marx, Karl. 'Critique of Hegel's Philosophy of Right', in *Marx: Early Political Writings*, ed. Joseph O'Malley (Cambridge: Cambridge University Press, 1994), 1–70.
Marx, Karl. *The German Ideology*, trans. C. J. Arthur (New York: International Publishers, 2007).
Marx, Karl. 'Theses on Feuerbach', trans. Loyd D. Easton and Kurt H. Guddat, in *Selected Writings*, ed. Lawrence H. Simon (Indianapolis: Hackett Publishing Company, 1994), 98–101.
Marx, Karl, and Friedrich Engels. *The Communist Manifesto* (London: Verso, 1998).
Meier, Heinrich. *The Lesson of Carl Schmitt*, trans. Marcus Brainard (Chicago: University of Chicago Press, 1998).
Mills, Catherine. 'Agamben's Messianic Politics: Biopolitics, Abandonment and Happy Life', *Contretemps* 5 (2004), 42–62.
Mills, Catherine. *The Philosophy of Agamben* (Montreal: McGill-Queen's University Press, 2008).
Monk, Ray. *Ludwig Wittgenstein: The Duty of Genius* (New York: The Free Press, 1991).
Morris, Michael, and Julian Dodd. 'Mysticism and Nonsense in the *Tractatus*', *European Journal of Philosophy* 17: 2 (2009), 247–76.
Mulhall, Stephen. 'Can There Be an Epistemology of Moods?', in Hubert

Dreyfus and Mark Wrathall (eds), *Heidegger Reexamined*, vol. 4 (New York: Routledge, 2002), 33–52.
Mulhall, Stephen. *On Being in the World: Wittgenstein and Heidegger on Seeing Aspects* (New York: Routledge, 1990).
Mulhall, Stephen. 'Words, Waxing and Waning: Ethics in/and/of the *Tractatus Logico-Philosophicus*', in Guy Kahane, Edward Kanterian and Oskari Kuusela (eds), *Wittgenstein and his Interpreters* (New York: John Wiley and Sons, 2007), 221–47.
Murray, Alex. *Giorgio Agamben* (London: Routledge, 2010).
Nancy, Jean-Luc. *The Creation of the World*, trans. François Raffoul and David Pettigrew (Albany: State University of New York Press, 2007).
Nancy, Jean-Luc. *The Experience of Freedom*, trans. Bridget McDonald (Stanford: Stanford University Press, 1993).
Nancy, Jean-Luc. 'The Inoperative Community', trans. Peter Connor, in *The Inoperative Community* (Minneapolis: University of Minnesota Press, 1991), 1–42.
Nancy, Jean-Luc. 'The Insufficiency of Values and the Necessity of Sense', *Journal for Cultural Research* 9: 4 (1997), 127–31.
Nancy, Jean-Luc. 'Literary Communism', trans. Peter Connor, in *The Inoperative Community* (Minneapolis: University of Minnesota Press, 1991), 71–81.
Nancy, Jean-Luc. 'Myth Interrupted', trans. Peter Connor, in *The Inoperative Community* (Minneapolis: University of Minnesota Press, 1991), 43–70.
Nancy, Jean-Luc. 'Originary Ethics', trans. Duncan Large, in *A Finite Thinking* (Stanford: Stanford University Press, 2003), 175–95.
Nancy, Jean-Luc. *The Sense of the World*, trans. Jeffrey Librett (Minneapolis: University of Minnesota Press, 1997).
Negri, Antonio. 'Giorgio Agamben: The Discreet Taste of the Dialectic', in Matthew Calarco and Steven DeCaroli (eds), *Giorgio Agamben: Sovereignty and Life* (Stanford: Stanford University Press, 2007), 109–25.
Nietzsche, Friedrich. *Beyond Good and Evil*, trans. Walter Kaufmann, in *Basic Writings of Nietzsche* (New York: Modern Library, 2000), 179–435.
Nietzsche, Friedrich. *The Birth of Tragedy*, trans. Walter Kaufmann, in *Basic Writings of Nietzsche* (New York: Modern Library, 2000), 1–144.
Nietzsche, Friedrich. *The Gay Science*, trans. Josefine Nauckoff (Cambridge: Cambridge University Press, 2001).
Nietzsche, Friedrich. *On the Genealogy of Morals*, trans. Walter Kaufmann, in *Basic Writings of Nietzsche* (New York: Modern Library, 2000), 437–599.
Nietzsche, Friedrich. 'On Truth and Lie in an Extra-Moral Sense', trans. Walter Kaufmann, in *The Portable Nietzsche* (New York: Penguin, 1976), 42–7.
Nietzsche, Friedrich. *Thus Spoke Zarathustra*, trans. Graham Parks (Oxford: Oxford University Press, 2005).
Nietzsche, Friedrich. *Untimely Meditations*, trans. R. J. Hollingdale (Cambridge: Cambridge University Press, 1997).

Nietzsche, Friedrich. *The Will to Power*, trans. Walter Kaufmann and R. J. Hollingdale (New York: Vintage Books, 1968).
Norris, Andrew. 'Sovereignty, Exception, and Norm', *Journal of Law and Society* 34: 1 (2007), 31–45.
Noys, Benjamim. 'Apocalypse, Tendency, Crisis', *Mute Magazine*, 3 February 2010, available at <http://www.metamute.org/editorial/articles/apocalypse-tendency-crisis> (last accessed 21 May 2013).
Noys, Benjamin. *The Persistence of the Negative: A Critique of Contemporary Continental Theory* (Edinburgh: Edinburgh University Press, 2010).
Owen, David. *Maturity and Modernity: Nietzsche, Weber, Foucault and the Ambivalence of Reason* (London: Routledge, 1994).
Parker-Starbuck, Jennifer. 'Becoming-Animate: On the Performed Limits of the "Hun"', *Theatre Journal* 58: 4 (2006), 649–68.
Peperzak, Adriaan. *To the Other: An Introduction to the Philosophy of Emmanuel Levinas* (West Lafayette: Purdue University Press, 1993).
Philipse, Herman. 'Heidegger's "Scandal of Philosophy": The Problem of the *Ding an sich* in *Being and Time*', in Steven Crowell and Jeff Malpas (eds), *Transcendental Heidegger* (Stanford: Stanford University Press, 2007), 169–98.
Plato. *Theaetetus*, trans. M. J. Levett and rev. Myles Burnyeat, in *Collected Works*, ed. John Cooper (Indianapolis: Hackett Publishing Company, 1997), 157–234.
Proust, J., and J. Buroker. 'Formal Logic as Transcendental in Wittgenstein and Carnap', *Noûs* 21: 4 (1987), 501–20.
Prozorov, Sergei. 'Why Giorgio Agamben is an Optimist', *Philosophy and Social Criticism* 36: 9 (2010), 1,053–73.
Prozorov, Sergei. 'X/Xs: Toward a General Theory of the Exception', *Alternatives* 30: 1 (2005), 81–112.
Prynne, J. H. 'On the Matter of Thermal Packing', in *Poems* (Highgreen: Bloodaxe Books, 2005), 84.
Prynne, J. H. 'Resistance and Difficulty', *Prospect* 5 (1961), 26–30.
Prynne, J. H. *Stars, Tigers, and the Shapes of Words: The William Matthew Lectures 1992* (London: Birkbeck College, 1993).
Rampley, Matthew. *Nietzsche, Aesthetics and Modernity* (Cambridge: Cambridge University Press, 2000).
Rée, Jonathan. 'Subjectivity in the Twentieth Century', *New Literary History* 26: 1 (1995), 205–17.
Reinhard, Kenneth. 'Toward a Political Theology of the Neighbor', in Slavoj Žižek, Eric Santner and Kenneth Reinhard, *The Neighbor: Three Inquiries in Political Theology* (Chicago: Chicago University Press, 2005), 11–75.
Riera, Gabriel. *Intrigues: From Being to the Other* (New York: Fordham University Press, 2006).
Riera, Gabriel. '"The Possibility of the Poetic Said" in *Otherwise than Being*', *Diacritics* 34: 2 (2006), 14–36.

Rosen, Stanley. *The Elusiveness of the Ordinary: Studies in the Possibility of Philosophy* (New Haven: Yale University Press, 2002).
Rosenzweig, Franz. *The Star of Redemption*, trans. William W. Hallo (Boston: Beacon Press, 1972).
Rosenzweig, Franz. *Understanding the Sick and the Healthy*, trans. Nahum Glatzer (Cambridge, MA: Harvard University Press, 1999).
Rubenstein, Mary-Jane. *Strange Wonder: The Closure of Metaphysics and the Opening of Awe* (New York: Columbia University Press, 2008).
Russell, B., and A. N. Whitehead. *Principia Mathematica* (Cambridge: Cambridge University Press, 1999).
Santner, Eric. *My Own Private Germany: Daniel Paul Schreber's Secret History of Modernity* (Princeton: Princeton University Press, 1996).
Santner, Eric. *On Creaturely Life: Rilke, Benjamin, Sebald* (Chicago: Chicago University Press, 2006).
Santner, Eric. *On the Psychotheology of Everyday Life: Reflections on Freud and Rosenzweig* (Chicago: Chicago University Press, 2001).
Santner, Eric. *The Royal Remains: The People's Two Bodies and the Endgames of Sovereignty* (Chicago: Chicago University Press, 2011).
Sartre, Jean-Paul. *Nausea*, trans. Lloyd Alexander (New York: New Directions, 1964).
Schapiro, Meyer. *Theory and Philosophy of Art: Style, Artist, and Society* (New York: George Braziller, 1994).
Schmitt, Carl. *The Leviathan in the State Theory of Thomas Hobbes*, trans. George Schwab (Chicago: Chicago University Press, 2008).
Schmitt, Carl. *Political Theology*, trans. George Schwab (Chicago: University of Chicago Press, 2005).
Sharpe, Matthew. 'Only Agamben Can Save Us? Against the Messianic Turn Recently Adopted in Critical Theory', *The Bible and Critical Theory* 5: 3 (2010), 1–20.
Snyder, Verne. 'Kafka's "Burrow": A Speculative Analysis', *Twentieth Century Literature* 27: 2 (1981), 113–26.
Stevens, Wallace. 'Notes Toward a Supreme Fiction', in *The Collected Poems* (New York: Vintage Books, 1990), 380–408.
Strathausen, Carsten. 'A Critique of Neo-Left Political Ontology', *Postmodern Culture* 16: 3 (2006).
Sullivan, Arthur (ed.). *Logicism and the Philosophy of Language: Selections from Frege and Russell* (Peterborough: Broadview Press, 2003).
Taubes, Jacob. *The Political Theology of Paul*, trans. Dana Hollander (Stanford: Stanford University Press, 2004).
Taylor, Charles. 'Theories of Meaning', *Man and World* 18 (1980), 281–302.
Thoreau, Henry David. *Walden and Other Writings* (New York: Modern Library, 2000).
Thurschwell, Adam. 'Cutting the Branches for Akiba: Agamben's Critique of Derrida', in Andrew Norris (ed.), *Politics, Metaphysics, and Death* (Durham, NC: Duke University Press, 2005), 173–97.

Thurschwell, Adam. 'Specters of Nietzsche: Potential Futures for the Concept of the Political in Agamben and Derrida', 1 September 2004, available at <http://ssrn.com/abstract=969055> (last accessed 21 May 2013).
Vaneigem, Raoul. *The Revolution of Everyday Life*, trans. Donald Nicholson-Smith (London: Rebel Press/Left Bank Books, 1994).
Vatter, Miguel. 'In Odradek's World: Bare Life and Historical Materialism in Agamben and Benjamin', *Diacritics* 38: 3 (2008), 45–70.
Vatter, Miguel. 'Strauss and Schmitt as Readers of Hobbes and Spinoza', *The New Centennial Review* 4: 3 (2004), 161–214.
Wall, Thomas Carl. *Radical Passivity: Levinas, Blanchot, and Agamben* (Albany: State University of New York Press, 1999).
Watkin, William. *The Literary Agamben: Adventures in Logopoesis* (London: Continuum, 2010).
Weigand, Hermann. 'Franz Kafka's "The Burrow" ("Der Bau"): An Analytic Essay', *PMLA* 87: 2 (1972), 152–66.
Whyte, Jessica. 'A New Use of the Self: Agamben on the Coming Community', *Theory & Event* 13: 1 (2010).
Wittgenstein, Ludwig. *Culture and Value*, ed. G. H. von Wright and H. Nyman, trans. P. Winch (Oxford: Basil Blackwell, 1980).
Wittgenstein, Ludwig. 'Ethics, Life and Faith', in *The Wittgenstein Reader*, ed. A. Kenny (Oxford: Blackwell Publishers, 2006), 251–66.
Wittgenstein, Ludwig. *Notebooks 1914–1916*, ed. G. H. von Wright and G. E. M. Anscombe, trans. G. E. M. Anscombe (New York: Harper & Row, 1961).
Wittgenstein, Ludwig. *Philosophical Investigations*, trans. G. E. M. Anscombe (Massachusetts: Blackwell Publishing, 2001).
Wittgenstein, Ludwig. *Tractatus Logico-Philosophicus*, trans. David Pears and Brian McGuiness (London: Routledge, 2001).
Wolin, Richard. *Walter Benjamin: An Aesthetic of Redemption* (Berkeley: University of California Press, 1994).
Zartaloudis, Thanos. *Giorgio Agamben: Power, Law and the Uses of Criticism* (Oxford: Routledge, 2010).
Ziarek, Krzysztof. 'After Humanism: Agamben and Heidegger', *South Atlantic Quarterly* 107: 1 (2008), 187–209.
Žižek, Slavoj. 'Divine Violence and Liberated Territories', interview with *Soft Targets Journal*, 14 March 2007, available at <http://www.softtargetsjournal.com/web/zizek.php> (last accessed 21 May 2013).
Žižek, Slavoj. *Gaze and Voice as Love Objects* (Durham, NC: Duke University Press, 1996).
Žižek, Slavoj. 'Neighbors and Other Monsters: A Plea for Ethical Violence', in Slavoj Žižek, Eric Santner and Kenneth Reinhard, *The Neighbor: Three Inquiries in Political Theology* (Chicago: Chicago University Press, 2005), 134–90.
Žižek, Slavoj. 'Odradek as a Political Category', *Lacanian Ink* 24/25 (2005), 136–53.

Index

abandonment, 14, 101, 118
accelerationism, 11n
Adorno, Theodore, *Minima Moralia*, 24–5
affirmation
  of the beast, 133, 138
  of life, 10n, 76n, 100, 123–4, 135–6
  of the will to power, 137
affirmationism, 9–10n
Agamben, Giorgio
  hyperbole, 10n, 19–20, 197n
  lack of historical nuance, 10n
  paraconsistent dialetheist logic, 104n, 185
  pessimism, 10n, 24
  WORKS
  'Form-of-Life', 23–4
  Homo Sacer, 2, 18–19, 22, 30n, 85, 135, 180
  'In This Exile', 137–8
  Infancy and History, 30n, 33, 34, 58, 159
  Language and Death, 22, 75, 80–1, 83–6, 92, 100, 106, 183
  'On Potentiality', 136
  Remnants of Auschwitz, 20–1
  Stanzas, 161n
  State of Exception, 19, 100, 118
  The Coming Community, 74, 86, 97, 99, 118, 122n, 147, 159–60n, 191–2, 193
  'The Idea of Language', 86
  The Kingdom and the Glory, 198n
  The Open, 59, 129, 135
  'The Passion of Facticity', 96, 99
  The Sacrament of Language, 75n
  The Time That Remains, 7, 73, 184, 192, 193
animality / the animal, 117, 121n, 123–4, 134–5, 137, 139
  forgetting of, 116, 128, 129–30, 139n, 142n
  unassumability of, 6, 124, 138–9, 184
anthropological machine (of humanism), 124, 129, 133, 135, 138
Aristotle, *Nichomachean Ethics*, 8
art, 27, 59, 60, 73, 75n, 139–40n
attentiveness, 116, 139, 159, 196
Augustine, 82
Ayer, A. J., 146

Badiou, Alain, 68–9, 77n, 181, 182
Bambach, Charles, 67, 76n
banishment, 5, 92, 95, 101
bare life (pure being), 4, 18–19, 20–2, 28, 107, 128–9, 141n, 183
'bare' sound, 62, 82
beast, the, 132, 133, 138
being
  escape from, 89, 90
  falleness of, 97
  forgetting of, 129–30
  generosity of, 26
  gratuity of, 73
  negation of, 92
  pure *see* bare life

question of, 2, 44, 59, 81
unbearable and unbareable, 99–100, 101
vs beings, 90
see also existence
being there / being in the world *see* Dasein
Benjamin, Andrew, 21
Benjamin, Walter, 3, 5–6, 32n, 106–18, 133, 184, 188, 189, 192–3, 198n
  materialism, 121–2n
  messianism, 2, 7, 118, 187
  WORKS
  'Critique of Violence', 5, 106, 106–10, 111, 113–14, 119n
  'Franz Kafka', 114–15
  'On the Concept of History', 186, 195–6
  The Arcades Project, 187
  'Theologico-Political Fragment', 185
Bernstein, Jay, 21
biopolitics, 3, 5, 11n, 23, 113, 117, 128, 129, 134, 141n
Bishop, Elizabeth, 143n
Black, Max, 145
Blanchot, Maurice, 56–7n, 72, 88, 132, 133
Bloch, Ernst, 70
Boulby, Mark, 132
Braver, Lee, 38
breakdown, 46, 49, 50–1, 62, 65, 91
Brentano, Franz, 36
Brod, Max, 133
Bruns, Gerald, 50

capitalism, 189, 190, 191, 192, 194, 198n
Carnap, Rudolph, 181
category mistakes, 17, 20, 28, 163
Cavell, Stanley, 54–5n, 154, 155–6, 158, 172–3, 175, 176, 187
Celan, Paul, 34
Cezanne, Paul, 66, 76n
change
  ontological, 5, 7, 137, 188
  political, 3, 11n, 15, 28
  possibility of, 171

circularity, 59–60
civilisation, emergence of, 127, 128
commonality, 193, 194–5
community, 21, 77–8nn, 185
  linguistic, 43, 61, 69
  mythical, 71, 72
Conant, James, 147, 149–50, 152, 156
conscience, bad, 126, 127, 130, 134
consciousness, reflective, 126
constitutivity thesis, 37, 38
contemplation, 4, 8, 9, 14, 190
coping, 55n
creation, 62–3, 65, 112
creatureliness, human, 112
Critchley, Simon, 32n, 88, 91, 92

Dasein (being there), 34, 37, 38–9, 40, 45, 47, 50, 51–2, 60, 66, 73, 81, 96, 96–7, 100, 129
  as being the there, 81
  impropriety of, 98, 99
  and ontological difference, 90–1
  and poetry, 70
  powerlessness of, 172
DeAngelis, William James, 178n
death, 80, 88, 156
death penalty, 111
Debord, Guy, 7, 9, 189, 190–1
Deleuze, Gilles, 181
democracy, parliamentary, 109–10
Dennet, Daniel, 193
Derrida, Jacques, 84, 102, 109, 113–14, 119nn, 143n, 181, 183
Diamond, Cora, 148, 152, 153–4, 170, 173
Dickinson, Colby, 83–4, 185, 200n
discourse
  hermeneutic vs apophantic, 53n
  world-constituting role, 46
Dolan, Frederick, 166
Dreyfus, Hubert, 40, 55n, 176
Durantye, Leland de la, 31–2n, 186, 198n

earth, 64–5, 67, 68, 70, 73–4, 76n, 78–9n; *see also* world
Emerson, Ralph Wardo, 12n

emotivism, 146
equipmentality, 4, 49, 51, 53, 63–4, 67
Ereignis (enowning/event of appropriation), 97–8, 99, 171
eternal return, 100, 136, 137
ethics
   and Agamben, 98, 99, 100
   and Levinas, 92, 93, 94
   of potentiality, 100, 141n
   and Wittgenstein, 148, 150, 154, 173
Euripides, 125
everyday life, 7, 9, 13, 27, 51, 105n, 116, 176, 196
evil, 94, 98, 126
exception / state of exception, 3, 4, 7, 25, 27, 31–2n, 113, 179, 180–1, 182, 195–6
existence
   gratuity of, 26, 101
   problem of, 76n
   see also being; *il y a*; thingliness; world
existentialism, 96
experimentum linguae, 58, 75n, 86, 159, 191–2

facticity, 41, 96, 99, 141n
Faye, Emmanuel, 77n
flesh, 130, 141n
forgetting, 116, 127–8, 129–30, 139n, 142n
form vs matter, 63, 75–6n
form-of-life, 20, 23–4, 25, 97, 159
formed matter, 61, 62–3
Foti, Veronique, 29–30n
Foucault, Michel, 18, 22–3
foundation, 2, 5, 8, 106, 107
   negative, 84, 86
freedom, 26, 190
Frege, Gottlob, 76n, 149, 158, 174, 180
Friedlander, Saul, 76n

games, 157–8
Glazebrook, Trish, 164, 165, 166
Gödel, Kurt, 182
gratuity
   of being, 73
   of existence, 26, 101
   of world, 27, 28, 71, 118
ground, negative, 5, 80, 84, 95, 101, 183; *see also* negativity
groundlessness, 26, 74, 75, 192, 195

Hallward, Peter, 32n
Hanssen, Beatrice, 117, 120n
happiness/ the happy, 6, 153–4, 158–9, 159–60n, 170, 185, 186, 187, 199n
Harman, Graham, 44–5
Hegel, G. W. F., 81
Heidegger, Martin, 2, 4, 5, 34–53, 58–75, 81, 96, 129, 173–4, 183, 188
   hermeneutic philosophy, 51
   kitchiness, 67, 76n
   Nazism, 67, 68
   quasi-transcendentalism, 37, 38, 39, 43, 44
   WORKS
   Being and Time, 3, 15, 34, 36, 37, 38–9, 40–1, 43, 47, 48, 51, 53n, 55–6n, 60, 61, 63, 68, 87, 90, 98, 99, 164, 176
   Elucidations of Hölderlin's Poetry, 69, 70, 73
   'Language', 35, 47, 48
   'Letter on Humanism', 90, 96
   Nietzsche, 16
   On the Way to Language, 69
   'Only God Can Save Us', 197n
   'The Age of the World Picture', 7, 163, 164–8, 171–2
   The Basic Problems of Phenomenology, 42
   The Metaphysical Foundations of Logic, 172
   The Nature of Language, 78n
   'The Origin of the Work of Art', 5, 59, 60–4
   'The Question Concerning Technology', 167
   'What are Poets For?', 69
   What is Metaphysics, 30n
Hejinian, Lyn, 187
Heller-Roazen, Daniel, 34, 140–1n
historicity, 37, 38, 39, 43, 61, 164

Hodges, Michael, 170–1
humanity, lack of vocation or historical destiny, 5, 73, 74
Husserl, Edmund, 96

idealism, 38, 39
il y a (fact of existence), 87–9, 91–2, 95, 183, 190; *see also* existence
immanence, 21, 78n
impropriety, 99, 100, 105n
inappropriable, the, 4, 99, 100–1, 184
inauthenticity, 105n, 176
inclusive exclusion, 17–18, 19, 20, 24, 92, 128, 138
incommensurabilism, 14, 35, 44, 50, 164
ineffable, the, 6, 34, 83, 84, 101, 145, 150
inner touch, 141n
inoperativity, 24, 51, 74, 134, 135
insomnia, 87–8, 91
irreparable, the, 97, 159n

Kafka, Franz, 111, 124, 184
  and animals, 114–16, 137–8
  and creatures, 114–16
  'The Burrow', 115, 130–3
  The Trial, 120n
Kant, Immanuel, 37, 39, 63, 75–6n, 126–7, 190
Kierkegaard, Søren, 154
Kishik, David, 11 n
Kosuth, Joseph, 66
Kuhn, Thomas, 164

Lacan, Jacques, 181
Laclau, Ernesto, 30n
Lacoue-Labarthe, Philippe, 67, 69
Lafont, Cristina, 36, 37, 40–1, 42, 43, 44, 46
language
  communicative function, 36
  concepts of, 4, 34–5
  and death, 80
  designative/instrumentalist function, 34, 35–6, 46, 47, 53n, 54n
  disclosive function, 34, 36, 41, 49
  and equipment, 41–2
  equipment function, 49, 51
  fact of, 33, 34; *see also experimentum linguae*
  functions, 33
  hermeneutic understanding, 53n
  materiality, 56–7n
  ordinary, 60, 175
  philosophy of, 33, 147
  picture theory, 6, 145, 150, 168
  poetic *see* poetic language
  primordial function, 36
  propositional, 151
  self-reference, 49
  and style, 173–4
law, 5, 85–6
  creaturely tie to, 112
  decay / mortification, 6, 110–11
  exceptionality, 116–17
  and modernity, 6, 110
  obscene dimension, 112, 113, 117, 120n
  positive vs natural, 107–8
  ungroundedness, 113
  and violence, 106, 108, 109–10
Lemm, Vanessa, 128, 134, 139n
Levinas, Emmanuel
  and *il y a* (fact of existence), 87–9, 183, 190
  and the other, 89–90, 92–5
  and the saying vs the said, 101
  and the subject, 93–4, 95–6
  WORKS
  'Ethics as First Philosophy', 92
  Existence and Existents, 88, 89
  On Escape, 89
  Otherwise than Being, 92, 93, 94, 95
  Time and the Other, 87, 89, 90, 91, 93, 195
  Totality and Infinity, 5, 91, 93, 94
Librett, Jeffrey, 105n
life
  affirmation of, 10n, 76n, 100, 123–4, 135–6
  bare *see* bare life
  contingency of, 4, 186
  everyday *see* everyday life
  mere, 11–12, 106, 107, 113, 116, 117, 120n
  moral, 126
  natural, 124–5

life (*cont.*)
　as passivity and receptivity, 136
　totality of, 89, 95, 100, 136
　as will to power, 135, 136
　see also zoē vs bios
Lingis, Alphonso, 95
linguistic idealism, 35, 41, 43–4, 46, 47, 51
Littell, Jonathan, 72
Livingston, Paul, 179–80, 181–2, 183
logic, 168, 178n
logical positivism, 146–7, 181
Lukács, György, 8–9, 189, 190

Maché, Britta, 132
McLoughlin, Daniel, 83, 85–6, 140n
Marchart, Oliver, 15, 31n
Marx, Karl, 8, 9, 196
Marxism, 8, 189
Meir, Heinrich, 13, 14
messianism, 2, 7, 11nn, 118, 184–6, 187
metaphysics, 2, 8, 15–16, 28–9, 30n, 73, 84, 105n, 129, 171, 182, 183, 188, 191
Mills, Catherine, 84, 198n
miracles, 25–7, 181
modernity, 6, 18, 20, 30n, 110, 123, 171, 182, 188, 189
Monk, Ray, 147
morality, slave, 125–6, 127
Mulhall, Stephen, 42–3, 52, 152
Murray, Alex, 133–4
Muselmann, 21, 93
mystical, the, 7, 147, 151
myth, 77–8n
　and literature, 71
　and poetry, 5, 69–70

Nachtwey, James, 21
Nancy, Jean-Luc, 21, 27, 71, 77–8nn, 94, 103n, 187
　WORKS
　'Myth Interrupted', 69, 71, 77–8n
　The Creation of the World, 29
　The Experience of Freedom, 26
　'The Inoperative Community', 21, 31n, 78n
　The Sense of the World, 8

Nazism, 67, 68, 69, 71, 76n, 78n, 113
negativity, 9n, 80–1, 83, 84, 86
Nietzsche, Friederich, 6, 120–1n, 123–30, 133–8, 139–40nn
　WORKS
　On The Genealogy of Morals, 124–5, 127–8, 141n, 142–3n
　'On Truth and Lie in an Extra-Moral Sense', 124
　The Will to Power, 140n
　Thus Spake Zarathustra, 142n
nihilism, 9n, 18, 26, 69, 73, 74, 75n, 86, 123, 163, 192
nonsense, 149, 150, 152, 153
Norris, Andrew, 28
Noys, Benjamin, 9–10n, 11n

ontological difference, 6, 15, 19, 37, 42, 90–1, 129, 143n
ordinary, the, 7, 27, 32n, 174–5
　exceptionality of, 3, 28, 194, 195–6, 199n
　see also everyday life
orientation
　constructivist, 181
　generic, 181, 182
　ontotheological, 181
　paradoxico-critical, 181, 182, 183, 184
overhuman, the, 134–5, 137, 138, 143n

paradox, 72, 119n
　and animal life, 133
　of Benjamin's philosophy, 122n
　of inclusive exclusion, 85, 92
　of insomnia, 88
　of institutionalised violence, 72, 110, 113
　and language, 191
　of law, 107, 113
　Meno's Paradox, 59
　of modernity, 182
　paradoxico-critical orientation, 181–2
　and picture concept, 181, 196
　Russell's paradox, 174, 179, 180
　of sovereignty, 180, 181, 183
　of Western *polis*, 17, 128
　of world, 196

passivity, 89, 93, 94, 96, 97–8, 100, 136, 137, 170, 172–3, 182
Paul, Saint, 7, 184, 192–3
Peperzak, Adriaan, 89
perception, 37, 43, 66, 76n, 191
Philipse, Herman, 39–40
philosophical beguilement, 7, 158, 176
philosophy
  auto-critical mode, 2
  hermeneutic transformation, 36, 37
  and poetry, 48, 68–9, 77n, 157
  scandal of, 39
picture-concept, 7, 144, 153–6, 162, 163, 169, 173, 174, 176, 180–1, 182, 188–94, 196; see also world picture
poetic experience, 35, 49, 50–1, 52, 53, 59, 68, 70, 72, 73, 74
poetic language, 4, 34, 48–50, 52–3, 68
poetry, 4, 5, 47, 51, 73
  and myth, 5, 69–70
  and philosophy, 48, 68–9, 77n, 157
police, 110, 112
political ontology, 1, 3, 9, 13–15, 16, 17, 23, 123–4, 133–5, 137, 183, 188
political theology, 4, 13, 14
politics
  concrete, 7, 19, 23, 114
  prescriptive, 32n
  subjunctive, 4, 29
Ponge, Francis, 50
potentiality, 38, 44, 85, 96, 97–8, 100, 136, 140n, 141n
power, constituting vs constituent, 106
pre-predictive vs pre-linguistic, 55n
pre-understanding, 42
pronouns, demonstrative, 81–2
Prozorov, Sergei, 31n
Prynne, J. H., 51
psychoanalysis, 141n, 161n
Putnam, Hilary, 154

rationality, 25, 58, 125
reconciliation, 121n, 133, 135, 138–9
redemption, 6, 107, 118, 186, 188, 196
  atheist, 123, 127, 134
  Pauline, 137
  see also messianism
Rée, Jonathan, 152
relativism, 35, 44, 164, 167
remnant, the, 7, 63, 184–5, 193
representation (*Vorstellung*), 29–30n, 144, 165–6
research, 164, 165, 166
Riera, Gabriel, 95, 103n
Rorty, Richard, 181
Rosen, Stanley, 32n
Rosenzweig, Franz, 154–5
Rubenstein, Mary-Jane, 103n
Russell, Bertrand, 180, 181, 182
Russell set, 179, 180

sacred, the, 85–6, 101
sacrifice, 69, 75, 78n, 83–4, 85, 86, 106
salvation, 3, 6, 89–90, 92, 171
  redemption from, 11n, 118, 127
Santner, Eric, 111–12, 113, 141n, 155, 161n
Sartre, Jean-Paul, 96, 104n
Schapiro, Meyer, 77n
Schmitt, Carl, 4, 13–14, 25–6, 28, 182
Scholem, Gershom, 29
science, 39–40, 46, 58, 163–6
scientism, 163, 173
self-referentiality, 168, 180, 181
sensations, unity of, 61–2
sentence structure, subject–predicate, 61, 62, 63
separation *see* ontological difference
shadow, 171–2
sovereignty, paradox of, 180, 181, 183
speakability, 52, 101
spectacle, 7, 32n, 190–1, 194, 198n
Stein, Gertrude, 187
Strathausen, Carsten, 14
strife, 65, 70
subjectivity / the subject, 93–4, 95, 95–6, 126, 127, 166, 172
suicide, 88, 170

Taubes, Jacob, 137
theory vs practice, 8, 188, 198n
thingliness, 60–3, 64, 65
Thurschwell, Adam, 102n

tool: phenomenology of broken tool, 44, 45–6, 50–1, 52, 65
totality, 7, 93, 158, 176–7, 181–2, 183, 184, 185
   of being / life, 89, 95, 100, 136
   of facts, 144, 145, 146, 151, 156, 166, 193
Trakl, Georg, 'A Winter Evening', 48, 50
transcendence, 89, 91
transformation, possibility of, 6, 66, 123, 135
truth, correspondence theory, 54n, 145–6

unhappy, the, 7, 145, 153, 157, 159n, 170, 172
unrepresentable, the, 48

value, absolute / ethical, 148–9
Van Gogh, Vincent, 63, 64, 66
Vatter, Miguel, 25, 141n
verbum incognitum, 82
vigilance vs attention, 88
violence, 75, 84, 173
   divine, 107, 113–14, 117–18
   just vs unjust, 108
   law-making vs law-preserving, 106, 109–10
   mythical, 5, 106, 111, 114
   ontological, 5, 72
   sanctioned vs unsanctioned, 108
voice, 22, 82–3, 84

Wall, Thomas Carl, 98
Watkin, William, 32n
Whitehead, A. N., 180
Whyte, Jessica, 188

will, 169–70, 171, 172
Wittgenstein, Ludwig, 2, 3, 58, 76n, 144–59, 172, 181, 194
   therapeutic goals / methods, 144, 150, 154, 162–3, 169
   WORKS
   Culture and Value, 179
   Philosophical Investigations, 7, 150, 156, 157–8, 162, 173, 174, 199n
   Philosophical Remarks, 173
   Tractatus Logico-Philosophicus, 6–7, 145, 146–7, 148–50, 156, 168, 169, 173, 176, 199n
wonder, kinds of, 158
work, concept of, 71
world, 38–9, 40, 43, 52
   as disclosure of beings, 43
   figure of, 28, 191, 193, 196
   gratuity of, 27, 28, 71, 118
   as inappropriable, 5, 100–1
   objectification of, 166–7, 190
   as representable, 7, 165, 167, 168, 176, 178n, 193
   as totality of facts, 72, 144, 145, 146, 151, 156, 166, 176–7, 186, 193
   wonder / mystery of existence, 27, 28, 66, 72, 147, 148, 151, 152–3; *see also* earth; world picture
world picture (*Weltbild*), 163, 167–8, 171, 172, 176–7, 180, 183, 184, 187; *see also* picture concept

Zartaloudis, Thomas, 198nn
Žižek, Slavoj, 11n, 120n
zoē (fact of life) vs *bios* (politically qualified life), 17, 19, 143n

EU representative:
Easy Access System Europe
Mustamäe tee 50, 10621 Tallinn, Estonia
Gpsr.requests@easproject.com

www.ingramcontent.com/pod-product-compliance
Lightning Source LLC
Chambersburg PA
CBHW051057230426
43667CB00013B/2332